Intellectual Property Asset Management

How to identify, protect, manage and exploit intellectual property within the business environment

David Bainbridge and Claire Howell

LONDON AND NEW YORK

First published 2014
by Routledge
2 Park Square, Milton Park, Abingdon, Oxon OX14 4RN

and by Routledge
711 Third Avenue, New York, NY 10017

Routledge is an imprint of the Taylor & Francis Group, an informa business

© 2014 David Bainbridge and Claire Howell

The right of David Bainbridge and Claire Howell to be identified as authors of this work has been asserted by them in accordance with sections 77 and 78 of the Copyright, Designs and Patents Act 1988.

All rights reserved. No part of this book may be reprinted or reproduced or utilised in any form or by any electronic, mechanical, or other means, now known or hereafter invented, including photocopying and recording, or in any information storage or retrieval system, without permission in writing from the publishers.

Trademark notice: Product or corporate names may be trademarks or registered trademarks, and are used only for identification and explanation without intent to infringe.

British Library Cataloguing in Publication Data
A catalogue record for this book is available from the British Library

Library of Congress Cataloging in Publication Data
Intellectual property asset management : how to identify, protect, manage and exploit intellectual property within the business environment / Claire Howell, David Bainbridge.
   pages cm
1. Intellectual property–Economic aspects–Great Britain. 2. Intellectual capital–Great Britain–Management. I. Bainbridge, David I. II. Title.
KD1269.H69 2014
346.4104'8–dc23
                                                                                            2013026874

ISBN: 978-0-415-52791-0 (hbk)
ISBN: 978-0-415-52792-7 (pbk)
ISBN: 978-1-315-84989-8 (ebk)

Typeset in Joanna
by Wearset Ltd, Boldon, Tyne and Wear

Contents

Preface	vii
Table of Cases	ix
Table of Legislation UK and International Legislation	xiii

1 Introduction to Intellectual Property Rights — 1
- What are intellectual property rights and what do they protect? — 2
- How are intellectual property rights classified? — 3
- The scope of intellectual property rights — 3
- Must intellectual property rights be registered? — 4
- I have created/invented a new 'thingamajig'. Can it be protected by more than one intellectual property right? — 5
- How long do intellectual property rights exist for? — 5
- How do I get protection in other countries? — 6
- How do I grant rights to others to use my intellectual property? — 8
- How can I sell my intellectual property rights or acquire someone else's intellectual property rights? — 9
- What are the pitfalls of disregarding intellectual property rights? — 9
- Summary — 10
- Management tips — 11
- Exercise — 11

2 Business Goodwill and Reputation — 12
- Trade marks in context — 12
- What are the forms of trade mark protection? — 21
- Someone is using a trade mark the same or similar to mine – can I do anything about it? — 25
- Defences — 29
- Remedies — 31
- How do I get protection outside the EU? — 32
- Passing off — 33
- Summary — 36
- Management tips — 37
- Exercise — 37

3 Confidentiality — 40
- Confidentiality in context — 40
- What are the requirements for information to be regarded as confidential? — 41
- For how long does confidential information last? — 43
- Employees have access to my secret information – what should I do? — 44
- Sharing secrets with third parties and non-disclosure agreements — 46

	Are there any circumstances where people may use my confidential information?	48
	What remedies are available to me if confidence is breached?	48
	Can I get protection for my secrets outside the EU?	49
	Summary	49
	Management tips	49
	Exercise	50
4	**Patents**	**52**
	Patents in context	52
	What are the requirements for protection?	55
	Who owns or is entitled to the rights in a patent?	67
	If an employee created the patent, to whom does it belong?	68
	Someone else is using something that is the same or similar to my patent – can I do anything about it?	68
	Alternatives to obtaining a patent	74
	Summary	75
	Management tips	76
	Exercise	76
5	**Copyright and Rights in Performances**	**78**
	Copyright in context	78
	What are the requirements for protection?	80
	What does copyright protect?	83
	Who owns or is entitled to copyright in a work?	89
	An employee created the work – to whom does it belong?	90
	I have engaged a consultant to create a work – who owns or is entitled to the copyright?	91
	How long does copyright last for?	92
	Moral rights	92
	You think there has been copying – what can be done about it?	95
	There are some things you are allowed to do even though it looks like infringement	102
	Remedies	104
	Crime in the workplace	106
	How do I get protection outside the EU?	106
	Rights in performances	106
	Summary	109
	Management tips	110
	Exercise: copyright	110
	Exercise: rights in performances	111
6	**Databases**	**112**
	'Sweat of the brow'	112
	Twin-track approach	113
	Common provisions	113
	Copyright	114
	Database right	116
	Summary	120

	Management tips	121
	Exercise	121
7	**Design Rights**	122
	What are design rights?	122
	What are the forms of design right protection?	122
	The unregistered Community design	124
	The registered Community design	130
	The UK registered design	133
	How do I maximise protection of designs?	138
	How do I get protection outside the EU?	139
	Summary	139
	Management tips	140
	Exercise	141
8	**Exploitation of Intellectual Property**	143
	What is an assignment?	143
	What is a licence?	143
	Why do I want to take or grant a licence?	143
	What do you want to license?	144
	How may the IP be used?	145
	Other terms	146
	Summary	146
	Management tips	147
	Exercise	147
9	**Strategy, Audit, Due Diligence and Valuation**	148
	Why does an organisation need an intellectual property strategy?	148
	What type of strategy is right for your business?	150
	What strategies are available?	152
	To create an IP strategy	157
	You need a vision of your strategic objectives	160
	Keep revising the strategy	162
	Audits	162
	Due diligence	166
	Valuation of IP	170
	Summary of key points: strategy	176
	Summary of key points: audit	176
	Summary of key points: due diligence	177
	Summary of key points: valuation	177
	Management tips	178
	Exercise	178
10	**Infringement of Intellectual Property Rights**	179
	Summary of intellectual property rights and infringement	179
	Summary of infringement of intellectual property rights	180
	What can I do to strengthen my position in relation to my intellectual property rights?	184
	Management tips	191
	Exercise	191

11	**Remedies**	193
	Summary of main remedies	194
	Preliminary actions	195
	Main remedies available for infringement of intellectual property rights	199
	Criminal offences	204
	Management tips	205
	Exercise	205

Bibliography	207
Index	208

Preface

When the authors of this book were students, intellectual property (IP) law was rarely taught at undergraduate level at law schools. Even at postgraduate level it was still a subject that was taught only at selected universities. Since then, however, the importance of IP law has been recognised and it is now found on the syllabus of most good law schools. However, in practice lawyers usually only get involved in IP issues when there has been infringement or some dispute. Surprisingly, IP rights (IPR) and how to protect innovation are generally not taught to engineers or scientists, the actual innovators, the people who have the new ideas or who create the novel products. Likewise, IP is generally not taught to the people who will manage the innovators, the people who we expect to create value from the products or processes that are the result of the creative process.

In the nineteenth and twentieth centuries land, labour and capital were the crucial factors in wealth creation. This has changed: today it is IP. Intellectual or intangible assets are now recognised by many organisations in today's knowledge-intensive economies as their most important resource. Without IPR many innovative organisations have nothing to sell or license. From the largest, most powerful companies to the smallest small to medium-sized enterprises (SMEs) the commercialisation of intellectual assets, copyright, patents, trade marks, designs and know-how are essential to success. Producing IP is the fastest-growing field of economic activity. In this digital age a company's IP portfolio represents on average 60–70 per cent of its business value. US companies now invest more than US$1.1 trillion per year in intangible assets. There is good evidence that companies with large, well-managed IP portfolios are more profitable than those that are IP passive.

IPR are intended to reward and encourage innovators and their effective use will promote commercial success. How well a company captures and uses innovation is crucial to its business success and so the aim of any innovative organisations should be to turn their intellectual assets into value. In this time of global communication it is not the company with the best product but the company with the best strategy that becomes the market leader. Whether an SME, start-up or international organisation, all firms need an IP strategy in line with their business strategy. Managing the IP strategy effectively allows an organisation to increase asset value, assess risk, reduce liabilities, improve its competitive position and increase the return to shareholders. Using IP effectively is the route to financial success.

Having taught intellectual property at Aston Business School for many years, the authors decided that the time was right for a book of this kind. We hope that by using this book you will not only find out about the various IP rights, but that you will also understand how they can be used to best effect.

You will make better decisions if you are well informed.

We would like to thank Damian Mitchell from Routledge who demonstrated saintly patience during the production of this book.

David Bainbridge, Emeritus Professor, Aston University
Claire Howell, Senior Lecturer, Aston University
Birmingham, June 2013

Table of Cases

A

Aerotel/Macrossan Patent Application [2006] EWHC 705, CA ... 58

American Cyanamid Co v Ethicon Ltd [1975] AC 396 ... 196

Anneka Bain [2001] EIPR 162 ... 29

Apis-Hristovich EOOD v Lakorda AD [2009] (Case C-545/07) ECR I-1627 ... 119

Arsenal Football Club plc v Matthew Reed [2003] RPC 144, ECJ ... 26

Asprey & Garrard Ltd v WRA (Guns) Ltd [2002] FSR 487 ... 30

Auchincloss v Agricultural & Veterinary Supplies Ltd [1997] RPC 649 CA ... 72

B

Baigent v Random House Group Ltd [2007] FSR 24 ... 84

Ball v Eden Project Ltd [2002] FSR 43 ... 18

Bang & Olufsen A/S v OHIM (Case T-508/08) ... 17

Blair v Osborne & Tomkins [1971] 2 WLR 503 ... 91

Bravado Merchandising Services Ltd v Mainstream Publishing [1996] FSR 205 ... 26

Bristol Conservatories Ltd v Conservatories Custom Built Ltd [1989] RPC 455 CA ... 35

British Horseracing Board Ltd v William Hill Organisation Ltd [2001] RPC 31 ... 112

British Horseracing Board Ltd v William Hill Organisation Ltd [2004] (Case C-203/02) ECR I-10415 ... 117, 118

British Sugar plc v James Robertson & Sons Ltd [1996] RPC 281 ... 20

C

Campbell v Mirror Group Newspapers [2004] UKHL 22 ... 47

Canon Kabushiki Kaisha v Metro-Goldwyn-Mayer Inc [1998] ECR I-5507 ... 19

Carflow Products (UK) Ltd v Linwood Securities (Birmingham) Ltd [1996] FSR 424 ... 185

Catnic Components Ltd v Hill & Smith Ltd [1982] RPC 183 ... 70

CBS Songs Ltd v Amstrad [1988] 1 AC 1013 ... 100

Celaya Empranza y Galdos Internacional SA v Proyectos Integrales de Balizamiento SL (Case C-488/10) 16 February 2012 ... 131

Churchill Retirement Living v Luard [2012] EWHC 1479 (Ch) ... 44

Coco v Clark [1969] RPC 41 ... 41, 42

CODAS Trade Mark [2001] RPC 14 ... 20

Commissioners of Inland Revenue v Muller & Co's Margarine Ltd [1901] AC 217 ... 34

Confetti Records v Warner Music [2003] EWHC 1724 ... 94

Conor Medysystems Inc v Angiotech Pharmaceuticals Inc [2008] 4 All ER 621; [2008] RPC 28 HL ... 53, 65

Cramp (GA) & Sons Ltd v Frank Smythson Ltd [1944] AC 329 ... 83

Crate & Barrel Euromarket Designs [2001] FSR 288 ... 25

D

D Green & Co (Stoke Newington) Ltd v Regalzone Ltd [2002] ETMR 22 ... 23

David Murray v Big Pictures (UK) Ltd [2008] EWCA Civ 446 ... 47

Designers Guild Ltd v Russell Williams (Textiles) Ltd [2000] 1 WLR 2416 HL ... 97

Deutsche Krankerversicherung AG v OHIM (COMPANYLINE) [2002] ECR I ... 24

Directmedia Publishing GmbH v Albert-Ludwigs-Universitat Freiburg [2008] (Case C-304/07) ECR I-7565 ... 118

Dramatico Entertainment Limited and others v British Sky Broadcasting Limited and others [2012] EWHC 1152 (Ch) ... 99

E

eBay Inc. v MercExchange LLC 547 (2006) US 388 ... 74, 199
Eli Lilly & Co v Human Genome Sciences Inc. [2012] RPC 6 SC ... 60
EMI Records Ltd v British Sky Broadcasting Ltd [2013] EWHC 379 (Ch) ... 200
Emma Delves-Broughton v House of Harlot [2011] EWPCC 29 ... 94
Essex Trading Standards v Singh [2009] EWHC 520 ... 29
Eurolamb Trade Mark [1997] RPC 279 ... 16
Exxon v Exxon Insurance [1982] 1 Ch 19 ... 80, 82

F

Faccenda Chicken Ltd v Fowler [1986] 1 All ER 617 CA ... 44
Feist Publications Inc. v Rural Telephone Service Co Inc (1991) 499 US 340 ... 112
Fraser v Thames Television [1983] 2 All ER 101 ... 42
Fundación Española para la Innovación de la Artesanía (FEIA) v Cul de Sac Espacio Creativo SL [2009] (Case C-32/08) ECR I-5611 ... 128

G

General Motors Corp v Yplon SA [1999] ECR I-5421 ... 21
George Hensher Ltd v Restawhile Upholstery Ltd [1974] AC 64, HL ... 86
Granada Group Ltd v Ford Motor Company Ltd [1973] RPC 49 ... 35
Griggs Group Ltd v Evans [2005] FSR 31 ... 91

H

Haberman v Jackel International Ltd [1999] FSR 683 ChD ... 57
Halliburton Energy Services Inc.'s Patent Application [2011] EWHC 2508 ... 57
Hodgson v Isaac [2012] ECC 4 ... 98
Hoffman v Drug Abuse Resistance Education (UK) [2012] EWPCC 2 ... 105
Human Genome Sciences Inc. v Eli Lilly & Co [2011] UKSC 51, SC ... 57
Hyde Park Residence Ltd v Yelland [2000] RPC 604, CA ... 103

I

IDA Ltd v University of Southampton [2006] RPC 21 ... 67, 77
Improver Corp v Raymond Industries Ltd [1991] FSR 223 ... 71
Independiente Ltd v Music Trading Online [2007] FSR 525 ... 98
Infopaq International A/S v Danske Dagblades Forening [2009] ECR 1–6569 ... 80
Intel Corp Inc v CPM UK Ltd [2009] RPC 15 EC ... 27
Interflora v Marks & Spencer plc [2012] (Case C-323/09) FSR 3 ... 27
Interlego AG v Tyco Industries Inc. [1989] 1 AC 217 ... 82
Irvine v Talksport Ltd [2003] FSR 619 ChD ... 35

K

Koninklijke Philips Electronics v Remington Consumer Products Ltd [2003] RPC 14 ECJ ... 17

L

Laboratoires Goemar SA's Trade Mark (No.1) [2002] FSR 51 (Mr Justice Jacobs) ... 23
LB (Plastics) v Swish Products Ltd [1979] RPC 551 ... 96
Lego Juris A/S v Office of Harmonization for the Internal Market (Trade Marks and Designs) (OHIM) [1020] ETMR 63 ... 16, 17
Leno Merken v Hagelkruis Beheer BV [2012] (Case C-149/11) ... 24
Libertel Groep BV and Benelux-Merkenbureau [2004] (C-104/01) FSR 4 ... 15
Lidl SNC v Vierzon Distribution SA [2011] ETMR 6 ... 28
Lion Laboratories v Evans [1985] QB 526 ... 48
L'Oréal (UK) Ltd v Johnson & Johnson [2000] FSR 686 Ch D ... 31
LTJ Diffusion SA v Sadas Vertbaudet SA [2003] ECR I-2799, ECJ ... 19
Lucasfilm v Ainsworth [2009] FSR 103 ... 85
Lux Traffic Controls v Pike Signals [1993] RPC 107 ChD ... 55

M

Marks & Spencer plc v One in a Million [1998] FSR 265 CA ... 36
Mars UK Ltd v Teknowledge Ltd [2000] FSR 138 ... 42, 47–8
Maxim's Ltd v Dye [1977] 1 WLR 1155 ... 7

TABLE OF CASES

Menashe Business Mercantile Ltd v William Hill Organisation Ltd [2003] RPC 31 CA ... 70
Michael Douglas v Hello! Ltd [2003] EWHC 786 (Ch) ... 47

N

Navitaire Inc v easyJet [2006] RPC 3 ... 102
Newspaper Licensing Agency Ltd v Meltwater Holding BV [2012] RPC 1 ... 82
Norowzian v Arks [2000] FSR 363 ... 87, 88
Norwich Pharmacal Co v Commissioners of Customs and Excise [1974] AC 133 ... 198
Nova Productions Ltd v Mazooma Games Ltd [2006] RPC 14 ... 102
Numatic International Ltd v Qualtex Ltd [2010] RPC 25 ... 33

O

Oasis Stores Ltd Trademark Application [1998] RPC 631 ... 21
Ocular Sciences v Aspect Vision Care [1997] RPC 289 ... 136

P

Pall Corp v Commercial Hydraulics [1990] FSR 329 ... 55
Parkes-Cramer Co v GW Thornton [1966] RPC 407 ... 56
Pepsico Inc. v Gruper Promer Mon Graphic SA (Case C-281/10P) 20 October 2011 ... 127
Perry v Truefitt [1842] 49 ER 749 ... 33
Pozzoli SpA v BDMO SA [2007] FSR 37 CA ... 56
Premier Brands UK Ltd v Typhoon Europe Ltd [2000] FSR 767 ... 19
Printers and Finishers Ltd v Holloway [1965] RPC 239 ... 44
Procter & Gamble Co v OHIM [2002] RPC 17 ... 16
Procter & Gamble Co v Reckitt Benkiser (UK) Ltd [2008] FSR 8 ... 126

R

R. v Boulter (Gary) [2009] ETMR 6 ... 29
Reckitt & Colman Ltd v Borden [1990] 1 All ER 873 ... 35
Reckitt & Colman Products Ltd v Borden Inc. [1990] 1 All ER 873 ... 33
Reed Executive plc v Reed Business Information Ltd [2004] RPC 40 ... 19

Rockwool Ltd v Kingspan Group plc [2011] EWHC 250 (Ch) 02 ... 28
Rodi & Wienenberger AG v Henry Showell Ltd [1969] RPC 367 HL ... 70

S

Salomon v Salomon and Co Ltd [1897] AC 22 HL ... 18
Samsung Electronics (UK) Ltd v Apple Inc [2012] EWCA Civ 1430 ... 193, 202
Schutz (UK) Ltd v Werit UK Ltd [2013] 2 All ER 177 ... 72
Shelfer v City of London Electric Lighting Co [1895] 1 Ch 287 ... 200
Shield Mark BV v Joost Kist [2004] RPC 315 ECJ ... 14
Sieckmann [2002] C-273/00 ECR I-11737 ... 15
Slater v Wimmer [2012] EWPCC 7 ... 90
Sociedad General de Autores y Editores de España (SGAE) v Rafael Hoteles SA [2006] ECR I-11519 ... 98
Stevenson, Jordan & Harrison v Macdonald and Evans [1952] RPC 10 CA ... 90
Symbian Ltd v Comptroller-General of Patents [2009] RPC 1 CA ... 58

T

Temple Island Collections Ltd v New English Teas Ltd [2012] EWPCC ... 97
Twentieth Century Fox Film Corp v Harris [2013] EWHC 159 (Ch) ... 200

U

United Wire Ltd v Screen Repair Services (Scotland) Ltd [2001] RPC 439 HL ... 72
University of London Press Ltd v University Tutorial Press Ltd [1916] 2 Ch 601 ... 80

W

Walter v Lane [1900] AC 539 ... 83
WEBSPHERE Trade Mark [2004] FSR 39 ... 19
White Hudson & Co Ltd v Asian Organisation Ltd [1964] 1 WLR 1466 ... 189
Williams v Settle [1960] 1 WLR 1072 ... 202
Windsurfing Chiemsee [1999] ECR I–2779 ... 16
Windsurfing International Inc v Tabur Marine Ltd [1985] RPC 59 CA ... 55

Table of Legislation UK and International Legislation

Companies Act 2006
   s 69 ... 30
Copyright, Designs and Patent Act (CDPA) 1988
      79, 114
   Part III ... 135
   s 4 ... 85
   s 4(1)(c) ... 86
   s 5A ... 87
   s 5B ... 88
   s 6 ... 88
   s 8 ... 88
   s 11 ... 89
   s 16(2) ... 99, 100
   s 17 ... 99
   s 18   98
   s 20(1)(b) ... 99
   s 50A-C ... 104
   ss 77–79 ... 93
   ss 80–83 ... 94
   s 84 ... 94
   s 85 ... 94
   s 96(2) ... 195
   s 97(1) ... 186
   s 97A ... 200
   s 103 ... 195
   s 107A ... 105
   s 111 ... 198
   s 116A ... 92
   s 116B ... 92
   s 178 ... 90
   s 191L ... 195
   s 194 ... 195
   s 205N ... 195
   s 213 ... 135
   s 213(1) ... 136
   s 213(2) ... 135
   s 213(3) ... 135
   s 215 ... 137
   s 216 ... 137
   s 226 ... 138
   s 239 ... 195

Data Protection Act 1998 ... 40
Digital Economy Act 2010 ... 198

Human Rights Act 1998 ... 46

Patents Act 1977 ... 52
   s 1(1) ... 57
   s 2 ... 55
   s 2(4) ... 186
   s 2(4)(b) ... 59
   s 2(4)(c) ... 59
   s 3 ... 56
   s 4 ... 57
   s 39 ... 68, 77
   s 60 ... 72
   s 60(1)(a) ... 69
   s 60(1)(b) ... 69
   s 60(1)(c) ... 69
   s 62(1) ... 186
   s 70 ... 72

Registered Designs Act 1949 ... 125, 134
   s 24A(2) ... 195

Statute of Anne 1709 ... 79

Trade Marks Act 1994 (TMA 1994) ... 189
   s 1 ... 14
   s 3 ... 21, 30
   s 3(1)(b) ... 15
   s 3(2) ... 16
   s 3(3)–(6) ... 16, 17
   s 4 ... 18
   s 5 ... 18
   s 5(1) ... 18
   s 5(2) ... 18
   s 5(3) ... 20
   s 14(2) ... 194
   ss 14–19 ... 31
   s 18(2) ... 18
   s 21 ... 31
   s 889 ... 198

Trade Marks Registration Act 1875 ... 12

Statutory Instruments
Patents Regulation 2000 (SI 2000/2037) ... 58

International instruments
Directives
Directive 84/450 concerning misleading advertisements as amended by Directive 97/55 (Misleading Advertisements Directive) ... 28
Directive 89/104/EEC of 21 December 1988 to approximate the laws of the Member States relating to trade marks (Trade Mark Directive) ... 189
Directive 96/9/EC of the European Parliament and of the Council of 11 March 2006 on the legal protection of databases, OJ L 77, 27 March 1996 (Database Directive) ... 115
  Art 1(2) ... 113
Directive 2000/31/EC of the European Parliament and Council of 8 June 2000 on certain legal aspects of information society services, in particular electronic commerce, in the Internal Market (OJ 2000 L 178 (E-Commerce Directive)
  Art 15 ... 99
Directive 2001/29/EC of the European Parliament and of the Council of 22 May 2001 on the harmonisation of certain aspects of copyright and related rights in the information society (Information Society Directive)
  Art 3(1) ... 99
Directive 2004/48/EC of the European Parliament and of the Council of 29 April 2004 on the enforcement of intellectual property rights (IPR Enforcement Directive) ... 200
  Art 3(2) ... 193
  Art 15 ... 202

Regulations
Council Regulation (EC) No 6/2002 of 12 December 2001 on Community designs (Community Design Regulation)
  Art 3(a) ... 124
  Art 3(b) ... 124
  Art 3(c) ... 124
  Art 4(1) ... 125
  Art 5 ... 125
  Art 6 ... 126
  Art 10 ... 129
  Art 11 ... 127
  Art 14 ... 128
  Art 19 ... 129
  Art 21 ... 129
  Art 25 ... 133
Council Regulation (EC) No 1383/2003 of 22 July 2003 concerns customs action against goods suspected of infringing certain IPR and the measures to be taken against goods found to have infringed such rights (Customs Regulation) ... 198

Treaties and Conventions
Agreement on Trade-Related Aspects of Intellectual Property Rights (TRIPS Agreement) 1993 ... 7, 79, 107
Berne Convention for the Protection of Literary and Artistic Works 1886 ... 6, 106
European Patent Convention (EPC) 1973 (Convention on the Grant of European Patents) of 5 October 1973 ... 52, 59
  Art 52(3) ... 57
  Art 52(4) ... 57
  Art 54 ... 55
  Art 56 ... 56
  Art 57 ... 57
  Arts 60–61 ... 68
European Patent Convention (EPC) 2000 (Convention on the Grant of European Patents) of 29 November 2000 ... 7
Hague Agreement Concerning the International Registration of Industrial Designs 1925 ... 8, 139
Paris Convention for the Protection of Industrial Property 1883 ... 7, 130, 139
Rome Convention for the Protection of Performers, Producers of Phonograms and Broadcasting Organisations 1961 ... 107
Treaty of Rome 1958 ... 25

Chapter 1

Introduction to Intellectual Property Rights

Intellectual property rights (IPR) are of vital importance in all forms of business and commerce, industry and manufacturing, creativity and the arts, pure and applied science and engineering, and marketing and advertising. In many cases, intellectual property (IP) is one of an organisation's most important assets. In some cases, it is the most important asset and the organisation would soon go out of business without its IPR. The music and film industries would not exist in anything like their present form without IPR. Why go to all the trouble and vast expense of making a film if anyone can copy it and distribute the copies, perhaps using the internet to do so?

Without patent protection pharmaceutical companies would not invest enormous sums of money in their pursuit of new pharmaceutical products. Without protection for trade marks, counterfeiters would have a field day and consumers would lose the ability to tell a genuine product from a fake. We could end up driving around in our cars on substandard counterfeit tyres. Without IPR, the creative arts and innovation would be stifled. Given the importance of IPR, it is essential that we all know something about them and acquire and use them to protect our creativity, innovation and business name and reputation. The purpose of this book is, therefore, to give the reader some understanding about these rights and how they are acquired and maintained, how they may be exploited and their nature and limitations.

This introductory chapter gives an overview of IPR and explains their basic nature and differences between them. This sets the scene for the other chapters in this book. By the end of this chapter, you should be able to answer the following questions.

What are intellectual property rights?
What sort of things are protected by each intellectual property right?
How are intellectual property rights classified?
What is the scope of each intellectual property right?
Do I have to register my intellectual property rights?
Can a given thing be protected by more than one intellectual property right?
How long do intellectual property rights exist for?
How do I get protection in other countries?
How do I grant rights to others to use my intellectual property?
How can I sell my intellectual property rights or acquire someone else's intellectual property rights?
What are the pitfalls of disregarding intellectual property rights?

The purpose of this book is to give readers an understanding of IPR so that they will be able to manage them more effectively and gain maximum economic benefit from them. Only with a reasonable understanding can one hope to manage IP successfully and proactively so as to maximise its value; to know how to identify it, acquire it, transfer ownership of it or license it; and to be able to assess the value of an IP portfolio.

What are intellectual property rights and what do they protect?

The term 'intellectual property' covers a number of rights, some of which are quite different in their nature and scope to others, that protect creativity, innovation and business reputation.

Generally, they are treated just as other property rights and can be transferred to another person, and rights to others to use the protected subject matter can be granted. They can even be mortgaged and used as security for a loan.

Before proceeding further, it is worth briefly describing each of the IPR. The main ones for the purposes of this book are as follows.

- Registered trade marks – the names, logos and other identifiers of trading undertakings are protected by registering them as trade marks, which prevents others using signs that are identical to or similar to the registered marks. Examples of well-known registered trade marks are Pentium®, KODAK, Routledge, Coca-Cola® (the ® denotes that the mark is registered); in many cases, trade marks consist of words, sometimes in stylised form, and/or images.
- The law of passing off protects business goodwill that has been built up in relation to a trading name or 'get-up'. This gives an informal form of protection that overlaps with trade mark law, but the protection can be weaker although it can have more extensive scope. Older examples include the shape of the Jif lemon and the words Advocaat and champagne (this is now a protected designation that can only be used by producers in the Champagne region of France).
- The law of confidence protects secret information such as trade secrets; these can vary from secret industrial processes to relatively mundane information about customers and clients.
- Patent law protects inventions for products or processes that are new, involve an inventive step and have industrial application. The range of inventions protected by patents is quite breathtaking, from mechanical inventions (see the Dyson Technology patent for an upright vacuum cleaner patent No GB 2495125) to leading-edge biotechnological inventions (see the US patent No US 8,329,170 B2, belonging to Janssen Biotech Inc.).[1]
- Copyright protects creative and derivative works such as literary and artistic works, music, films and broadcasts; the sorts of thing protected by these rights are undoubtedly the most familiar to us.
- There are other rights described as rights related to copyright such as a special form of protection for databases (some of which may be protected by copyright) and rights in performances. Databases may be computer databases or a manual database such as a card index; rights in performances are given to persons making a live performance (for example, singers or stand-up comedians) and to recording companies that have exclusive licences with them.
- Designs are protected by registration and/or by unregistered design rights. These rights protect new shapes applied to articles, graphic designs, ornamentation and such like, which may be applied to a vast range of articles from toys to furniture to motor vehicles to household goods to computers and mobile phones. Almost every form of technology and craftwork can be protected, providing they are unlike existing designs or are not commonplace.

---

1 Patent specifications are available through the UK Intellectual Property Office using the Espacenet patent search system.

There are other forms of protection, such as for plant varieties and a special extended form of patent protection for medicinal products, but these very specialised rights are not discussed further in this book.

How are intellectual property rights classified?

IPR are a mixed bunch and some are completely unlike others. Therefore, classifying these rights is not easy. Some distinctions may be made to separate some of the rights from others. For example, some of the rights are only available after registration, whereas other rights come into being automatically, once the subject matter has come into existence. Table A sets them out on this basis.

A number of points may be made.

- For the registered rights, the process to obtain registration can be quite different. For example, patents are granted only after an extensive search and examination process. As they are the most powerful form of IP, giving strong monopoly rights, patents are reserved for those inventions conforming to very strict rules as to novelty and inventive step. In contrast, most trade marks and designs will be accepted for registration, providing the basic requirements are satisfied, only if they are not opposed by others having similar marks or designs.
- Registered rights are normally monopolistic in nature. The justification for this is that the registrations are held in publicly available registers that can be consulted by the public or potential competitors.
- The rights not subject to registration, 'informal rights' or 'soft IP', normally require proof of copying to show infringement of the right. Thus, it is permissible to create a work of copyright, such as a photograph, that looks very similar to an existing work, providing it has not been copied from that work but has been created independently.
- Some of the informal rights last much longer than others: for example, most works of copyright are protected for the life of the author of the work plus 70 years. The maximum duration of a patent is usually 20 years only.

The scope of intellectual property rights

IPR work by giving their owners certain specific things that they can do in relation to the protected matter to the exclusion of everyone else.

Table A

Rights which must be registered (often referred to as 'hard IP')	Rights which come into being automatically (often referred to as 'soft IP')
Trade marks	Goodwill protected by the law of passing off
Patents	Information protected by the law of breach of confidence
Registered designs	Copyright
	Database protection
	Rights in performances
	Unregistered designs

For example, the owner of a registered trade mark is given the right to use that trade mark for goods or services specified in the registration. He can prevent anyone else using an identical sign for the same goods or services or using an identical or similar sign for identical or similar goods or services if this causes confusion among consumers as to the origin of the goods or services concerned.

The owner of a patent for an invention can prevent someone else making, importing, selling, etc., a patented product where the patent is for a product or using a patented process.

The owner of the copyright in a literary work can prevent anyone copying the work, making it available or communicating it to the public, performing it in public, broadcasting it or making an adaptation of it.

These are just some examples showing the scope of the rights. However, the rights are not absolute. The rights will only be infringed if the act complained of falls within the scope of the right *and is not otherwise permitted*. For example, it is not an infringement of a trade mark to honestly use one's own name. It is not an infringement of a patent to carry out a repair on a patented product such as where a bearing in a patented motor has worn out. There are many 'permitted acts' under copyright law. These are acts that may be carried out without the permission of the owner that do not infringe copyright. One example is making an accessible copy of a literary work for a blind person, such as a Braille version. Another is making use of a work for criticism or review or for the purpose of reporting current events.

Apart from such acts that do not infringe, there are numerous defences to infringement actions. For example, it is a defence to a copyright action to show that the amount copied was not a substantial part of the work in question.

Other areas of law may also limit the scope of IPR, such as competition law. For example, if a person buys up all the patents covering a particular technology in order to prevent competition and drive up prices, he may be fined heavily under EU law. If a patent is not being worked sufficiently to meet demand, third parties may apply for compulsory licences under the patent.

These controls are not solely the domain of monopoly rights and may apply to informal rights such as copyright: for example, in the case of the Microsoft corporation bundling its own internet software with its computer operating system software.

Must intellectual property rights be registered?

The short answer is 'no'.

The informal rights ('soft IP') cannot be registered at national registration offices. That does not stop the owner depositing copies with third parties who can provide evidence of the existence and form of a work at a certain date. This can prove useful in an infringement action where the defendant claims his work pre-dated that of the claimant.

The right that can be registered may be protected in other ways. Instead of applying for a patent, it may be possible to keep the invention secret: for example, by imposing an obligation of confidence on each and every person, including employees, who has access to the invention.

Rather than registering a trade mark, it is possible to rely on the law of passing off. However, that is less desirable as it will be necessary to show that goodwill has been established in the name or logo or whatever, that the defendant has made a relevant misrepresentation and that damage to the goodwill has been or will be caused.

Instead of registering a design, one could rely on unregistered design protection. This only gives a right against copying rather than a monopoly right and only lasts for three years as opposed to a maximum of 25 years if registered. (The UK's unregistered design right is anomalous and can give up to 15 years' protection but applies to a narrower range of designs.)

Taking all of this into account, and as will be shown in the subsequent chapters, if you can register an IP right, then do so. Apart from the obvious desideratum of maximising the scope of protection, it will make it easier and more profitable to deal with the rights as a commodity in the future. A registered right is easier to value than an unregistered right where registration is possible. The only question then becomes one of deciding on the territorial scope of protection that you desire.

I have created/invented a new 'thingamajig'. Can it be protected by more than one intellectual property right?

Take an invention for a new product. It may be patented if it involves an inventive step and has industrial application. Drawings and written specifications and details will be protected by copyright. Patent specifications are published, usually 18 months after the date of the application. Until then it is vital that the details of the patent are kept secret, and the law of confidence protects the invention. But as well as seeking patent protection, it may be possible to register the product or some elements of it as designs. Furthermore, when copies of the product are sold commercially, they may be sold under a trade mark. This may be a company generic trade mark or one applied for specifically for that product.

Say I have an idea for a new dramatic play. At that stage, the idea may be protected by the law of confidence. When I get round to writing the play, it become a work of copyright and is protected accordingly. If the play is performed live, the performers and any recording company having an exclusive recording contract will also accrue rights in that performance. If the play is eventually made into a blockbuster movie, it will be protected as a film.

If an established retailer has registered its name as a trade mark, it has also probably built up a goodwill protected by the law of confidence.

This shows that IPR do not stand in splendid isolation from each other. A number of rights may apply in relation to a particular 'thing' and some or all of these may co-exist or exist for a period of time before being replaced by other IPR.

How long do intellectual property rights exist for?

The duration of the various IPR can be seen as a reflection of the cultural dominance of art over science in the recent history of the modern world, particularly in the UK. It was not always so. The Victorian era saw a massive growth of and admiration for industry at a time when the UK ruled a large part of the world. But towards the end of that time and subsequently, the creative arts have enjoyed much longer protection than industrial inventions and designs. But this is balanced by the fact that the latter usually give monopoly rights.

Most IPR, in their modern form, originated in and developed in the UK. Towards the end of the nineteenth century there were significant international conventions that now shape much of our modern system of IP laws. Thus, the duration of rights in the UK is much the same as in most other countries, especially within the EU. Even then, there is much similarity with the rest of the world.

Table B gives a guide as to the duration of the IPR described in this book.

Trade mark registrations can be renewed every five years without upper limit providing the mark is still used. The UK's first registered trade mark, the Bass Red Triangle Mark, is still registered today.[2]

---

[2] To see the trade mark, now owned by Brandbrew SA, go to the UK Intellectual Property Office website at www.ipo.gov.uk and carry out a trade mark search by number for UK00000000001.

Table B

Right	Duration	Comments
Trade mark	Indefinite	Subject to renewal every 5 years and must be used as can be revoked for non-use
Passing off	Unlimited	Providing goodwill has been built up and continues to exist
Confidence	No limit	Providing the confidential nature of the information can be maintained
Patents	20 years	Initial registration for 4 years then renewed annually for up to 20 years
Copyright (including copyright databases)	Up to life plus 70 years	Some works have a lesser duration, such as sound recordings, broadcasts and typographical arrangements
Database right	15 years	If published before the end of that period, the 15 years runs from the end of the year of publication
Rights in performances	Generally 50 years	
Registered designs	25 years	Initially 5 years renewable in 5-year periods up to a maximum of 25 years
Unregistered Community design	3 years	
UK unregistered design	15 years	Reduced to 10 years from end of year of commercial use if started in first 5 years

How do I get protection in other countries?

It is important to understand that IPR are territorial. As a general rule, they only apply in the country in which they were created, first published or registered.

Copyright

There are some exceptions to the general rule. The major exception is that a work of copyright can qualify for protection by virtue of the nationality of the author or the country in which the work is first published. Thus, a work created by a British citizen will have UK copyright no matter where he or she was at the time the work was created. As far as qualifying for protection by publication is concerned, there is a rule that simultaneous publication in a number of countries will attract copyright protection in each of those countries. There is a 30-day period in which publication in another country will be regarded as simultaneous publication.

In any case, territorial limitations are of no real consequence for copyright works because of the Berne Convention for the Protection of Literary and Artistic Works 1883. By this convention, each of the convention countries must give equal treatment to citizens of the other convention countries as they do their own nationals. At present there are 166 convention countries.

However, in other cases, the territorial limit applies, subject to what is said below.

Trade marks

A UK registered trade mark is protected in the UK alone. If protection is required in other countries, application can be made to those countries individually or collectively through the Madrid System, which is administered by the World Intellectual Property Organization (WIPO), normally by applying through a national trade mark office, such as the UK Intellectual Property Office (UK IPO).

The European Union also has a Community trade mark that applies throughout the Member States of the EU. This is a single registration and is obtained by application to the Office of Harmonization for the Internal Market (Trade Marks and Designs) (OHIM), which is situated in Alicante.

Passing off

It is fairly self-evident that this form of protection only applies in the country where the goodwill exists. However, goodwill can exceptionally exist in more than one country. For example, the then English owners of the famous Parisian restaurant, Maxim's, were able to prevent the use of that name for a restaurant in Norfolk.[3] Although Maxim's did not trade in the UK, its reputation, and hence goodwill, extended to the UK.[4]

Not every country has a law of passing off. The action tends to be limited to some of the countries that are members of the British Commonwealth. Other countries may use other forms of protection such as a law against unfair competition.

Confidence

This is clearly territorial inasmuch as the country concerned recognises the confidentiality of the information in question. The nationality of the person who seeks to bring an action for breach of confidence is not an issue.

Patents

Each country has its own patent system. Basic patent law tends to be similar in most countries because of international conventions that set out fundamental principles. These are the Paris Convention for the Protection of Industrial Property 1883 and the Agreement on Trade-Related Aspects of Intellectual Property 1993. However, some significant differences exist. For example, the USA bases entitlement to a patent on the basis of the person who is the first to invent, whereas almost every other country uses the test of the first to file the application for a patent.[5]

Patent law throughout Europe is very similar, especially as regards the requirements for patentability and the scope of protection because of the European Patent Convention (EPC). All EU Member States belong, plus a number of other countries, including Albania, Iceland, Norway and Turkey. Currently there are 38 contracting states.

The way the EPC works is that a single application can be made, electing for protection in three of more of the contracting states. The European Patent Office (EPO) is responsible for the grant of the patents and dealing with opposition to grant. However, once granted, the patents devolve to each of the contracting states named in the application. For example, if you apply through the EPO for patents for the UK, France, Italy and Ireland, when granted you will have a UK patent, a French patent, an Italian patent and an Irish patent. Each will have effect in each of

---
3 *Maxim's Ltd v Dye* [1977] 1 WLR 1155.
4 Subsequently, Maxim's opened restaurants in other countries, including the UK.
5 The USA is considering changing to a first to file approach.

those respective territories only. If someone makes the patented product or uses the patented process in Germany, there is nothing you can do about it except prevent the import of those products into the UK, France, Italy or Ireland.

As yet there is no Community patent system, although we are moving closer to this very desirable goal. Such a patent would have effect throughout Europe. It would be a single patent with cross-border effectiveness. This would be far easier to enforce than a bundle of national patents. For example, if our UK, French, Italian and Irish patents, all for the same invention, were infringed in each of those countries, four parallel sets of legal proceedings would have to take place, even if it was the same person infringing those patents. The only time this would not be the case is if the infringer did not challenge the validity of those patents. This is quite rare as the best form of defence in a patent infringement action is usually to attack the validity of the patent. If it is found to be invalid wholly, that would provide a complete defence as well as wrecking the patent.

Designs

As with trade marks, there is an EU-wide design. Registration as a Community design gives five years' protection, renewable in five-year-periods up to a maximum of 25 years. Application is made to OHIM. However, if a design is not registered, if it complies with the basic requirements it will have protection as an unregistered Community design. This lasts for three years only.

Protection in other countries can be achieved by application to those countries (normally through the UK IPO).

There is a unified system of registering designs in several different countries under the Hague Agreement 1925. Presently there are 60 countries party to the agreement.

How do I grant rights to others to use my intellectual property?

IP is just like any other form of property. The owner can sell it (see below) or grant rights to others to use the subject matter. For example, the owner of the copyright in a work of literature can grant the right to publish copies of the work in return for royalty payments or a fee. The owner of a patent, known as the proprietor, can grant a third party the right to make and sell products made to the invention, if it is a patent for a product.

The most common form used is a licence agreement. Some licences are exclusive licences, which means that the person granted the licence, the licensee, has the right to carry out the licensed rights to the exclusion of everyone else, including the owner of the right.

A non-exclusive licence is appropriate where the owner of the right, the licensor, intends to grant equivalent rights to others and/or carry out the relevant acts himself. This is common in the case of popular software packages and apps.

Licence agreements are complex documents and have to fully cover all aspects of the licensed activities, but also have to include details about other rights such as royalties and payments, indemnities and warranties, responsibilities to notify and take appropriate action in cases of alleged infringements of the rights, termination, etc. Account must be taken of legal controls on licence agreements, such as those relating to competition law, for example, where the agreement is overly restrictive or requires the licensee to purchase raw materials needed from the licensor.

Where the licence is exclusive, it is required to be in writing and signed by the owner to take effect at law. For some forms of IP, especially patents, the fact of the licence must be registered. Failure to do so may result in a court refusing to award costs to the owner or licensee if the right is found to infringe.

A golden rule in granting rights under a licence (the same applies where the ownership of an IP right is being transferred) is never grant more than is required for the purposes of the licence. For example, if the owner of a musical work grants a licence to a band to play the music live on stage and make recordings on disk for sale, he should grant those rights only, retaining the rest of the copyright. For example, he may want to sell copies of the sheet music or allow another band to make an arrangement of the music and play it for an online broadcast.

Licences, as with transfers of IPR, may be partial and can be limited to specific acts, territories or in time. Thus a licence can be granted to perform a work in public in Scotland only for a period of two years.

The advice of a lawyer experienced in drafting IP licences is vital.

How can I sell my intellectual property rights or acquire someone else's intellectual property rights?

If I pay a fortune to buy an oil painting by a famous artist, that does not automatically mean that I will own the copyright in the painting. Of course, I can hang the painting in my living room, show it to friends and enjoy it. But I cannot take a photograph of it and sell copies of the photograph, or even put a photograph of it on my website, without the artist's permission. If I wanted to go beyond simple enjoyment of the painting, I should have obtained a transfer of ownership of the copyright.

It might have been sufficient if I had been given a receipt signed by the artist that carried a form of words indicating that all the rights in the painting were being transferred to me.

A transfer of ownership of IP is called an assignment. As with exclusive licences, these are required to be in writing and signed by the previous owner. Again, with registered rights, the assignment must be registered.

Again, as with licensing, an assignment may be partial and cover some of the rights only or be limited in time or territory. For example, with a product patented in the UK and France the licence may grant rights to make and sell the product in France for a period of five years. At the end of that period, the rights assigned will revert back to the original owner.

What are the pitfalls of disregarding intellectual property rights?

Failure to properly understand IPR and to manage them appropriately may have dire consequences.

A very common mistake is to fail to obtain an assignment of a copyright in a work created by a self-employed consultant or other third party. You may have paid for the work of creation as if you would own all the rights in it but unless you ensure there is a valid assignment of the rights in place, you will run into difficulties. The person creating the work may decide to exploit it himself or a third party may be infringing the copyright in the work. This could mean an expensive court case is required to resolve the situation, which may not necessarily be resolved in your favour. It may be that the court only orders that you be granted a licence rather than an assignment of the copyright.

Failure to protect your confidential information – for example, by ensuring employees and others having access to the information know about the confidential nature of the information and are under a duty not to disclose it or use it for their own benefit – will soon mean the information gets out into the public domain and all protection will be lost.

Failure to register a patent may mean that someone else applies to patent the technology. Although if you were already using it or had made serious and effective preparations to do so previously, you will be allowed to use the technology. However, had you patented it you could have exploited it by granting licences under the patent or by assigning it to a third party. Of course, you could also have used the patent to bring legal proceedings to enforce it. The infringer would be stopped and you would receive financial compensation, even if the infringer was not aware of your patent.

If you have a new design and don't register it, you would have to prove that an infringer copied your design, whereas had you registered it, you would have monopoly protection in the relevant territory or territories. You would also have the advantage of longer potential protection.

If you have built up goodwill in a name or logo and you haven't registered it as a trade mark, if you bring a legal action against someone using it without your permission, you would have to prove the existence of goodwill in the name or logo as well as damage to that goodwill. If someone uses a registered trade mark for the same goods, he will be found to infringe without further proof. In other cases, all that is needed is evidence that consumers are likely to be deceived or that one of the essential functions of the trade mark will be harmed by the defendant's activities.

Without knowing about IP you will not even know what you have or what you could acquire by taking appropriate steps such as registration.

Without knowing how to manage IP you will not achieve the greatest economic benefit from it.

Without knowing how to value IP you will not know how much yours is worth, how much can be obtained from it by licensing or by assignment. You will not know how much someone else's IP is worth if you are thinking of taking rights in or under it. If you are acquiring an existing business, you will not know how much it is worth overall if you are not able to value the IPR owned by the business or licensed by it.

If you do not manage your IP effectively, you might forget to renew any registrations, which could mean that you lose them.

If you do not have a reasonable grasp of IP, you might commit criminal offences by dealing with counterfeit articles even if you do not have actual knowledge of their status. You may commit offences under patent law if you ignore the secrecy provisions or submit an application to a foreign country before the UK patent office has seen the specification for the invention.

Summary

Intellectual property rights protect all manner of things, from original literary and artistic works and new, industrially applicable inventions to trading names and logos.

There are several forms of IPR. Some are very different from others. Some come into being automatically, such as copyright, while others must be acquired through formal applications for registration, such as patents and registered designs.

Some IPR, particularly those subject to registration, provide the owner with a monopoly in the subject matter of the right, such as in the case of a patent. Other rights require that the defendant has made some use of the protected work, such as by making copies of a photograph.

Some things can be protected by more than one IP right. For example, drawings of a new product will be protected by copyright, the product itself may be patented and the shape or appearance protected by registered and unregistered design rights and a trade mark may be applied to copies of the product made for sale. Before the product is patented, it is essential that details of it are kept confidential, otherwise the product's novelty could be prejudiced.

Registered IPR are relatively limited in their duration compared with the informal rights. Thus, a patent can only be renewed up to 20 years maximum, whereas a literary, artistic or musical work can be protected by copyright until 70 years after the death of the creator.

Unless you are happy to restrict your activities to the UK, it is important to gain protection in other countries. Even if your activity is limited to one country, it may be worthwhile getting protection in other countries so that you can assign or license those rights to others.

Management tips

Senior managers must ensure that they have a good awareness of IPR and arrange for more junior managers and other key employees to have appropriate training in IP.

When commissioning the creation of a work, design, invention or logo, make sure that you or your organisation has provided for ownership of the associated IPR.

Make sure that employees' contracts of employment impose obligations of confidentiality in relation to the employer's trade secrets. Also, if dealing with customers, suppliers, distributors and the like, make sure they are under a duty of confidence where they will be given access to confidential information.

Seek the advice of professionals such as lawyers and patent agents at appropriate times, such as when granting licences or assigning or acquiring IPR. Similarly, if you think you have something that may be protected by registration, check with your advisers to see if this is possible, and if so, what steps should be taken. For example, if you have made an invention which may be patentable, it is vital that you do not publish information about it before an application for a patent is submitted.

Organisations should identify key individuals responsible for liaising with professional advisers in relation to the organisation's IPR.

Carry out regular IP audits and understand how to value intellectual property.

Exercise

Look around your workplace and home and consider how many things are protected or could be protected by IPR and which rights might apply to which sort of object or subject matter.

If you are an employee, does your contract of employment mention a duty of confidentiality?

Look for products that carry the term 'patent' or 'pat applied for' or 'pat pending'.

How many articles can you find with the symbol ® after the name of the article or maker? Can you find any with the sign ™? What is the distinction between them?

What is the usual form of sign denoting copyright?

How much do you think the IP belonging to Dyson Technology Ltd is worth? What would happen to the company if it lost all its IPR?

Chapter 2

Business Goodwill and Reputation

In this chapter we will explore the nature, acquisition and scope of trade marks and the tort of passing off. By the end of the chapter you should be able to answer the following questions.

- What are trade marks?
- What are the forms of trade mark protection?
- What are the requirements for trade mark protection?
- For how long do trade marks last?
- Someone else is using a mark the same or confusingly similar to mine – can I do anything about it?
- How do I get trade mark protection outside the UK?
- What is passing off?
- What are the requirements for protection under the tort of passing off?
- What are some problems with domain names?

Trade marks in context

Marks or brands have been used to distinguish one trader's goods from those of others for hundreds of years. Branding allows both businesses and consumers to know who manufactured or supplied goods and can also help to establish and protect business goodwill and reputation.

If you take a trip into the countryside you will see that branding is commonly found on animals. Branding allows people to identify which farmer owns which cow or sheep when they have strayed. The distinguishing function of trade marks was initially to inform those working in the distribution network. Before the advent of container shipping, if bales of cotton were being shipped by sea from foreign lands they would pass through numerous ports in various countries before reaching their final destination. It was important that when goods were stored in the hold along with similar goods of other traders, they could be distinguished. Rarely would workers at these ports to be able to read in their native language let alone a foreign tongue, so it became common practice for logos, simple pictures or distinctive marks to be branded or printed onto products so that each trader's goods could be easily identified. With the growth of industrialisation in the nineteenth century there was an influx of cheap, shoddy goods into the UK. These imported goods often used the logos of existing, higher-quality British goods in an attempt to trick retailers and consumers into buying inferior-quality or even dangerous products. To counter this the first Trade Marks Registration Act was introduced in 1875, which established formal registration of these marks or logos. The oldest registered trade mark in the UK is the Bass Red Triangle Mark, which was first registered in 1876. Once registered, a trade mark can prevent other traders using confusingly similar marks on similar goods. A registered mark allows suppliers to build up a reputation for quality (or not, as the case may be) and also gives consumers confidence that they are buying genuine goods from a particular source. Over the years various health and safety regulations improved the quality and safety of goods available to the consumer. This reduced the consumer protection role of trade marks but a new function was to take its place. Supermarkets arrived in the 1960s. Rather than being served by a shopkeeper from behind a counter, goods were now laid out before consumers who could choose which of various competing products they wanted to buy. If a mark was both memorable and attractive consumers would be encourage to buy and then re-buy the goods of one trader rather than those of a competitor. Today, trade marks have become a marketing tool to attract customers. Companies now spend a great deal of money advertising and promoting an image to create a brand. Due to extensive advertising, a highly branded product such as an Apple computer commands a premium over similar, non-branded products. A person's status is increasingly measured by the brands they purchase. Hopes, aspirations, a lifestyle are purchased with the brand.

A brand is not the same thing as a trade mark. A trade mark identifies the origin of goods or services, while a brand captures the image, social values and emotional attachment associated with the mark. Consumers are loyal to brands and their value can be increased if transferred to new products and markets via licensing agreements. Calvin Klein was originally a clothes designer but the brand has expanded into numerous additional markets including, among others, fragrances, sunglasses and household furnishings. In developing a brand the trader, say Cadbury the chocolate manufacturer, as part of their marketing strategy supplies information about their goods or services along with the values and integrity of the business. They will advertise the core trade mark Cadbury and any other trade marks of goods such as Picnic, Twirl or Crunchie that are sold under the Cadbury brand. In order to create the desired brand image they will carefully consider the company name and any trade name (a trade name, such as Roses, does not need to be the same as the company name Cadbury), domain names, the packaging and shelf displays of the goods and how and where the goods are to be advertised. All of these aspects of the brand may be protected by passing off (see later). Today a company's brand can be one of the most valuable assets it owns. The Coca-Cola brand in 2012 was worth nearly US$78 billion.[1]

According to research carried out by the British Brands Group, one million people are employed in the UK creating and building brands. It is also estimated that £33 billion a year is invested in creating brand recognition, which contributes £16 billion to the UK economy (12 per cent of all intangible investment). A 2011 report suggested that firms using trade marks are 21 per cent more productive than those that do not.[2] Such firms also employ more people on higher wages, they are more innovative and that innovation leads to lower prices and a greater variety of products of better quality to the benefit of consumers.

But a brand is a delicate thing that needs to be nurtured or it will die. The 168-year-old popular British newspaper the *News of the World* had a very strong brand and a readership of over five million people. In July 2011 it was discovered that employees had hacked into the mobile phone of a 13-year-old murdered teenager. Within hours of the news of the hacking being made public millions of pounds worth of advertising had been cancelled and within a few days the paper was closed down. It was felt that the brand could not regain the trust of either its readership or its advertisers.

The aim in registering a trade mark is to acquire a monopoly right in that mark but it only gives protection in the class or classes of goods or services for which it is registered. Under the NICE classification system there are 45 classes of goods and services. The name Lloyds is used in various classes of good or services: a pharmacy chain, a bank and an insurance market, but only

---

1 www.interbrand.com/en/best-global-brands/2012/Best-Global-Brands-2012.aspx.
2 Trade Mark Incentives: www.ipo.gov.uk/ipresearch-tmincentives-full-201107.pdf.

one bank, one pharmacy chain, etc. can register the mark Lloyds. Once registered the trade mark can last indefinitely but a renewal fee must be paid every ten years.

You may want people to recognise what your product is on seeing or hearing your trade mark. Be careful, however, as you will not be able to register a mark if it is too descriptive of your goods. A good mark will stand out as being different from other existing marks but at the same time it will be easy to recognise, remember and pronounce. Not an easy task! It is sensible to use the same name in all the countries in which you intend to market your product but check the meaning of the name in different languages before you commit yourself. For example, Chevrolet named one of its cars Nova. This seemed like a good name in the English-speaking market but in Spain 'no va' means 'it won't go', an unfortunate name to choose for a car.

What are the requirements for protection?

A trade mark must be described in the *Trade Marks Journal*. You may use words or pictures but it must be clear enough for everyone to understand what your trade mark is so that they can avoid infringing it.

A trade mark must be a sign.[3] The sign may consist of words, including names such as Cadbury for confectionary, letters such as BT for telecommunications, numerals such as 501 used for jeans or a combination such as 3iii. You may register logos, colours, moving images, holograms, slogans such as *Vorsprung durch Technik*, shapes such as the Coca-Cola bottle, sounds such as the Microsoft boot-up sound or jingles. Most trade marks combine words with a logo.

Smells and sounds

A trade mark can be made up of sounds and smells but it is almost impossible to register a smell as a trade mark, so although in theory it is possible, in practice it is not. This is because a registered trade mark will stop all other traders using the same or a confusingly similar mark in their business for the same or similar goods. To be registered, a smell would have to be described clearly and accurately in the *Trade Marks Journal*. But each person perceives and describes smells differently – just think of the language of a wine taster! What is a 'generous full-bodied' wine to one person might be 'big and chocolaty' to another, but do they taste the same? It is impossible to be clear enough in depicting a smell to prevent confusion. In addition, although they can be registered there are problems associated with shape, sound or colour marks. Problems arise because, as well as being a sign, a trade mark must be capable of graphical representation.[4] This just means that they have to be capable of being recorded or described on paper.

You can use drawings or a photograph backed up with a written description where necessary. If you want to register a gesture such as tapping the side of your nose you would need to include a series of drawings showing clearly the movement involved. Everyone can inspect the *Trade Marks Journal* so that they can clearly see what marks are registered and ensure that they do not infringe the marks of others. People are wise to check the journal before they go to the expense of deciding on a name, colour or logo for their product to make sure that others have not already registered a mark that is the same or confusingly similar to theirs. If a description of the mark in words or pictures or other type of clear description cannot be entered into the journal it will not be possible to register it.

There was one case where a trader wished to register a community trade mark for the sound of a cockerel crowing. They used onomatopoeia, the imitation of the sound associated with the crowing cock. It was rejected, however, as it was not clear what the sound intended to be the trade mark was.[5] The onomatopoeic sound for a cock crowing is different in different languages.

---

3 Section 1 of the Trade Marks Act 1994.
4 Section 1 of the Trade Marks Act 1994 (TMA 1994).
5 *Shield Mark BV v Joost Kist* [2004] RPC 315 ECJ.

In English, the usual representation of a cock crow is 'cock-a-doodle-doo', but in Dutch it is 'kukelekuuuuu', while French cocks call 'cocorico'. Where did this cockerel come from? To be registered you cannot assume any prior knowledge on behalf of the person reading the journal; the description must stand on its own.[6] If you want the sound of a dog barking you must be clear whether it is a happy or an angry dog. Is it a big dog or a little dog; is the bark loud or soft?

The description must be clear and precise. If you want to register a piece of music or sound you may use musical notation, but if the instruments to be used are important and a necessary part of the mark this should made clear. Merely stating the title of the piece is not sufficient, even if it is a very well-known piece. Remember, a trade mark may last indefinitely; just because most people recognise a piece of music today does not mean that they will do so in 50 years' time.

Colours

The problem with colours is that merely using a description such as 'orange' is not accurate enough to be registered. Is it a yellowy orange or a reddy orange, dark or light? Providing a sample is not sufficient as colour samples may fade over time. It is, however, acceptable to describe the colour you want to register with reference to the number in an internationally recognised colour identification system[7] such as Pantone®, Focoltone® or Toyo®. BP, the petroleum company, for example, has registered green as a UK trade mark to be used on petrol stations.

Slogans

Slogans can be catchy and memorable and can make good trade marks. But the trade mark must not be merely descriptive. It must be capable of distinguishing your goods from those of other traders dealing in the same goods or services. There are three main types of registrable slogans. Fanciful, such as 'CATCH A WRINKLE IN TIME' for cosmetics in Class 3; impenetrable 'TAKING CARE OF CONTROL' for a business consultancy in Class 35; or an unusual combination of words such as 'OPEN POUR ENJOY LIFE ONCE MORE', in Class 30 for foodstuffs. You will not, however, be allowed to register 'NEVER CLEAN YOUR SHOWER AGAIN' in Class 21 for household cleaning materials because the slogan merely describes in plain language the intended purpose of the goods.

Items that absolutely cannot be registered

The purpose of a trade mark is to distinguish the goods or services of one trader from those of other traders; hence it must be able to do its job and distinguish.[8] This means that very common images, words or mis-spellings such as 'xtra' instead of 'extra' cannot be registered as they will not allow consumers to differentiate your goods from those of another. When choosing a trade mark businesses may want people to identify from the name, such as SOAPY for soap, what the product is, but this is descriptive not distinctive. A fruit and vegetable seller, unlike a telecommunications corporation, would not be allowed to register the word 'Orange' as that is descriptive of the goods they sell. The most distinctive trade marks like Kodak, Google or Intel stand out from others because they are made-up names.

In an attempt to overcome the problem of immediate recognition versus distinctiveness people often combine two words to create a new word (which is called a 'portmanteau' word). You would imagine that such a word would pass the distinctiveness test, but you have to be careful if you combine two descriptive words as the result may still be too descriptive to be registered. It is a fine line, however, and sometimes it is difficult to know which side you are likely to

---

6 *Libertel Groep BV and Benelux-Merkenbureau* [2004] C-104/01 FSR 4.
7 *Sieckmann* [2002] C-273/00 ECR I-11737.
8 Section 3(1)(b) TMA 1994.

come down on. The words 'Euro' and 'lamb' were combined to make the word Eurolamb. As this was for a product that was indeed lamb that came from Europe, the fact that 'Eurolamb' was not in the dictionary did not prevent it from being too descriptive to register.[9]

In another case 'Baby' and 'Dry' were combined to make the mark BabyDry for disposable nappies. It does, it is true, describe the product's main attribute, keeping babies dry, but it was not wholly descriptive as BabyDry could have referred to all sorts of things, such as baby wellington boots or baby raincoats or any other similar baby product, so registration was allowed.[10] Remember, just because you have not registered your mark does not mean that you cannot use it in business. If you have been using a descriptive mark for some time you may be able to register it if you can show that people now recognise it as your trade mark – that it has become distinctive though use.

People sometimes want a trade mark that indicates that their goods are superior in some way to other similar goods, but this again poses a problem. It is felt that laudatory words, such as 'best' or 'treat', should not be registered and monopolised indefinitely by one undertaking,[11] but should be free for all traders to use to promote their own goods.

Names and geographical locations

It is a good idea to register your company name such as Virgin® as a trade mark as it can then be combined with other marks. Be aware, however, that registering your company name at Companies House or registering a domain name gives you no trade mark rights. Trade marks must be registered separately. Some problems arise with personal names and geographical locations. If Mr Smith, a baker from Birmingham, wishes to register trade marks for two new types of biscuit, one to be called Smith and the other Birmingham, he will not be allowed to do so. Although there is a presumption that you may register your own surname or the name of your company you may only do so if it is unlikely that other people would want to use that name for similar products. As Smith is such a common name in the UK and as Birmingham is the second-biggest city in the country, these names should be free for others called Smith from Birmingham to use. Do not waste time trying to register a name that will be refused.

To decide if a name is too common, consult the telephone directory; that is what the intellectual property office (IPO) will do. The product is also relevant. If Mr Smith made not biscuits but aircraft, then as few people make aeroplanes and it is unlikely that many people would want to use the name Smith, Mr Smith would probably succeed with his registration. In the same way if Mr Smith chose Arctic rather than Birmingham as a trade name for biscuits, because few bakers would want to use the name Arctic this would be allowed.[12] It is worth getting good marketing advice when seeking a new trade mark.

Shapes

It is possible to register a shape as a trade mark, the triangular shape of the Toblerone chocolate bar being a perfect example, but the shape must be distinctive.[13] Most shape marks are registered for the shape of bottles, such as the famous Coca-Cola bottle. It is, however, quite difficult to make bottles look distinctive. To be useful bottles must be able to stand on their own, which usually requires a flat bottom, and a spout seems unavoidable. Apart from the practical difficulty of making a shape distinctive there are some legal restrictions on what shapes may be registered.[14] You may not register three types of shapes even if they have become very well known and

---

9 Eurolamb Trade Mark [1997] RPC 279.
10 Procter & Gamble Co v OHIM [2002] RPC 17.
11 Section 3(1)(c) TMA 1994.
12 Windsurfing Chiemsee [1999] ECR 1–2779.
13 Section 3(2) TMA 1994.
14 Section 3(2) TMA 1994.

consumers recognise them as coming from you. First, you may not register a mark that consists exclusively of the shape that results from the nature of the goods themselves. This means that if you make chocolate Easter eggs you will not be able to register an egg shape as a trade mark. This is because it would be unfair to stop others using an egg shape for their Easter eggs. Second, you are not allowed to register the shape of a good that is necessary to obtain a technical result or a function.[15] Allowing such a shape to be registered would give the proprietor of the functional mark an indefinite monopoly over that technical function and this, as a matter of policy, is not allowed. Patent that last for up to 20 years and not trade marks that may last indefinitely are the appropriate protection for inventions (see Chapter 4). In the *Philips* case the company tried but failed to register the triangular image of their three-headed rotary shaver as a trade mark. If they had succeeded no other shaver company would have been able to manufacture a similar shaver without infringing even if they had a very different trade mark and name.

In the same way, registration for the shape of the Lego brick, the children's plastic toy, was not allowed.[16] Although distinctive, the shape of the brick was made by two rows of studs on the upper side of the brick. These studs are purely functional allowing the bricks to be joined together; consequently, if the shape was registered the trade mark would indefinitely prevent other traders marketing a brick that functioned in the same way. Finally, you are not allowed to register a shape that gives substantial value to the goods in question. Bang & Olufsen A/S have a reputation for producing visually attractive sound systems. They failed to register the shape of a speaker as a trade mark as the design[17] was held to be an important selling point that increased the value of the product.[18] If people are buying something for the shape rather than for the good itself the trade mark is not doing the job of differentiating one trader's goods from those of another and so is outside the scope of trade mark law. If consumers do not recognise a shape as a trade mark then it cannot be one.

Other things you are not allowed to register

You will also fail in an attempt to register a trade mark if the mark is contrary to public policy or to accepted principles of morality, or of such a nature as to deceive the public (for instance, as to the nature, quality or geographical origin of the goods or service). Registration will be denied if the trade mark conflicts with other laws such as passing off or anti-competition laws or if the application is made in bad faith.[19]

Morality

When morality is considered it must be remembered that what may have been immoral in one decade will not be regarded as immoral in another. Although even today it is doubtful whether COCAINE would be regarded as an acceptable trade mark for a soft drink, OPIUM has been registered by Yves Saint Laurent for a perfume. For the IPO to reject an application on the grounds of morality they must feel that the mark would be likely to cause public outrage generally and not just be offensive to a small section of the public, and that it will undermine social or religious values.

Deception

A mark will not be registered if it is deceptive. Using the trade mark Silver-Silk for a polyester shirt made neither of silver nor of silk would not be describing the goods, as they are made out of neither silk nor silver, but it would be deceptive.

---

15 Koninklijke Philips Electronics v Remington Consumer Products Ltd [2003] RPC 14 ECJ.
16 Lego Juris A/S v Office of Harmonization for the Internal Market (Trade Marks and Designs) (OHIM) [1020] ETMR 63.
17 Bang & Olufsen A/S v OHIM Case T-508/08.
18 It is suggested that passing off could be a remedy if the shape of the speaker was copied.
19 Section 3(3)–(6) TMA 1994.

Bad faith

Marks should not be registered if the application is made in bad faith. Various circumstances will give rise to an accusation of bad faith but all require some evidence of dishonesty or standards that fall short of acceptable commercial behaviour. Many traders would love to monopolise marks, registering them defensively so that competitors do not have access to them. If a mark is registered with no intention of using it in a particular class of goods this will be regarded as acting in bad faith. You will also be in bad faith if you register a mark knowing that it rightfully belongs to another trader. You may want to do this either to cash in on their reputation or to prevent them from registering the mark themselves.

By way of example, in one case Mr Ball had been the inspiration behind the eco garden attraction The Eden Project in Cornwall.[20] He had been a director of the company running the venture but had become disillusioned with the way the project was developing. Mr Ball registered the trade mark 'The Eden Project' under his own name. This registration was held to be in bad faith as it was the company, a separate legal entity,[21] that was entitled to register the mark, not a single director acting in his own right.

Specifically protected emblems

There are further marks that you will not be allowed to register.[22] These include state emblems, official signs and devices owned by various organisations. You may not register flags of countries or any devices associated with the Royal family. Also protected are such signs as the Red Cross or Red Crescent. In addition, Olympics symbols are out of bounds for anyone other than sponsors. The owner of Café Olympic, in London, for example, got into trouble in 2011 when he tried to use that name in the run-up to the London Olympic Games. In rare circumstances you may not be allowed to register the mark of a very well-known foreign mark for similar goods even if the mark has not been registered in the UK.

Other existing marks or the 'relative grounds for refusal'

Before seeking to register a trade mark you should check either for a Community Trade Mark (CTM)[23] or a national mark at the relevant website[24] to ensure that a similar sign has not already been registered for that type of good or service. The whole point of having a trade mark is to let consumers know the source of goods. Registration of the same or a similar mark for similar goods is not allowed if confusion as to source would arise in the minds of consumers.[25]

Registration gives notice of your mark or logo and should discourage other traders from using something confusingly similar. Registration will also allow you to oppose[26] any attempt by other traders to register identical or similar marks for identical or similar goods.

There are three issues to look at. Identical marks and identical goods; similar marks and similar goods; and marks with a reputation. Both the Directive and the Trade Marks Act state[27] that without the consent of the owner of the prior mark you may not register an identical mark for identical goods or services. Consumers need not be confused; you are just not to do it. Second, you may not register a similar mark for similar goods or services if the similarity would cause confusion in the minds of the consumers of the goods in question.[28] If you do discover that

---

20 Ball v Eden Project Ltd [2002] FSR 43.
21 Salomon v Salomon and Co Ltd [1897] AC 22 HL.
22 Section 4 TMA 1994.
23 http://research.oami.europa.eu/copla/index.
24 www.ipo.gov.uk/tm.htm.
25 Section 5 TMA 1994.
26 Section 38(2) TMA 1994.
27 Section 5(1) TMA 1994.
28 Section 5(2) TMA 1994.

someone is applying to register a similar mark for similar goods you can object by bringing opposition proceedings to prevent them from doing so. But that does pose the question: what are identical and similar marks?

Identical mark

To be identical does a mark have to be exactly the same? The answer is no, not in every respect. An identical mark is one where an average consumer, when thinking about the two marks (they are not expected to have the marks sitting side by side allowing them to make a detailed comparison), would not be *aware* of any differences in the marks.[29] Identical marks are those where any differences are so insignificant that consumers just would not notice them. It has been held that the average consumer would not notice the difference between Origin and Origins or Cannon and Canon;[30] they might not notice that websphere and web-sphere[31] were different but they are sure to notice that, although similar, Reed Elsevier and Reed Business Information are not identical marks.[32]

Similar mark

To decide if two word marks are similar you need to consider the initial impact on the average consumer of the look, sound and conceptual similarity of the words. But you must also take into consideration the goods to which the marks are applied. If an expensive purchase is being made the average consumer is unlikely to be confused into buying the wrong good despite a similarity in marks. They are unlikely to buy a Mitsubishi Cordia thinking that it was a Ford Cortina. If, however, a Penguin chocolate biscuit was sitting side by side with a Puffin chocolate biscuit at the checkout of a crowded supermarket, both packaged in a similar style, the average consumer would give the purchase little attention and may well be confused into buying the wrong chocolate biscuit.

You must, however, understand that confusion does not arise merely by the consumer seeing the marks, they may also hear them. The words may look similar but if they are pronounced very differently there will be no confusion. The two words 'cut' and 'cute' look very similar but no one would be confused if they were used on similar goods as they sound so different when pronounced. Also, the meaning of two apparently very similar words could prevent confusion arising. TYPHOON and TYPHOO[33] are both aurally and visually similar but as they conjure up such different images in the mind of the consumer they are unlikely to cause confusion. However, Penguin and Puffin are both sea birds and both begin with 'P' and so conceptually could easily be confused. The nature and kind of customer is also relevant. A child who had only recently learned to read would be more likely to be confused than an adult. A trade customer would be less likely to be confused as to origin than a consumer, especially if ordering goods from a trade catalogue or website with the company's name prominently displayed.

Similar goods

After you have considered the similarity of existing registered marks you then need to turn your attention to what is a similar good. Unfortunately, it is not as easy as just establishing in what class of goods the mark is registered. Each class may cover a very wide variety of goods and so is not an accurate reflection of whether the goods are similar. Class 29 of the NICE classification includes meat, fish, poultry and game; meat extracts; preserved, frozen, dried and cooked fruits and vegetables; jellies, jams, compotes; eggs, milk and milk products' edible oils and fats. Could you really say that meat is a similar good to jam? To help answer our question we look at British

---

29 LTJ Diffusion SA v Sadas Vertbaudet SA [2003] ECR I-2799, ECJ.
30 Canon Kabushiki Kaisha v Metro-Goldwyn-Mayer Inc. [1998] ECR I-5507.
31 WEBSPHERE Trade Mark [2004] FSR 39.
32 Reed Executive plc v Reed Business Information Ltd [2004] RPC 40.
33 Premier Brands UK Ltd v Typhoon Europe Ltd [2000] FSR 767.

Sugar plc v James Robertson & Sons Ltd, where a toffee-flavoured syrup, sold in a bottle, was using the same name as a toffee-flavoured jam-like food, sold in a jam jar.[34] Both were registered in Class 29. There was no issue regarding the similarity of the name but were these similar goods? To decide you must ask yourself various questions. How are the goods used? Here the syrup was to be used on top of ice cream while the jam was to be spread on toast. Who uses them and when? The ice cream would be a treat at any time and often eaten by children, while the toast would be eaten at breakfast by anyone. Where would you buy the goods? If bought in a self-service shop, are they likely to be on the same shelf? Here the answer was no. But the most important question is: are the goods in competition – would the consumer buy one instead of the other?

Even if the marks and goods are very similar there will be no problem with having both on the register if consumers will not be confused into thinking that the goods come from the same source. It was said in *CODAS Trade Mark*[35] that to determine confusion you look at the average consumer of the goods concerned. That here would be an average ice-cream-buying consumer who is reasonably well informed and reasonably observant (and not a 'moron in a hurry'). If the goods are very similar there is more likely to be confusion even where the marks are not that similar and vice versa. The more similar the marks, even if the goods are less similar; the more likely there is to be confusion.

Marks with a reputation

Very strong trade marks that have become very well-known brands are especially vulnerable to others wanting to poach the value that has been created in the mark. If a great deal of money has been spent creating an original and distinctive brand it can justifiably be argued that the proprietor of the mark is entitled to prevent its effectiveness and exclusivity being impaired by others. As Schechter has famously commented, 'if you allow Rolls-Royce restaurants and Rolls-Royce cafeterias, and Rolls-Royce pants and Rolls-Royce candy, in 10 years you will not have the Rolls-Royce mark any more'.[36] If others are allowed to use a famous mark whenever they wanted to on any sort of good it could very well result in 'the gradual whittling away or dispersion of the identity and hold upon the public mind'.[37]

Due to this, vulnerably famous marks or marks with a reputation have been given greater protection against use by others even on non-similar goods or services and even if no confusion will arise. This is significant protection and could give a monopoly in a word, shape or logo for all goods of any type. Great care must therefore be taken if proprietors of these famous marks want to prevent others using their mark. Although such marks with a reputation may receive extra protection,[38] they will only do so if it can be proved that the mark has indeed got a *reputation*, that the use of the famous mark by the other trader is *without due cause* and that the use would also take *unfair advantage* of or be *detrimental* to the famous mark. Note that when we are talking about these special marks no confusion is necessary. Consumers do not need to feel that they are buying toothpaste made by Rolls-Royce but consumers must make a link between the goods that will affect the uniqueness of the Rolls-Royce brand by either blurring, making it less distinct or tarnishment, losing its shine.

Reputation

The well-known mark must have a reputation but how much of a reputation is needed? Does *everyone* need to know about the mark? Does it have to be a household name? The reputation

---

34 [1996] RPC 281.
35 [2001] RPC 14 at para 19.
36 F.I. Schechter (1927), 'The Rational Basis of Trademark Protection', Harvard Law Review 40 at 813.
37 Ibid.
38 Section 5(3) TMA 1994.

needed has been deliberately left flexible so we can in many ways say, 'Well, it all depends on the circumstances'. It has, however, been held that the trade mark must have acquired a reputation with a 'substantial' part of the relevant public.[39] A substantial part does not have to mean everyone, but no fixed percentage is put on what it might be. Who the relevant public are depends on the product. If you are talking about four-wheel-drive cars the reputation must be among people who are involved with four-wheel-drive cars. If you are talking about a computer manufacturer you look at people who may be either retailers or consumers of computers. The market share, intensity of sale, geographical location, duration of use and the advertising of the mark must also be considered.

Harm

Once it is established that the mark has indeed got a reputation there are some uses that can without hesitation be seen as harming a famous mark. In one case the battery producer Eveready wanted to stop a condom manufacturer selling condoms under the EVEREADY mark.[40] Eveready claimed that such use would tarnish the image of their batteries. I think you can understand the battery producer's concern. The condom manufacturer retorted that theirs was a perfectly legitimate use of the mark as it was indicating that with their condoms you were 'ever-ready'. The court felt that the EVEREADY mark of the battery would not be damaged or tarnished as consumers would not make the mental link to batteries when they saw the mark on condoms, and people would not stop buying batteries due to an association with condoms. Tarnishment could result, however, if a liquid toilet cleaner was given the name IRN BRU, which is the same mark as a famous drink. It could well be that people would make a link between the two liquids and be put off buying the drink due to an association with disinfectant and toilets.

What are the forms of trade mark protection?

Trade marks must be registered where you want protection so before registering you must decide where you intend to market your goods. If you intend to trade in the UK only, you can apply to the UK Intellectual Property Office (UK IPO) for a UK trade mark under the Trade Marks Act 1994.[41] This will protect you in the UK only. If you are going to trade within Europe you can apply for a CTM, which is almost exactly the same but gives you protection in all the countries in the EU. For protection further afield you must use the Madrid Protocol (see later).

UK

If you have done your homework properly registering your trade mark should not be a problem. You should have decided that the sign you have chosen to register is unlikely to be denied registration under the 'absolute grounds for refusal'.[42] This means that the mark is not descriptive of your goods or services or of their characteristics. You have also established that your mark is distinctive and will allow consumers to tell that the goods sold under the sign come from you. To reduce the likelihood of your application being opposed you will have completed a search of the register (which can be found at www.ipo.uk.gov or http://esearch.oami.europa.eu) to check that no one else has registered the same sign for the same or similar goods. It is quite difficult to find confusingly similar marks, however, and you may wish to ask a trade mark attorney to help you

---

39 General Motors Corp v Yplon SA [1999] ECR I-5421.
40 Oasis Stores Ltd Trademark Application [1998] RPC 631.
41 Section 3 TMA 1994.
42 Section 3 TMA 1994.

with this. As it is possible for anyone to use the title 'trade mark attorney', whether or not they have been examined and have a qualification in trade marks, you should check that the adviser you choose is a 'registered trade mark attorney'[43] or a 'patent attorney'.[44]

Assuming all is well you are now ready to go ahead and apply to register your sign as a trade mark. If you are registering at the UK IPO you need to fill in the appropriate form (TM3) with any description and illustration of your mark in words and pictures. You must state in which class or classes you want your mark to be registered and pay the appropriate fee. It costs £200 to register a mark in one class of goods or services and an additional £50 for each additional class (although there is a discount if you register online at www.ipo.gov.uk). Depending on how straightforward your application is, a registered trade mark attorney will probably charge you between £450 and £750 (plus VAT) to prepare and file a single class application.

The UK IPO will examine your application within about ten days of receiving it. They will check that you have applied to register your mark in the correct class or classes of goods or services. Assuming you have, and if your mark does not fall foul of the absolute grounds of refusal, your application will be accepted and published in the *Trade Marks Journal*.[45] During the next two months it will then be open for anyone, not just people who may own a similar mark, to make comments or observations or oppose your mark. If after two months there is no objection and it has not been opposed it will take about six months for your mark to be registered. You will then be sent a registration certificate. You may now put the sign ® with your mark to indicate that it is a registered trade mark. It is a criminal offence to put ® with your mark if it is not registered. If you use an unregistered mark you may put the ™ sign on your goods or packaging.

The registry may, however, decide that your mark has not met their criteria for registrability. They may conclude it is a laudatory word or that it is not distinctive. You may be able to persuade the examiner that although yours is quite a descriptive mark, because you have been using it for some time it has acquired distinction through use. If you are using a geographical location as part of your mark it may be rejected. However, you may change the examiner's mind if you can demonstrate that you are not using the location to indicate where your goods are coming from. After all, people do not think that Bristol Street Motors are always to be found in Bristol or always on Bristol Street. If there is a problem you will get two months to try to sort it out with the office. If you cannot convince the examiner, your mark will be rejected and you will have lost the fee you paid.

The IPO will also look at earlier UK, Community and International trade marks. If there is a similar mark for similar goods, they will not reject your mark but they will tell you of the earlier mark in an examination report. You might decide at this early stage and before you have spent too much money on marketing your product that you do not wish to go ahead with the application as there is a chance it will be opposed.

Opposition

After your mark has been published in the *Trade Marks Journal* there is a two-month period in which it may be opposed. There are two main reasons for opposition. First, anyone may object to your mark if they feel that it should not be registered due to the absolute grounds for refusal: if it is, for example, descriptive or immoral. Second, it may be opposed if it is confusingly similar to an earlier mark even if that mark has not been registered. Opposition hearings can cost thousands of pounds to defend and if you lose you will have to pay not only your legal costs but some of the costs of the other side – and you will still not be able to register your mark.

---

43 www.itma.org.uk.
44 www.cipa.org.uk/pages/home.
45 www.ipo.gov.uk/tm/t-journal/t-tmj.htm.

If you decide to defend your mark you will probably need professional advice. Be careful to get proper advice. Do not be tempted to engage a firm that you found in a Google search as they may not be qualified. It is much better to choose from a list of professionally qualified attorneys, which you can find from the Chartered Institute of Patent Attorneys (CIPA; www.cipa.org.uk) or the Institute of Trade Mark Attorneys (ITMA; www.itma.org.uk). You can appeal the decision but this might be the time to seriously reconsider your choice of sign. Alternatively, you may be able to come to an arrangement to license the earlier mark. Also remember, if you become aware that someone is trying to register a trade mark that is similar to yours for similar goods you should get legal advice as to whether you should oppose their registration or grant them a licence to use your mark.

Revocation

Revocation proceedings can be taken even after you have been granted your trade mark. The main grounds for revocation are (1) that you should not have been granted the mark in the first place, (2) that for no good reason you have not been using the mark for five years, or (3) that it has become generic or misleading.

It is unlikely that anyone would attack your mark unless they want to remove you from the scene so they can register a similar mark themselves. It will be costly to defend your mark but if you do nothing your mark will be removed from the register. It is in the public interest to remove unused trade marks from the trade mark registers. It has been said that unused marks are 'abandoned vessels in the shipping lanes of trade'.[46] They clog up the register, preventing other traders registering similar marks. If you have registered a mark in more than one class of goods but are not using it in all the classes in which it is registered it is vulnerable to revocation in the unused classes. Not only must you use the mark in the classes in which it is registered but you must ensure that the use you are making of your mark is *proper* use; that is, you use it just as you registered it. If you had registered the mark MERCEDES but only used the mark MERC or had registered the word BUDWEISER but only use BUD you are not using it as registered and are again open to revocation proceedings for non-use.

The aim of most advertising campaigns is for a mark to become a household name. If, however, a trade mark has become generic it may be revoked. 'Generic' means that is has become the common name in the trade for the goods or services of that type. This happened to the mark 'Hoover', which is often used to describe all vacuum cleaners, 'Escalator' to describe a moving staircase and 'Aspirin' for painkillers. In one case a company had created an item of cutlery that is a combination of a fork and a spoon.[47] It was sold under the trade mark 'Spork'. The fork/spoon product quickly became known as 'a spork' even when made by other manufacturers. The name 'spork' had become descriptive of the goods and was no longer capable of indicating the source of the product. The proprietors should have referred to their product as the 'SPORK' fork or the 'SPORK' spoon or even the 'SPORK' scoop; anything but 'the spork'.

Some organisations promote the 'verbing' of their names, which may dramatically increase the value of the brand but may lead to a mark losing its identification function. Skype is often used as a verb, for instance 'Skype me', and was sold to Microsoft in 2011 for US$8.5 billion despite never having made a profit. However, unless it is part of your IP strategy it is wise to always indicate that your sign is a trade mark by, for instance, using capital letters, putting the mark in inverted commas or adding the ® sign to it. You may also have your mark revoked if it is likely to mislead the public, particularly as to the nature, quality or geographical origin of the

---

46 Mr Justice Jacobs, Laboratoires Goemar SA's Trade Mark (No.1) [2002] FSR 51 at para 19.
47 D Green & Co (Stoke Newington) Ltd v Regalzone Ltd [2002] ETMR 22.

goods or services on which it has been used. For example, if you allow your suppliers to use the mark WeRJustOrganic and you are not providing organic products you could have your mark revoked.

The community trade mark

Trade marks are territorial; that is, they apply only in the country where they are registered. If you intend to market your goods outside the UK you will need more protection than a UK trade mark can give. If you intend to market in more than two or three European countries it would be cheaper to apply for a CTM at the Office of Harmonization for the Internal Market (OHIM).[48] If you are an EU resident you can make the application yourself, but applicants from outside the EU must employ a representative. The CTM is a unitary mark. This means that it is the same in all the Member States, giving the same protection in all 28 EU countries. You only have to pay for one application and one renewal fee and you don't have to employ a lawyer or attorney in each country. The rules are almost identical to those of the UK trade mark, but having to apply them to 28 countries can create problems. Your mark must comply with the 'absolute grounds' in all the EU countries, which means it must be distinctive and not descriptive in all of them. This can cause a problem if you have been using a foreign language for your mark.

A German trader had registered Companyline as a trade mark in Germany.[49] Although unusual in Germany, in the UK Companyline is descriptive of the services being offered under the mark. The mark could not therefore be registered as a CTM as it was not distinctive in all the countries where the CTM applied. A mark may also fall foul of one of the other absolute grounds for refusal. Although the name Fitta for a Honda car was meaningless in the UK it was regarded as immoral in Scandinavia. Once a mark has been rejected in one of the EU countries it will be rejected for all of them. You can still apply for national marks but this will of course be far more expensive. If you want to register a CTM you can apply straight to OHIM, which is based in Alicante, Spain. You can also apply for a CTM via the UK IPO but it will cost £15 extra for their handling fee. Your application can be made in English but you must also select one other language – French, German, Italian or Spanish – which may be used if there are opposition proceedings. As with a UK mark there will be an initial examination for the absolute grounds for refusal. A search will be made for earlier CTMs and a report produced and sent to both the applicant and anyone with a similar earlier mark. The application will be published with observations and oppositions being made within three months. Opposition proceedings may be brought only by people with an earlier mark.

The cost of registering a CTM is €1,050 for an application containing up to three classes of goods. The cost to apply online is €900 plus €150 for each extra class. Just as with the UK trade mark, your mark may be revoked if it has become a common name or deceptive or if, with no proper reason, it has not been used for five years. But you do not need to use the mark in all countries of the EU; genuine use in just one country may be sufficient.[50] However, if you want to sell (assign) the mark the sale must apply to the whole of the EU. Infringement proceedings are usually brought in the country where the infringement has occurred.

How long will a trade mark last for?

As long as they have not been revoked both the UK and CTM will initially last for ten years, but on payment of a fee can be renewed every ten years indefinitely.

---

48 http://oami.europa.eu/ows/rw/pages/index.en.do.
49 Deutsche Krankenversicherung AG v OHIM (COMPANYLINE) [2002] ECR I.
50 Case C-149/11 Leno Merken v Hagelkruis Beheer B.V.

Someone is using a trade mark the same or similar to mine – can I do anything about it?

Civil infringement

Use of the same or a similar mark on the same or similar goods

As we have already seen, an application to register a trade mark can be opposed if there is already an identical or similar UK or Community trade mark for the same or confusingly similar goods. It may also be opposed if you apply to register a mark that is the same as a mark with a reputation and your registration would in effect be riding on the coat-tails of that mark, potentially causing it damage. The relative grounds of refusal of registration and the acts that amount to infringement of a trade mark are very similar and in essence require that you ask the same questions. Are the signs the same or similar, and, if so, will the consumer be confused into thinking that the goods or services come from the same source? There is one main difference, however: for infringement to occur there must have been use of the trade mark in the course of trade.

It is possible to infringe a trade mark not only by speaking or singing a word mark or playing a jingle, which could happen in advertising or on a website, but by graphically representing a pictorial logo. That would mean using it on packaging, trade literature or in advertisements. It is also an infringement to import or deal with infringing goods. Infringing goods are goods falsely carrying the mark. However, trade marks are territorial so to infringe a UK trade mark the use must be in the UK. To infringe a Community mark the use must be in the EU. Use of a trade mark in the USA or China cannot be prevented unless you have registered your trade mark there.[51] But what if you have a small business, say in Hong Kong, and it is your intention to sell only in your immediate area: does putting goods for sale on the internet, where they can be viewed anywhere in the world, mean that you are offering them for sale everywhere your site can be accessed? It has been held that if it appears that UK or Community customers were being targeted that would amount to trading in the UK or the EU. If goods are priced in pounds sterling or postage and packing to the UK is stated as part of the price, that would amount to offering for sale in the UK. If, however, you are in the UK and stumble across a website aimed at the USA with no mention of the UK or the EU and no mention of prices in pounds sterling or the euro, then there would be no offering for sale on the part of the advertiser and no infringement. It was once said that selling on the internet was like someone standing on the cliffs of Dover with a telescope looking at a shop in France.[52] It would be wrong to claim that the French shop was selling in the UK just because someone in the UK could see it. Stating your target audience on your website might avoid unnecessary problems. If you then abide by all the laws of those territories you have targeted, you may save yourself grief in the long run.

Imports and exhaustion of rights

One of the objectives of the European Common Market is to create a single trading market so that goods and people can move freely from one European country to another.[53] This means that if DVDs are cheaper in France than in the UK, a trader may legitimately buy DVDs in France and import them into the UK and resell them at a higher price, making a better profit. Due to the Common Market once a trader has put their goods on the market in the EU they may not stop this internal movement. But a trader does have the right to have exclusive distribution agreements with retailers that should be honoured as a matter of contract.

---

51 Either as a national mark or under the Madrid Protocol.
52 Crate & Barrel Euromarket Designs [2001] FSR 288.
53 Under the Treaty of Rome 1958.

A luxury brand such as Armani will usually have agreements according to which their distributors contract not to sell Armani items in discount stores, which could damage the luxury image of the brand. Although trade within the EU cannot be prevented, a trader does have the right to prevent importation from outside the EU. The trade mark holder has the right to be the first to distribute their goods within the community. A UK trade mark holder may sell their 'WHISHH'® chocolate bar in China, not yet having marketed them in the UK. If someone imports the 'WHISHH'® bars into the UK or any European country, the chocolate will be regarded as infringing goods. There is a growing trend for goods to be sold over the internet and the company selling the goods may be situated anywhere in the world. There will be infringement if goods are illegally imported into the EU.

Use in the course of trade

A trade mark will only be infringed if it is being used 'in the course of trade'. There is nothing to stop a private person embroidering their t-shirt with the Nike logo as long as they do not then enter into the business of selling such t-shirts. However, does any use of a trade mark in commerce or by a business amount to business use? The answer is not if the use is only to describe the goods or if one of the defences applies. A decided case concerned an unauthorised book about the 1980s pop group, Wet Wet Wet, who had registered their name as a trade mark.[54] The band sued for trade mark infringement but it was held that the mark, although being used in a business, was not being used in a 'trade mark sense'. The title did not indicate that the *origin* of the book was the group itself; it merely *described* what the book was about.

We know that an identical sign may never be used on identical goods, whether or not confusion is likely to arise, and an identical or similar sign may not be used on similar goods if confusion will result. Does this mean that if you put a sign on your goods saying 'these are not genuine Nike goods' you can then use the trade mark with impunity?

Such a thing happened to Arsenal Football Club.[55] Arsenal makes a huge amount of money from merchandising, and where there is a lot of money to be made there will always be someone who wants to cash in. Arsenal had registered the names ARSENAL and GUNNERS as trade marks, along with their associated logos, a gun and a shield. Arsenal sold hats, scarves and other football paraphernalia with the words and logos attached. Mr Matthew Reed became accustomed to setting up a market stall whenever the team were playing. He sold merchandise in the Arsenal colours and with their logos attached. At the point of sale Mr Reed displayed a sign saying 'non-official goods'. Fans bought these goods because they were cheaper than the official goods and wore them as a badge of allegiance to their team, not as a badge of origin indicating that the goods had come from Arsenal.

When Arsenal sued Mr Reed for trade mark infringement they had what seemed to be an impossible hurdle of non-confusion to overcome. The courts, however, concluded that the use Mr Reed was making of the trade marks damaged the function of the marks. Once the goods had been sold no one would know about the disclaimer; everyone would assume that the goods came from Arsenal. A trade mark is supposed to be a guarantee of origin and if Mr Reed was allowed to carry on selling such goods no one could be sure if their scarf was a legitimate Arsenal scarf or one of Mr Reed's unlicensed copies. In other words, if he had been allowed to continue selling the unauthorised merchandise it would have affected Arsenal's interests as owner of the mark. Remember, however, if your aunt knits you a scarf emblazoned with the Arsenal logo this is perfectly acceptable. So use in trade that is not descriptive use is likely to damage the main function of the mark because it would lead to the trade mark no longer guaranteeing origin. This will not be allowed – even if there is no confusion.

---

54 Bravado Merchandising Services Ltd v Mainstream Publishing [1996] FSR 205.
55 Arsenal Football Club plc v Matthew Reed [2003] RPC 144, ECJ.

Damage

If a mark has a reputation the proprietor of the mark does not need to show confusion but they do need to show that there has been some damage to their famous mark due to the use of the mark on someone else's goods. Damage will exist if it can be shown that there has been or is likely to be a change in the economic behaviour of the average consumer of the goods or services,[56] meaning that consumers will buy fewer of the famous products. This could be due to blurring if the mark no longer stands for the luxury image that it once did or that the image of the mark is tarnished in some way because of an unpleasant association, such as a disinfectant using the same name as a famous soft drink.

Internet service providers

Electronic marketplaces like eBay or search engine operations such as Google have created new ways for goods to be traded. They have in the process created new ways to infringe copyright and trade marks. It would be almost impossible for internet service providers (ISPs) to monitor everything that appears on their servers, and due to 'safe-harbour provisions' in the EU E-Commerce Directive they are not obliged to do so. If they do, however, discover or are told that some infringing or illegal activity is occurring on their server they must act quickly and remove or disable access to the information or they will lose their protection under the directive. EBay has filtering procedures to detect counterfeit goods or goods that are being illegally imported into the EU. They remove tens of thousands of illegal listings each month but nevertheless many trade mark holders feel that such sites should do far more to prevent illegal trade.

Sites such as Google sell trade marks as keywords or AdWords. If a competitor buys a trade mark as a keyword and a consumer searches on Google for the mark a paid advertisement for the competitor will appear. L'Oréal is a luxury brand of cosmetics and was not at all pleased to have their trade mark used as a keyword directing consumers to advertisement displaying illegal L'Oréal goods. L'Oréal brought proceedings, claiming that eBay itself was infringing their L'Oréal mark by allowing it to be used in the course of trade as a keyword. The European Court of Justice held that by allowing it to be used as a keyword eBay are not 'using' the L'Oréal trade mark in the trade mark sense as consumers will understand that these are merely sponsored links. However, in a later case it was held that if keywords led consumers to be confused about the source of the goods with the advertisement itself containing the trade mark,[57] or if the use of the keyword would adversely affect the investment function of the trade mark by dilution, free riding or by offering imitations of the goods, then this would be regarded as infringement and an injunction could be obtained to prevent it.

Comparative advertising

Something that you may want to take part in when advertising your own business is comparative advertising. We all know that adverts may say 'My soap power washes the whitest', but can you say 'My WHISHH washing power washes whiter than DAZ®'? Well, the answer is yes, as long as you abide by the rules.

You must be using DAZ® to identify that the washing powder is coming from your competitor and not from you. What you are doing is viewed as helping consumers make an informed choice, which is a good thing. In reality, if consumers were confused and thought you were actually advertising DAZ® your advertising campaign would be a failure and a waste of money.

---

56 Intel Corp Inc. v CPM UK Ltd [2009] RPC 15 ECJ; Interflora v Marks & Spencer plc [2012] FSR.
57 See Interflora v Marks & Spencer plc, Case C-323/09.

When using comparative advertising you must act in accordance with honest practices in industrial or commercial matters. You must also be careful not to without due cause take unfair advantage of, or be detrimental to, the distinctive character or repute of the trade mark you are using as a comparator.[58]

I think that you can see that there is a problem about deciding what commercially honest practice is. It is obvious that an entrepreneur, eager to sell as many goods as possible, may have a very different opinion about what is an honest practice in business than a judge may have. It has been held that in order to decide what use of a competitor's trade mark would be regarded as in accordance with honest practices you must try to think of what a reasonable consumer would think. If in their view your use of the mark was honest there will be no infringement. Consumers know that in such comparative advertising you will always try to make your own product look best and they will take that into account when looking at any comparisons you make. There was a case concerning comparison of prices of foodstuffs in supermarkets.[59] Lidl, a giant supermarket chain, complained when a rival supermarket, Leclerc, compared the prices of baskets of 34 items from each of the two chains, showing that that Lidl basket of items was more expensive. Lidl claimed that the advertisement was misleading not only because Leclerc only chose items that were more expensive in Lidl but that the goods were not identical as they were comparing Leclerc products with Lidl own brand. Lidl claimed their goods were nicer to eat. It was held that just because some of the Lidl goods might be nicer does not mean that they cannot be compared, but there should be something in the advertising letting the consumer know that the comparison is not between identical goods. So you can say 'Our Cadbury Crunchie bars are cheaper than Lidl's Cadbury Crunchie bars', but you may not say 'Our chocolate bars are cheaper than Lidl's' when you are comparing a Cadbury Crunchie from Lidl with an own brand of your own.

Malicious falsehood

Although in order to increase your sales it is perfectly acceptable to 'puff' or exaggerate the benefits of your own goods, you must not be untruthful. Sometimes in comparative advertising people can go further than mere untruth and maliciously try to create a false impression about their competitor's goods in order to cause them damage. This is sometimes called trade libel but more commonly it is termed malicious falsehood.

In the case *Rockwool v Kingspan*, both companies produced building panels.[60] Rockwool produced a video for a commercial showing both panels exposed to fire, but because the Kingspan panels were accidentally being used inappropriately the video falsely indicated that they were highly flammable. Kingspan unsuccessfully claimed that Rockwool was guilty of malicious falsehood. For a claim of malicious falsehood or trade libel to succeed the defendant must have maliciously published false information about the claimant, thus causing damage. Here the videos did indeed contain false representations that would cause damage to Kingspan, but to show malice Rockwool must have known that what they were saying was false. As Rockwool had relied on the advice of a reputable firm in conducting their tests and they did not know that what they were saying was misleading there was no malice and so no malicious falsehood.

---

58 Directive 84/450 concerning misleading advertisements as amended by Directive 97/55.
59 Lidl SNC v Vierzon Distribution SA [2011] ETMR 6.
60 (1) Kingspan Group plc (2) Kingspan Holdings (IRL) Ltd v Rockwool Ltd: Rockwool Ltd v Kingspan Group plc [2011] EWHC 250 (Ch).

Criminal infringement

Counterfeiting

One of the problems associated with success is that unscrupulous people will want to free ride on your good reputation. There is, however, a difference between one trader using a similar mark on their own similar goods so as to cause confusion and someone who is producing counterfeit goods, pretending their goods are those of another. In a study of almost 500,000 Tiffany jewellery products sold on eBay, 75 per cent were discovered to be counterfeit.[61] It is very bad for business to be constantly associated with the black market, fake brands and the criminality that is linked to it. People buy counterfeits either because they are tricked into thinking that they are the real thing or because they think the real goods are too expensive. A Business Action to Stop Counterfeiting and Piracy (BASCAP) report in 2009 estimated that the cost to the G20 governments of counterfeit goods was US$100 billion.[62] This includes the costs of deaths due to injuries caused by fake products such as dangerous electrical goods, fake dried egg and counterfeit drugs.

Customs and excise

Because of the damage in both human and economic terms that counterfeit goods can cause, criminal sanctions are available against people who make or deal in counterfeit goods. Where criminal sanctions exist Trading Standards Officers will be able to obtain a search and seizure warrant and take action against counterfeiters. If found guilty the penalties are a fine of up to £5,000 or ten years' imprisonment. A person will only be guilty of such an offence if he or she knew or had reason to believe that copyright or trade marks would be infringed. It is a defence if they honestly believed on reasonable grounds that they were not infringing a registered trade mark. But the belief must be both honest and *reasonable*. In one case Mr Singh on behalf of X was selling Nike sports shoes at a market from X's van.[63] Mr Singh knew the shoes were very cheap for such a brand but claimed that as X had assured him they were genuine he took his word for it that they were. In the court's view, because X was a notorious drug addict Mr Singh should not have trusted him so easily. He had not shown that his belief that the shoes were genuine was reasonable.

If you try to get round the law by putting 'brand copies' or 'genuine fakes' on your stall of counterfeit goods you are indicating that you have more than a reasonable suspicion that what you are doing is against the law. But what about very poor-quality goods? A Trading Standards Officer obtained a search warrant and, accompanied by the police, searched Mr Boulter's home, seizing thousands of counterfeit DVDs and CDs that had the EMI trade mark attached. Mr Boulter claimed that he could not be infringing as the goods and the logo attached to them were of such poor quality that no one would be confused into thinking that the goods came from EMI. The court decided, unsurprisingly, that despite the poor quality these were still identical marks used on identical goods and so Mr Boulter was guilty.[64]

Defences

There is a presumption that people should be allowed to use their own name, the name of their company or their address when running their business. It is also accepted that laudatory expressions or marks indicating the kind, quality, intended purpose value, geographical origin, the time

---

61 Anneka Bain [2001] EIPR 162.
62 www.iccwbo.org.
63 Essex Trading Standards v Singh [2009] EWHC 520.
64 R. v Boulter (Gary) [2009] ETMR 6.

of production of goods or rendering of services, or other characteristics of goods or services should not be monopolised by one trader but should be available for all to use.[65] If such marks have been registered, maybe because they have acquired distinction through use, there is a defence available if other traders honestly use them. There is also a defence available if you use a mark to show the intended purpose of the goods. This is particularly relevant for spare parts. It would be difficult to run a garage mending cars if you could not use the trade mark of the type of car that you are capable of working on.

Own name

The use of one's own private or company name is of particular importance to many businesses. When you register a company name at Companies House it may give the shareholders of the company limited liability but it does not in addition protect that name as a trade mark.[66] In the same way, registering an internet domain name does not give you the exclusive right to use that name or give you an automatic right to register it as trade mark. Although there is a presumption that your personal or company name may be registered as a trade mark it would be very easy to abuse the system, so you may only do so if you are acting honestly and in good faith. If you changed your name by deed poll to Rolls-Royce you will not be able to register your new name as a trade mark. In addition you will not be able to register a name if using it would amount to passing off (see later). In one case a family business, Asprey, was sold to a third party along with the trade mark.[67] A member of the Asprey family then set up a new business in competition using the Asprey name. It was held that even though it was their personal name, the right to use it had been sold. They were not acting in good faith when they started up the new company in competition. Because a company can choose to adopt any trading name, neither will the defence apply to a trade name or abbreviations of a name, as otherwise, the judge said, 'a route to piracy would be obvious'.

Descriptive use

Descriptive marks should not have been registered but if a mark has acquired distinctiveness through use registration may have been allowed. Nevertheless there will be a defence to infringement of such a descriptive mark if honest traders wish to use, but not register, such descriptive terms in their own business. You can see that descriptive marks are not as strong as highly distinctive marks as they do not create the same monopoly. They are not a good choice for a trade mark.

Intended purpose

It is acceptable to use another's trade mark in business where it is necessary to indicate the intended purpose of a product or service, provided the use is in accordance with honest practices in industrial or commercial matters. This is particularly important in relation to accessories or spare parts. If you run a garage it would be necessary to your business to show that, for example, you can mend BMW cars but you must not indicate that you have any association with BMW unless you really have. You may also say that your substitute spare parts will work on a BMW car but you must not say that they are BMW spare parts. In the same way a shopping centre may display the trade marks of goods or services to be found in their premises without infringing any of the marks.

---

65 Section 3 TMA 1994.
66 But see s 69 of the Companies Act 2006.
67 Asprey & Garrard Ltd v WRA (Guns) Ltd [2002] FSR 487.

Groundless threats of infringement proceedings

You should stay vigilant in detecting if others are using your trade mark but you must be very careful if you do think that your mark is being infringed. In the UK you may find yourself exposed to legal proceedings if you accuse someone of infringing when they are not.[68] The reason this provision has been introduced into the UK legislation is that some of the remedies available against an infringer can be quite draconian and may be open to abuse. It may be possible, for instance, to obtain a search and seizure order, which, if used against a retailer, could close their premises for a considerable time. This sort of action could, if left unchecked, be used by unscrupulous people against their competitors to try to force them out of business. It is important that if you do feel that your rights are being infringed you contact a lawyer immediately and do not take any action yourself. Even with a lawyer involved things can go very wrong. In one case Johnson & Johnson had the trade mark 'No more tears' for a baby shampoo.[69] L'Oréal was using the same mark on their baby shampoo. The solicitors of L'Oréal wrote to Johnson & Johnson asking whether Johnson was going to bring infringement proceedings against them as they were using a similar mark on a similar product. The letter in reply contained an enigmatic message but mentioned the possibility of future proceedings for trade mark infringement. This was held to be a threat. The test was whether it would be understood by the ordinary recipient in the position of L'Oréal as constituting a threat of proceedings for infringement. Because of this L'Oréal was entitled to: a declaration that the threats were unjustified, an injunction to stop further threats and damages for any loss suffered due to the threats.

Remedies

If you find that someone has infringed your trade mark you may not just appropriate the infringing goods, which could amount to trespass, but you may apply to the court for a search and seizure order. Trading Standards Officers and the police can then enter the premises of the defendant to obtain evidence of infringement. If they find infringing goods you can then get an order that the infringing sign be 'erased, removed or obliterated' from any infringing goods. You can also get an order that someone delivers up to you any infringing goods, materials or articles that are in their possession, custody or control in the course of business, but you must then get a further order that the goods be destroyed.[70] This order can apply to not only the primary infringer (the person who attached your trade mark to their goods) but also to an innocent shopkeeper who has the goods on their premises. It is also possible for a freezing order to be obtained that will freeze the defendant's assets so they may not be removed from the country.

The most useful and most widely sought remedy is an injunction to stop the defendant infringing a trade mark. There are different types of injunction. An interim injunction will order the defendant to stop using the trade mark immediately. Such an injunction will be granted if substantial loss will be caused to the owner of the trade mark if the defendant continues to use the mark. Commonly, if the defendant is ordered to stop using the trade mark they will change their business strategy and stop infringing. Hence it is rare for trade mark actions to come to full trial. A final injunction may be awarded where there is clear evidence that the defendant will continue to infringe and damages are not an adequate remedy to compensate the proprietor of the mark.

After an injunction, the next most common remedy is damages. An award of damages is intended to restore the trade mark owner's position to what it was before the infringement.

---

68 Section 21 TMA 1994. This provision is due to be reformed.
69 L'Oréal (UK) Ltd v Johnson & Johnson [2000] FSR 686 Ch D.
70 Sections 14–19 TMA 1994.

Damages will consist mainly of money due to loss of sales because of the infringement. If you cannot prove that you have lost sales damages could instead be assessed on the amount that you would have charged for a licence to use the trade mark lawfully. This could be a considerable sum if a famous brand had been infringed. Being unaware that you are infringing will not stop an award of damages being made against you.

An account of profits is an alternative remedy to damages. You cannot get both. An account of profits is not always the best remedy to seek and should only be considered if the defendant did indeed make a substantial profit. If the defendant had spent a great deal of money setting up a business and made little profit, the trade mark proprietor might be better off being compensated via damages for his own lost sales. Innocence is a bar to an order for account of profits. So if the defendant did not realise they were infringing, only damages can be awarded.

How do I get protection outside the EU?
Madrid Protocol, World Intellectual Property Organization (WIPO)[71]

You may want to trade in countries outside the EU. It is, of course, possible to apply for a national mark in each country in which you want protection but this can be both time-consuming and expensive. Each application would need a local professional adviser and would have to be translated into the relevant language. Different rules may apply and there may be different renewal dates in each country, causing a housekeeping nightmare. It became apparent many years ago that this was inefficient and a barrier to trade. The Madrid Agreement for the International Registration of Marks has been in existence since 1891 and applies to 87 countries including EU Member States, the USA, Japan and China, but not Brazil or India, where only national marks are available. If the country in which you are interested is a 'Contracting Party', that is, one that has ratified the Madrid Agreement or the Protocol, you may use this procedure. This will give you protection in your chosen countries using a single international application filed at your own national trade mark office.

If you have already registered a trade mark in one of the participating countries such as the UK you can use the Madrid system to gain protection for your mark in any of the other member countries. It is not, however, a unitary mark like the CTM applying in the same way in all the EU countries. Under the Madrid system you get a bundle of national trade marks from the countries you have selected. The international application *must* be filed via the national trade mark office where your basic mark is held. This would be UK IPO if you have a UK trade mark or OHIM if you have a CTM. An international trade mark must be translated into English (an advantage for owners of UK trade marks), French or Spanish. The mark will then be published in the *International Gazette*. No report is sent to the owners of existing marks but the Romarin (Read-Only-Memory of Madrid Active Registry Information) database contains information about international trade marks. If you have an international trade mark you should look at this regularly. There is also a free 'watch service' allowing you to monitor the status of certain international trade mark registrations.[72]

If no opposition is raised in any of the countries in which the mark was applied it should be registered within 12–18 months. Unlike the CTM, a refusal in one country does not destroy protection in all the other countries. Like the CTM, registration lasts for ten years, but one disadvantage is that the mark must be used in all the designated countries or it may be revoked in the countries where it is not used. For a CTM, use in just one Member State can be sufficient to

---
71 Headquartered in Geneva, Switzerland: www.wipo.org.
72 www3.wipo.int/login/en/mea/index.jsp.

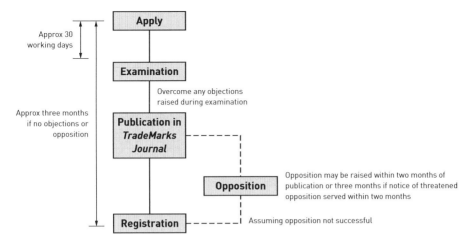

Figure 2.1 Basic trade mark application procedure.

keep the CTM alive in all territories. Another disadvantage is that unlike the CTM, which applies to all the EU countries for the same fee, the more countries in which you want international protection the more expensive it will be and the fee structure is quite complex. There will also be fees charged by the national office; UK IPO charges £320 for each international registration. It is, however, much easier to use this route than to apply directly to China, for example, where it is necessary to hire a local professional, or Spain, where the process is quite slow.

Passing off

What is passing off?

Unlike many other jurisdictions the UK does not have a law of unfair competition. We do, however, still feel that nobody has any right to present his goods as the goods of somebody else.[73] To that end we, along with other common law jurisdictions such as Australia, India and the USA, have the tort of passing off, sometimes called trade dress. Imagine that Ann Ltd is the manufacturer of a small, round, brightly coloured vacuum cleaner that is called 'Henry'.[74] Ann Ltd's cleaner is decorated with a black bowler hat top and it has a nose and a smiley face painted on the front. None of these features are protected as trade marks but the look of the cleaner is highly distinctive. Ann Ltd discovers that a rival manufacturer, Fred Ltd, has produced a vacuum cleaner of the same round shape with a black bowler hat top. Do you think that there would be a real likelihood that at least some members of the public would be confused and buy Fred Ltd's machine thinking that it was a 'Henry'? If so, there may be passing off. For passing off there needs to be three things: (1) a misrepresentation by the defendant (Fred Ltd), (2) the applicant (Ann Ltd) must have goodwill and (3) the applicant must have suffered damage.[75]

The misrepresentation is usually related to, but is not necessarily limited to, an exact copy of the name or get-up used for the applicant's product. Here there is no smiley face or nose on Fred Ltd's cleaner but consumers could still be confused by the hat and shape. There is a large overlap between passing off and trade mark infringement and it is not unusual for legal disputes to

---

73 Perry v Truefitt [1842] 49 ER 749.
74 Numatic International Ltd v Qualtex Ltd [2010] RPC 25.
75 Reckitt & Colman Products Ltd v Borden Inc. [1990] 1 All ER 873.

Figure 2.2 The Henry vacuum cleaner.

involve both actions. Passing off can be used if you have failed to register a trade mark but it provides wider protection than registration of a mark. Passing off can not only protect marks or signs used to indicate the origin of goods but it can also be used to protect such things as advertising campaigns or how goods or services are presented, packaged or described, which trade mark registration will not protect.

What are the requirements for protection?

Registration is not required for passing off but you do have to establish that you have business goodwill, that there has been a misrepresentation and that you have suffered damage as a result of the misrepresentation.

Goodwill

Goodwill has been described as 'the attractive force which brings in custom'.[76] Goodwill consists in not merely having a reputation but actually making sales in the UK. It usually takes time to create goodwill but it depends on the type of business and the geographical area involved how much time it would take. Goodwill can be local, so the proprietor of a café called 'Cloud 9' in the small English town of Ledbury could obtain an injunction to prevent another café calling itself 'Cloud 9' in the local area. Unless it was a very famous café with customers throughout the UK they could not prevent use of the name 'Cloud 9' on Ben Nevis in the Scottish Highlands. The use of the internet has extended the area in which some businesses may have goodwill. Extensive advertising could increase the range of goodwill from the purely local area and reduce the time it can take to acquire. Before Ann Ltd could succeed in a passing off action, they would have to demonstrate that they have goodwill in the 'Henry' product.

Misrepresentation

This goodwill, as you can see, is found not just in the name 'Henry' but the whole 'get-up' of the cleaner: the shape, nose, bowler hat and smiley face. In order to attract goodwill the mark, get-up, etc. must not be descriptive but must be distinctive of Ann Ltd's goods or services. I don't think that Ann Ltd would have much problem in showing that none of the attributes of 'Henry'

---

76 Commissioners of Inland Revenue v Muller & Co's Margarine Ltd [1901] AC 217.

that were used by Fred Ltd were descriptive of a vacuum cleaner. The misrepresentation needed for a passing off action to succeed is found if Fred Ltd takes some or all of these distinctive aspects of Ann Ltd's product. As with trade marks descriptive words may become distinctive if they are used in an unusual or unexpected context or have become distinctive through use.[77]

Although Fred Ltd copied the 'Henry' vacuum cleaner, that copying did not of itself amount to passing off. With passing off you are not talking about someone copying your product. As with trade marks, passing off is not intended to stop competition, just deception. Everyone is free to make or deal in vacuum cleaners, as long as they are not infringing copyright, a patent or design right, but they must in addition not present a vacuum cleaner in a way that would confuse consumers into thinking that they come from Ann Ltd. That is, they must not be round and have a black bowler hat top.

Damage

Normally, the damage suffered due to passing off would be that consumers bought the wrong goods, leading to lost sales. But damage is not limited to lost sales. Ann Ltd could also suffer damage to their reputation if Fred Ltd's cleaner was of poor quality and consumers thought the poor-quality cleaner came from Ann Ltd. Inverse passing off can also cause damage. This would be the case if Fred Ltd had shown customers photos of Ann Ltd's 'Henry' cleaner on their website, pretending that they were photographs of their vacuum cleaner.[78]

Damage could also extend to blurring of the plaintiff's goodwill, such as the unique brand of Rolls-Royce being eroded. Damage could also extend to the reputation of a famous person. One case involved Eddie Irvine, a well-known former Formula 1 racing driver.[79] Talk Radio, without consent, manipulated a photograph of Eddie Irvine taken while talking on a mobile phone. The image of the phone was changed to that of a radio with 'Talk Radio' written on the side and it was then used in an advertising campaign. It was held that as Eddie Irvine regularly sponsored items and had generated goodwill in his persona, this goodwill could be protected against a misrepresentation that he had endorsed Talk Radio. We can see here that doctoring images on webpages so as to suggest a famous person endorses a particular product could amount to passing off.

Confusion

If the goods or services are completely different, confusion and therefore passing off is less likely to occur. The Granada television group wanted to prevent the Ford Motor Company calling one of their cars Ford Granada.[80] Their passing off action failed as it was held that confusion between a television company and a car manufacturer was unlikely. Even if the products are similar, an expensive item, a product that needs to be fitted, an item with a specific model number or that needs to be ordered from a catalogue is unlikely to give rise to confusion. There are many lookalike products that take advantage of the look, get-up or packaging of a branded product. These are especially found in supermarkets as 'own brands'. Even if consumers buy the own brand rather than the branded product, if the own brand name has been clearly and prominently displayed so that no confusion results there can be no passing off.

How long does passing off last for?

You can bring an action in passing off to protect your name, get-up or logo for as long as you have goodwill. Goodwill can last even after you have stopped trading as long as people still think of you when seeing or hearing the distinctive aspects of your product.

---

77 Reckitt & Colman Ltd v Borden [1990] 1 All ER 873.
78 Bristol Conservatories Ltd v Conservatories Custom Built Ltd [1989] RPC 455 CA.
79 Irvine v Talksport Ltd [2003] FSR 619 ChD.
80 Granada Group Ltd v Ford Motor Company Ltd [1973] RPC 49.

How do I get protection outside the EU?
Passing off only applies in the UK.

Remedies for passing off
As with trade marks, the most commonly sought remedy is an injunction to prevent further passing off. This is followed by damages to compensate for any harm done to the claimant's goodwill or to make up for lost sales. An account of profits may be available as an alternative to damages.

Internet domain names
Domain names are registered on a first-come-first-served basis. No account is taken of existing trade marks, company names or whether the applicant had any right to register the name. Every internet domain name must be different, but merely inserting a hyphen will change a domain name. Malvernip.co.uk is not the same domain name as Malvern-ip.co.uk. If such 'different' names are registered by other traders, confusion and even passing off may result. Similar but 'different' registrations can be made innocently but there have been numerous cases where the domain names of famous people or organisations have been registered by 'dealers'. They then offer to sell the domain name to the 'rightful owner' at an extortionate rate.

In one early case a dealer in domain names had registered numerous names such as bt.org and marksandspencer.co.uk, offering to sell them to the relevant companies at a high price.[81] The court concluded that even though there had been no use of the names in the course of a business, the dealer had been using the domain names as a 'vehicle of fraud' and had been guilty of passing off. They were ordered to transfer the domain names to the claimants. Such confusing registrations are also made by people who seek profits by diverting internet traffic to their links in order to maximise 'click-through' revenue. When running a business it is advisable to register domain names as trade marks and trade marks as domain names. Register common mis-spellings to prevent others doing so. There are now dispute-resolution systems such as Nominet[82] and ICANN[83] in place to deal with disputes concerning the right to own a domain name. Under these procedures, if you are the owner of a registered trade mark there is no need to go to court as owning the trade mark shows that you have a right to the domain name covering the mark. Monitor your names regularly and make sure you renew them on time.

Summary

Trade marks
Brand is a much wider concept than trade mark and includes brand awareness, brand loyalty and perceived brand quality – in effect, all aspects of the presentation of the image of a business. These aspects may be protected by passing off. A trade mark is a sign that is registered for a particular class or classes of goods either as a national trade mark, a CTM or under the Madrid Protocol. A sign must be clearly and unambiguously represented in the relevant trade mark journal. A mark must be used or it will be lost.

---

81 Marks & Spencer plc v One in a Million [1998] FSR 265 CA.
82 www.nominet.org.uk.
83 www.icann.org.

A mark must not be descriptive of the goods or services, immoral or denied under any of the other 'absolute grounds of refusal'. The sign must not be the same or confusingly similar to any earlier mark for identical or similar goods or services. To decide if a mark is identical or similar you consider how the average consumer would view the marks. The average consumer will look at the marks as a whole, taking into account the look, sound and meaning of the mark. The more similar the goods, the more likely consumers are to be confused by similar marks. Marks with a reputation have special protection as they are more vulnerable to free riding. Trade marks can be infringed if they are used by another trader without consent in the course of trade. There are various defences to infringement, such as the own name defence or use to indicate the intended purpose of the goods. It is not an infringement to use another's trade mark in comparative advertising or as a keyword if the use is honest and does not give rise to confusion.

Passing off

If a trader A has goodwill in their distinctive get-up, sign or logo and trader B takes advantage of that goodwill to the detriment of trader A, this can lead to a successful claim in the tort of passing off.

Management tips

Register what you use, and use what you register.

- You may use the ™ symbol with an unregistered sign before you register it as a trade mark.
- It is a criminal offence to use the ® symbol unless a mark has been registered.
- Choose a trade mark that will distinguish your goods from those of other traders.
- Search the IPO and www.oami.europa.eu website for any existing marks. If you don't, you may be stopped from using your mark.
- A trade mark attorney will undertake a more comprehensive search than you can manage, but never employ someone unless you are sure that they are properly qualified.
- Trade marks must be used exactly as they have been registered in the class of goods for which they have been registered.
- Trade marks should be used as adjectives, not as nouns or verbs, or they run the risk of becoming generic.
- You must manage your trade marks properly with a named individual, preferably someone from the marketing department, keeping a list of what marks you have and ensuring that they are supported in line with the strategy of the business.
- Once registered, police your marks by studying newspapers and trade shows, looking for infringement. Take action immediately if you discover misuse but do not make any groundless threats in the UK.
- You must renew your registration every ten years.
- Any licensing of trade marks must be in writing and signed by the owner.

Exercise

Since 1932 Nasbro Plc has made a pre-mixed modelling compound called PLAY-DOH, which is used by children to make shapes, including pretend food. The Community Trade Mark 'PLAY-DOH' is registered in Class 16 of the NICE classification system.

The toy is sold in yellow plastic tubs with green stripes and the tubs have green lids with yellow stripes. The name PLAY-DOH is enclosed in a white cloud shape.

Mischer–Price Plc, a rival toy company, has produced a similar modelling compound but it is sold in a powdered form and needs to be mixed before use. Mischer–Price sells their product under the mark 'YUMMY PLAY DOUGH'. This product is sold in green tubs with yellow stripes and the lids of their product are yellow with green stripes. The name YUMMY PLAY DOUGH is also enclosed in a white cloud shape.

Nasbro plc want to bring trade mark infringement and passing off proceedings against Mischer–Price for the use of the name, the look of the tub and use of the cloud shape surrounding the name.

Mischer–Price claim that the 'PLAY-DOH' mark should be revoked as it is descriptive of the goods.

An expert witness gave evidence that the 'PLAY-DOH' product is very well known with a large market share of the toy modelling market.

What you should consider

The marks
- The marks are not identical. Visually, the average consumer would probably notice the difference between YUMMY PLAY DOUGH and PLAY-DOH, but phonetically 'doh' and 'dough' are identical. Conceptually consumers would probably just think that YUMMY PLAY DOUGH was a new version of PLAY-DOH. The marks are therefore not identical but they are similar.

The goods
- The Mischer–Price product is in powered form so the goods are not identical. However, if the goods are interchangeable, and the consumer would buy one in the place of the other, they will be regarded as similar.

Confusion
- As there is a similar mark for similar goods, one must then ask: would this cause confusion in the minds of the average customer?
- You must look at the type of purchase.
  - It is not an expensive product and is probably bought without a great deal of attention being paid to the actual name of the product.
  - The customer might be a child. Would they be aware of the subtlety of the difference in the names, as they might only hear the name pronounced and not read it?
  - Where would consumers purchase these goods? Both these toys would be found in the same part of a toy shop, increasing the likelihood of confusion arising.
- In conclusion, the overall impression made by these marks on these goods would be likely to give rise to confusion in the average consumer of the goods. YUMMY PLAY DOUGH would be thought to be a 'yummy' version of PLAY-DOH.

Revocation of trade mark
- The expert witness gave evidence that PLAY-DOH has a reputation and large market share so even if PLAY-DOH was originally descriptive it will have acquired distinction through use and would therefore not be revoked.

Passing off

For a claim of passing off to succeed you need goodwill, misrepresentation and damage.

- The Nasbro name, logo or get-up must have acquired goodwill in the market. We have evidence that the name had a reputation, having been used since 1932, and so goodwill is certain. The get-up of the tubs using stripes and the colours yellow and green with the use of the cloud shape around the name are all aspects of the get-up of the product that could also acquire goodwill.
- There must have been a misrepresentation by Mischer–Price, whether intentional or not, that would lead the public to believe that the goods were those of Nasbro. Placing the name in a cloud, the use of stripes, the green and yellow colouring are all misrepresentations that could lead to consumers being confused into buying the wrong product.
- Had or was Nasbro likely to suffer damage? Yes; consumers would in all probability buy the YUMMY PLAY DOUGH thinking it was PLAY DOH, but it would be helpful to have evidence to show this was the case.

Chapter 3

Confidentiality

In this chapter we will explore the nature of confidential information and trade secrets. By the end of the chapter you should be able to answer the following questions:

> What type of information can be protected under the law of confidence?
> What are the requirements for information to be regarded as confidential?
> How long does confidence last?
> Can you legally prevent employees taking or using your confidential information?
> Can you talk to other people about your secrets without losing their confidential status?
> Can I always protect my secrets in all circumstances?
> What remedies are available if there is a breach of confidence?

If you say that you will keep a secret, then you must.

Confidentiality in context

There are likely to be some information or ideas, no matter how wacky or bizarre, exciting or innovative, that you have within your business that you want or need to keep confidential. Confidential information may well give your business an edge over your competitors and may turn out to be the most valuable asset that you have. Confidential information does not always have to be highly innovative and might include what appears to be routine information about addresses of customers or employees. Such information might be contained in a photograph, a letter or a drawing. It may be something that was said during the course of a conversation or an idea that was batted around between colleagues and then quietly stored in the mind. You may be under a legal obligation to keep some information secret under the Data Protection Act 1998, or you may want to retain confidentiality for purely commercial or business reasons. It may be absolutely essential that some information be kept confidential to give your business that important competitive advantage.

Such information could be a new design, manufacturing process, marketing strategy or source code. Such essential information is referred to as a trade secret. Research has shown that firms increasingly rely on secrecy rather than patents to provide lead time for innovative products.[1] If you have trade secrets these must be carefully protected or they will be lost and with them any value they may have had to your business. After all, once a secret is out it is no longer a

---

1 W.M. Cohen, R.R. Nelson and J.P. Walsh (2000) 'Protecting Their Intellectual Assets: Appropriability Conditions and Why U.S. Manufacturing Firms Patent (or Not)', February 2000, NBER Working Paper No. w7552.

secret. To help keep such information secret you should practise a 'need to know' policy, where only a few select employees who do actually 'need to know' about these secrets are entrusted with this key knowledge.

It must also be stressed that anyone with access to trade secrets should be aware of the importance of this information and should be bound by strict confidentiality agreements. Not only should a confidentiality agreement be used if discussing an inventive concept before a patent is filed but the law of confidence can also be used to protect additional information such as the valuable know-how that surrounds the production of patented processes. Some things such as business methods and creative concepts cannot be patented in the EU. If you cannot or do not want to patent your invention you may be able to use the law of confidence as an alternative but you will be successful only if you are able to keep the inventive concept secret.

The law concerning confidential information and trade secrets has not been harmonised in the EU but there is protection for 'undisclosed information' under the Trade-Related Aspects of Intellectual Property Rights (TRIPs) agreement. In some countries there is unfair competition legislation to protect such sensitive information, while in others, such as the UK, it is dealt with under case law. In France, Spain, Italy and Japan stealing or receiving a stolen business or industrial secret can be a crime. In the UK confidential information covers more than commercial information or trade secrets protecting an inventive concept before a patent is filed or the idea of a tune before it is put into tangible form. It may also be applicable where there has been misuse of private information or government secrets. In this book we are going to concentrate on commercial secrets used in business in the UK. Similar criteria will be used to determine whether other personal secret information is eligible to be protected by the law of confidence.

What are the requirements for information to be regarded as confidential?

In *Coco v Clark* the basic requirements needed for information to be regarded as confidential were established.[2] The claimant, with the delightful name of Marco Polo Coco, had had an idea for a new moped engine. He did not have the resources to make such an engine and approached A.N. Clark, an engineering company, hoping that they would be willing to enter into an agreement with him to manufacture the engine and pay him royalties on each engine sold. Mr Coco explained the mechanics of the engine to Clark but he did so without the protection of any confidentiality or non-disclosure agreement (NDA). Talks broke down but some time later Clark produced a moped engine of their own. Mr Coco claimed that the Clark engine was based on his idea. If a contract or confidentiality agreement had existed he could have sued them for breach of contract; as it was, he had no alternative but to sue them for breach of confidence. The court stated that for a breach of confidence action to succeed three things must be established.

Quality of confidence

First of all, the information must have the necessary quality of confidence about it. It does not have to be particularly special information but it must not be commonplace, trivial gossip or consist merely of vague ideas. Also, to be regarded as confidential the information must not be freely available to the public or in the public domain. It must actually be secret. Limited disclosure under a confidentiality agreement will not deprive information of its secret status but even if disclosed in confidence it must not be disclosed too widely. Putting a 'confidential' notice on top

---

2 [1969] RPC 41.

of a document and then distributing it to everyone in a firm would be regarded as publishing the document. Finally, for information to be categorised as confidential it must be identifiable and certain.

Let us assume I have an idea for a new television show and I unsuccessfully and unwisely pitch it to a production company without using an NDA. Some time later I see a similar show being produced by the company. Can I sue them for breach of confidence? I will only be protected if mine was not a common idea and if I explained it in great detail, not just enthusing about a vague idea. It cannot just be something like: there is pop group made up of three young women who live in the same house. Every week they do something silly and say funny things.[3] To be regarded as the right sort of information it would need to be more specific, with a well-developed and well-formed idea. Including unusual details of the young people's characters with any idiosyncrasies and various storylines for the different episodes outlined would be needed before this 'idea' could be solid enough to have the necessary quality of confidence about it.

Obligation of confidence

Second, the information must have been imparted in circumstances imposing an obligation of confidence. Under UK law a written contract is not needed if the circumstances surrounding the disclosure indicate the existence of a confidential relationship. If we are travelling on a bus and I tell you of my new inventive concept with no mention of confidentiality this would not be regarded as a circumstance where an obligation to keep that information secret would be imposed upon you. If, however, we have a confidential relationship, you are a patent attorney and I am your client, due to the relationship between us any disclosure made in furtherance of this professional relationship would be regarded as having been made in circumstances imposing an obligation of confidence upon you. The position may, however, be murky if your patent attorney is a friend and you are talking on a golf course. You must in these circumstances ask whether a reasonable person would think that the information was being imparted in circumstances imposing an obligation of confidence.

It is common for manufacturers, where it is possible to do so, to encrypt their products in an attempt to prevent third parties from reverse-engineering them. Does this encryption indicate to people that the product is confidential, that their consciences are bound and that they are not to reverse-engineer the product? In one case Mars Ltd created a new vending machine.[4] The machine incorporated sensors that created signals that identified coins and then provided the correct change. Mars Ltd encrypted the machine to prevent people working out how it functioned but Teknowledge Ltd managed to reverse-engineer the product. Mars Ltd claimed that Teknowledge Ltd was bound by confidence as the encryption indicated that this information was intended to be confidential. The court held that once a product has been purchased, the new owner is entitled to reverse-engineer it despite knowing that the encryption was incorporated in an attempt to prevent them from doing do. Encryption does not amount to imparting information under an obligation of confidence as required in *Coco v Clark*.

What about if there is some uncertainty concerning imparting information under circumstances imposing an obligation of confidence? If, for instance, a secret has been stolen or lost and then divulged to an innocent third party, is the third party then free to use or disclose it? If a file of confidential letters is accidentally left on a train, can the owner prevent the publication of the information within the letters? (The letters themselves would be protected by copyright but copyright does not protect mere ideas or facts.) This is a very difficult area and the outcome depends on the exact facts of each case. If mobile phone messages or emails are obtained illegally

---

3 Fraser v Thames Television [1983] 2 All ER 101.
4 Mars UK Ltd v Teknowledge Ltd [2000] FSR 138.

by a private detective and sold to a newspaper it may be felt that the newspaper must have known that the information had been obtained illegitimately. If the newspaper had turned a blind eye to how the information was obtained they should, it is felt, be bound by confidentiality. If the information, however, was found abandoned on a bus it might be felt that sufficient care had not been taken to protect its confidential status and the owner would not be able to complain about its use and reuse by others.

In a business environment any disclosure should ideally be via an express written and signed contractual agreement, an NDA. However, if there has been no confidentiality agreement and it is necessary to make a contract work it may be possible to go to court and ask for an obligation to be implied into a contract. It is, however, unwise, uncertain and expensive to rely on this route.

Unauthorised use

Third, to succeed in a claim for breach of confidence there must be an unauthorised use of the information to the detriment of the party communicating it. So Fred merely being in possession of confidential information is not enough; he must be threatening to disclose or use it in some way that had not been agreed when the information was imparted to him. If instead of, as agreed, producing a prototype of your invention for your use, Fred takes the prototype to a large manufacturer and tries to license it himself he will be making an unauthorised use of your confidential information and will be in breach.

For how long does confidential information last?

A secret will last until it is disclosed to the public and so can last indefinitely. The benefits of secrecy over patenting can be seen when looking at the Coca-Cola recipe. Coca-Cola was first produced in 1886 and the recipe was successfully protected by secrecy for many years. If all those years ago a patent had been obtained for this famous soft drink, things would be very different. Not only would the 'secret' recipe have been published to the world, allowing everyone to discover how it was made, but the protection from copying that the patent gave would only have lasted at the most 20 years from the date of filing. It would then have fallen into the public domain and everybody would have been entitled to use it. Sometimes secrecy is the only option. There are some things for which no satisfactory formal intellectual property (IP) protection is available. In the EU for instance, unlike in the USA, you cannot get patent protection for some software or business methods, but secrecy may give you some protection.

Keeping a process or product secret may in many circumstances be much easier and cheaper than obtaining a patent and if you are lucky a secret can last forever. It must be kept in mind, however, that secrecy will only be successful if it is difficult to find out what the inventive concept is by reverse-engineering. It is much easier to keep information secret about a process than about a product that can easily be reverse-engineered. A process for making a product would in all likelihood take place in a factory where public access to that information can be restricted and monitored. But products are freely available for inspection by the public when sold and the inventive concept may easily be discovered. Secrecy also requires that no employees leave and divulge secrets to their new employers. With the use of digital technology secrets are highly vulnerable to theft. Stealing them is often just a one-click procedure, with much information being easily stored on a memory stick. But do take note that a patent or a registered design will give you a monopoly over your invention or design. If someone else independently comes up with the same idea that you have been using in secret, not only can you not prevent them from using their product or process but they may be able to obtain a patent or design right for it.

Employees have access to my secret information – what should I do?

Employees will often have access to confidential information and trade secrets. This must be managed carefully. The most common cause of trade secrets being leaked is via ex-employees going to work for a competitor and then divulging the information to their new employer. There are numerous types of sensitive information used in a business and employees should only have access to information necessary for the job they do. Confidential or sensitive information should be stored so that it can only be accessed by people who are authorised to deal with it. Some sensitive information may be intended for internal use only. Although valuable and not to be disclosed outside the business it is not, unlike a patentable idea, regarded as so essential to the business that it be kept secret. Some information will be regarded as confidential or highly confidential and of such importance that it is categorised as a trade secret.

A trade secret is information that, it would be obvious to a reasonable person, would cause real harm to the owner of the information if it were disclosed to a competitor. This information should be locked up when not in use. If it is highly sensitive information there should be only a limited number of copies and these copies should be tracked so that it is always possible to trace who has what copy and when they had it. Any disclosure of this highly sensitive information even under an NDA should only be taken after serious consideration, trade secrets are the most valuable category of information that employees are likely to have access to. Even if there are no express terms in the contract of employment there is an implied duty on employees during the course of their employment to further the interests of their employer, but this duty may continue after employment ceases if the information is regarded as a trade secret.

This duty is more onerous the more senior the employee. We do not practise slavery in our society so employees cannot be prevented from leaving their employment. Employees should be made aware that they are in possession of sensitive information and that they should not 'steal' this information when they leave.[5] When changing jobs what duties are they under and what information may they take? It has been decided by the courts that ex-employees may make use of the know-how and skills they have learnt but they must not use their ex-employer's trade secrets, the most sensitive category of information.[6]

In a recent case L, one of C's employees, went to work for a competitor.[7] Before leaving L copied onto a memory stick an Outlook contact list, information for calculating building costs and an Excel spreadsheet containing information about sites C wished to purchase. When C tried to obtain an injunction to prevent the use of this information it was held that, although after he had left C's employment L was entitled to contact people he had dealt with when working for C, he could not take a detailed list of customers and contact details with him. The fact that L copied the Outlook contacts list of names showed that they were not part of his general knowledge as he could not remember them without copying and the list was confidential information. The calculation of C's potential profit margin (and therefore by how much it would need to improve its offer to succeed in purchasing sites) was held to be a trade secret and was protectable even after the end of L's employment. L was also under an express contractual obligation that had been contained in his employment contract to return all documents relating to C's business. He was in breach of that term by making copies of documents before he handed in his notice.

We can see from this that there should always be a clause in all contracts of employment dealing with the protection of confidential information especially after employment ceases. But this must be worded carefully. Employers must not be too restrictive when trying to control the

---

5 Faccenda Chicken Ltd v Fowler [1986] 1 All ER 617 CA.
6 Printers and Finishers Ltd v Holloway [1965] RPC 239.
7 Churchill Retirement Living v Luard [2012] EWHC 1479 (Ch).

behaviour of ex-employees. It is not a wise move to try to prevent an employee from taking away and using *all* sensitive information in his future employment. If an employer is too restrictive in an employment contract and the ex-employee disputes the clause with the matter coming before a court, the court may well find that as the claims were too wide the entire clause in the contract will be ignored. In that case none of the employer's information will be protected as confidential, no matter how important it might be to their business.

It is a good idea to conduct exit interviews for employees who are likely to have access to sensitive information. They can then be reminded of their duty to keep secrets confidential and any sensitive material they have can be returned at this point so that it cannot be passed on to a new employer. You must also be aware of cultural differences in the approach to confidential information. If you have employees or a manufacturing arm in countries like China there is a more urgent need to educate the workforce in the concept of confidentiality, what is important, how to store it, etc., as the ownership of ideas is not part of the traditional Chinese culture or way of doing business.

Covenants in restraint of trade

Another clause that may be incorporated into a contract of employment is a restraint of trade clause. Here an employee agrees that on leaving their present employment they will not work for a competitor for a specified period in a particular geographical or commercial area. What this period might be depends on the type of employment. Such a clause will be enforced by the courts but only if it is reasonable and only to protect the employer's legitimate interests – not merely to prevent competition.

It may be reasonable to expect an employee not to work for a competitor or set up in business in competition with their ex-employer in the same area for a six-month period but it would not be reasonable to say that they could never work for a competitor of their ex-employer anywhere in the world. Such a restriction may in effect make them unemployable, unable to use their skills and know-how for the rest of their working life. If the court regards such a clause as unreasonable they will strike it out altogether, so it is sensible for an employee to ensure that such a clause is reasonable and therefore enforceable.

Gardening clause

It is common, when you have senior employees with access to highly sensitive confidential information, to include a 'gardening leave' clause into their contract of employment. This clause in essence says that if the employee wants to leave their present employment they should leave immediately rather than working out any period of notice. During a notice period employees carry on working as normal, but with such a 'gardening leave' clause they will stop work immediately, receive full pay but not work for anyone else during the stated period. They will stay at home 'gardening' (although there is unlikely to be a stipulation that they must actually tend their garden). The intention of such a clause is that by the time their notice period has worked through any confidential information in their possession would, it is hoped, have grown old or stale and be of no use to a competitor. The employee will then be free to use their skills and know-how for the benefit of their new employer but will no longer be in possession of fresh secrets that could harm the competitive position of their ex-employer.

Sharing secrets with third parties and non-disclosure agreements

Everyone would accept that the best way to keep a secret is not to tell anyone about it. However, when dealing with creative businesses that produce patentable ideas or new designs it is often necessary to involve others with complementary skills in the development or manufacturing process. If, as we discuss in Chapter 4, you want to obtain a patent for a new product or process, the product or process must be new. New in this context means that it has not been previously disclosed or made available to anyone, at any time, anywhere in the world. Telling even one person, not in confidence, before filing could destroy novelty. However, before you commit yourself to filing for a patent or registering a design you would be well advised to discuss with potential customers whether there is a market for your type of product. You may want to create a prototype of an invention before filing as this can often be the only way to prove that a principle works. It may even be possible to find someone who is willing to license your innovation at this early stage. This may of necessity involve telling a manufacturer and their employees full details of your invention. In the UK this problem can be overcome if the disclosure was made in confidence. If you are disclosing confidential information, the information should be imparted using a formal contract, a know-how licence, technology transfer agreement or NDA. As we know, confidential relationships may be implied in certain circumstances but it is much better, cheaper (if there is a dispute) and more reliable to have a properly constructed signed agreement. However, keep in mind that these are *agreements*. You may not *impose* an obligation to keep something secret upon someone else. I may not, for instance, send you a letter with my confidential information in it and say, 'You are bound to keep this secret and not use it for your own purposes'. Allowing this to happen would enable unscrupulous people to abuse confidentiality.

However, do not just rely on your NDA; you must always be sure that the other party will keep their word. If you do need to discuss your information with anyone else, only divulge what is required and no more. If you don't trust them not to tell then don't trust them with your secret. If, however, you do decide that you can do business with them, it may be wise to contact a patent attorney or a lawyer to draw up a non-disclosure or confidentiality agreement. You can also find model agreements on the UK Intellectual Property Office (UK IPO) website at www.ipo.gov.uk/nda.pdf.

An NDA should be clear, dated and signed. It should stipulate the names of the owner of the confidential information and the recipient of the information. There should be a brief description of what information is covered by the agreement, how the information is to be used – sometimes called the permitted purpose – and a statement that it is not to be used for any purpose other than the one agreed, such as creating a prototype. There should also be agreement about how the recipient is to look after the information in order to retain its confidential status and finally the length of the agreement (usually 2–5 years) should be specified.

It must be stressed that this is the law in the UK. In some countries an offer to sell or license a patentable invention even under an NDA is regarded as prior use and will destroy novelty, preventing you from gaining a patent for your invention.

Privacy

There is no right of privacy in English law but the law of confidence has often been used in its place. Since 1998 the Human Rights Act has applied to the misuse of private personal information in the UK and Europe. The Human Rights Act states that everyone has a right to respect for his private and family life, his home and his correspondence. There are exceptions that apply to national security, the prevention of crime and the protection of rights or freedoms of others. Most of the privacy issues raised in the courts involve media snooping relating to famous people.

There had for many years been an assumption that if you seek publicity when it shows you in a good light you cannot then complain of an invasion of privacy by the press that shows you in an unfavourable light.

There has, however, been a move by the courts towards greater protection for famous people. In one case, Naomi Campbell, a well-known fashion model, sued Mirror Group Newspapers.[8] The *Daily Mirror* had printed a photograph of her coming out of a drug rehabilitation clinic alongside an article indicating that she was a drug addict. This is the sort of private information protected by the Human Rights Act. The Mirror Group, however, disputed her right to anonymity in this matter. Campbell, they claimed, was regarded by many as a role model and had often been quoted claiming that she was strongly anti-drugs. The newspaper claimed that there was a public interest defence in their publication. They claimed that the public had a right to know that she was a hypocrite and that she had lied about her drug-taking habits. It was accepted by the Court that the newspaper was justified in exposing her hypocrisy, there was a public interest in this, but she nevertheless had a reasonable 'expectation of privacy' for 'private' activity. Although the photographs had indeed been taken in a public place it was held that the newspaper had overstepped the mark by printing them along with an article exposing her addiction. The article telling of her treatment would have been sufficient to reveal her hypocrisy. The details of her treatment alongside the photographs added nothing more and although they were undoubtedly interesting to the public, it could not be said that it was in the public interest to publish them.

Another case involved David, the baby son of J.K. Rowling, the author of the Harry Potter books.[9] Photographs of David in his pram were taken in the street and were published in a newspaper. Although the public might have been interested in seeing the baby there was no public interest defence or any other reason than to increase the sales of the newspaper in publishing photographs of the child. The newspaper had breached the child's privacy and was ordered to pay damages. The defence of public interest did, however, almost succeed after photographs were published of the Formula 1 boss Max Mosley 'frolicking' with five 'lap dancers' in his hotel bedroom. The newspaper claimed that there was a Nazi theme associated with the sado-masochistic orgy in which Mosley was participating and that it was in the public interest that this be exposed. On the facts, however, the Nazi angle was not proved and it was held that Mr Mosley had a reasonable expectation of privacy in relation to his sexual activities, however unconventional.

Although private information and business information are treated differently by the courts, sometimes there is an overlap. People in the public eye often use their image as a commodity and indeed many have registered a trade mark of their likeness. The celebrities Michael Douglas and Catherine Zeta Jones are no exception in exploiting their fame, having used the occasion of their wedding to make £1 million by selling *OK!* magazine the exclusive rights to publish their wedding photographs. The couple had gone to great lengths to keep the wedding celebrations highly confidential and only *OK* magazine photographers were allowed to attend the wedding. A rogue photographer managed to infiltrate the reception and sold the resulting photographs to the rival *Hello!* magazine. Although the photographs involved a commercial arrangement, the court held that the couple had the right to keep the photographs secret until they chose to make them public. Because the couple had gone to such great lengths to ensure that their wedding was to be private (all the guests were searched for cameras), it was obvious to all third parties that this was a confidential situation.[10]

This approach could be contrasted with encrypting a product. Where in *Mars UK Ltd v Teknowledge*,[11] despite the fact that the encryption of the product demonstrated that the creators

---

8 Campbell v Mirror Group Newspapers [2004] UKHL 22.
9 David Murray v Big Pictures (UK) Ltd [2008] EWCA Civ 446.
10 Michael Douglas v Hello! Ltd [2003] EWHC 786 (Ch).
11 See note 4 above.

wanted this information to be regarded as confidential, the owner of the product was held by the Court to have themselves destroyed confidentiality by putting the product into the public domain by marketing it.

Are there any circumstances where people may use my confidential information?

There are times when the courts will not prevent people using the confidential information of others. These are called defences. The main defence to an action for breach of confidence is that disclosure of the information is in the public interest. The courts will not protect secret information where there has been wrongdoing. If you have been illegally tapping people's phones you will not have the support of the law to keep this information confidential. If it is felt by the court that the public should have access to your information despite its confidential nature it will not be legally protected. Public interest does not just mean, however, that the public would be interested to know your secret; it means that it is in the public interest that it becomes public knowledge. If, for instance, an employee knows that their employer is running a dangerous business it would be in the public interest that people know this in order to protect the public.[12] It must always be kept in mind, though, that this defence should not be overused. In such a situation the employee should inform the appropriate authorities of the danger, not just go rushing off to the newspapers with the story.

What remedies are available to me if confidence is breached?

If you find that your confidential information has been disclosed first of all you should make sure that any confidentiality agreement is still in force. Was there a time period attached to your NDA and has that time now been reached? Did the contract of employment stipulate a six-month period where the employee was not to work for a competitor and are we now into the seventh month? If so, the defendant is free to use all the information for their own benefit as they have your consent. Do not start expensive legal proceedings until you are sure you have a case.

The main weakness of the law of confidence is that once the information has been disclosed the value of that information is destroyed and there is little that the owner of the information can do to prevent anyone from using it. It is therefore essential to act before a breach occurs. The main remedy sought by claimants when there is a threatened breach of confidence is an injunction. An injunction is a court order that directs someone to do or not do something. Here, because the owner wants to stop their confidential information entering the public domain and losing its value to them they will want the order to state that the other party must not disclose the confidential information.

If there is a threatened breach of an NDA the issue should be quite clear-cut and an injunction can be easily granted. If there has already been a disclosure of the confidential information damages will be awarded to compensate the claimant for losses due to the loss of confidentiality. An injunction can have a significant negative impact upon a defendant. If the issues are not clearly defined in an NDA and the judge is not sure that the owner of the information has a strong enough case they may be reluctant to make such an order. It may be felt by the court that if an injunction is denied damages may be a perfectly adequate remedy for use of the information even

---

12 Lion Laboratories v Evans [1985] QB 526.

if it later turns out that the information has been wrongly allowed to be published. Alternatively, if the discloser has made a great deal of money out of exploiting the confidential information, an account of profits may provide more appropriate compensation to the owner of the information. However, whatever remedy you get, whether damages or an account of profits, your competitive advantage due to your confidential information will have gone forever.

Can I get protection for my secrets outside the EU?

In some countries there are criminal laws against stealing valuable business information. However, confidence is often a matter of contract and so protection can be obtained easily in other countries via this method. It is wise to include a choice of law clause in any legal documents. This allows you to stipulate which law will govern the contract and you can choose the law that suits you best.

Summary

All TRIPs-compliant countries have a minimum standard of protection for undisclosed information that has commercial value and where the owner has taken reasonable steps to keep the information secret. Firms increasingly use secrecy rather than other forms of IP protection. Under UK case law information to be regarded as confidential: (1) must not already be in the public domain, (2) must not be trivial or commonplace and (3) the information must have been imparted in circumstances imposing an obligation of confidence. A confidential situation exists if a reasonable person would think that the information was being imparted in circumstances imposing an obligation of confidence. To be confidential the agreement does not have to be in writing but writing does provide good evidence. To bring a successful action there must have been unauthorised use of the information to the detriment of the party communicating it. Employees are the main route to losing confidential information and confidentiality clauses should be included in their contracts of employment. Although you cannot prevent ex-employees using their know-how and skills in their future employment you can prevent them using your trade secrets. To be a trade secret the information must have a commercial value and the owner must have taken reasonable steps to keep the information secret. All disclosures or negotiations with third parties relating to sensitive information should be made under an NDA.

Management tips

Loose lips sink ships.

- Make sure employees know their obligations and what information is to be protected.
- Make sure that all covenants in restraint of trade are reasonable.
- Only divulge as much sensitive information as necessary and only to people who need to know.
- Before any meeting where confidential information is to be disclosed make sure that a non-disclosure agreement is signed by both parties.
- Keep an accurate note of what information is discussed.
- At the end of the meeting agree the information that is regarded as confidential.

Exercise

Jeremy had a business named 'Sand-witch' that provided light lunches to office workers in the city centre of Birmingham. Each morning either Jeremy or one of his staff went to the participating offices and took orders from the individuals working there. The lunches were then prepared in the Sand-witch kitchens. Each individual customer's likes and dislikes were carefully recorded so that Jeremy was able to estimate what food was likely to be ordered each day. Every week on his computer, Jeremy or, if he was on holiday, his assistant Sam prepared an invoice for each office based on the record of its orders. The invoices were closely guarded and protected by a password to avoid the risk of the names and preferences of the customers being discovered by competitors who could then entice away their customers by undercutting the Sand-witch prices. Only Jeremy and Sam knew the password to the invoice records.

Sam had worked for Sand-witch for three years. Her contract of employment had stipulated that termination was subject to six months' notice and thereafter she was restricted from disclosing trade secrets, from soliciting business from any of Sand-witch's customers or from having any involvement worldwide in any business in competition with Sand-witch for a year after her employment with Sand-witch ended.

In June, Ian from Lunches-R-Us, a rival of Sand-witch, approached Sam and asked her to come and work for him at a much higher salary than she was currently receiving. Ian suggested that if Sam was able to access Sand-witch's customer lists, customer preferences and the prices the customers paid for their lunches, this knowledge would increase the sales of Lunches-R-Us substantially and that she would earn a large percentage bonus if sales were increased in that way.

Sam told Jeremy that she wanted to leave Sand-witch as she kept eating the leftover sandwiches and was gaining a great deal of weight as a consequence. She told Jeremy that she did not want to work out her notice period and he agreed that she could leave immediately. Jeremy threw a leaving party for her during which she crept into the office and accessed the customer invoices, copying them onto her memory stick.

Shortly afterwards Sam started to work at Lunches-R-Us. She used Sand-witch's invoices to contact their customers to try to persuade them that Sand-witch was no longer delivering to their area and that customers should in future buy their lunches from Lunches-R-Us. Using the information from the invoices Lunches-R-Us was, in addition, able to undercut Sand-witch's prices.

Discuss

Jeremy, on behalf of Sand-witch, is likely to claim that both Sam and Lunches-R-Us were in breach of confidence. He would also want to seek an injunction to enforce the breach of the restrictive covenant contained in Sam's contract of employment preventing her from working for Lunches-R-Us.

1 Is the information confidential?

Both Sam and Lunches-R-Us are likely to claim that the information in the invoices is neither confidential nor of any value because the prices being paid and the likes and dislikes of the customers could be found out simply by asking the customers.

We should look at *Coco v Clark*.

2 Does the information have the necessary quality of confidence about it?

PUBLIC DOMAIN

No. The information in the invoices was not in the public domain, being found only in the invoices, from the knowledge of the employees or from the customers themselves.

WAS IT TRIVIAL INFORMATION?

No. Both Sam and Lunches-R-Us were well aware of the commercial advantage that competitors could obtain from such information. The fact that the information about likes and dislikes could be obtained by asking the customers would not be a reason for concluding that the information was not confidential to begin with.

WAS THE INFORMATION IMPARTED IN CIRCUMSTANCES IMPOSING AN OBLIGATION OF CONFIDENCE?

Is Sam bound?

Sam would say that the information was not a trade secret but was of the kind that an employee had to treat as confidential only while employed. She would claim that once learned, such information remained in the employee's head and became part of their own skills, experience and knowledge, which they could not be restrained from using after their employment ended.

Only Jeremy and Sam had the password to the invoices. It was clear that when Sam took the invoices she knew that it was Sand-witch's commercially valuable information, and that she had no right to it or to pass it on to Lunches-R-Us.

Is Lunches-R-Us bound?

After encouragement Sam had stolen the invoices and given them to Lunches-R-Us. They must have known that the information was stolen and that was sufficient to impose a duty of confidentiality on them.

3 There must be an unauthorised use of that information

There had been an unauthorised use of the information. Sam had approached Sand-witch's customers and undercut their prices and that use had been to the detriment of Sand-witch.

4 Is the restrictive convent enforceable?

As the restrictive covenant was worldwide and for a year it would be regarded as too wide and therefore would be struck out as being unreasonable.

Chapter 4

Patents

In this chapter we will explore the nature, acquisition, entitlement and scope of patents. By the end of the chapter you should be able to answer the following questions:

- What are patents?
- What are the requirements for protection?
- In what territories and at what stage should you file for a patent?
- How to file and how long do the rights last for?
- Who owns or is entitled to the patent?
- Someone is using an invention that is similar to mine – can I do anything about it?
- How do you avoid infringing others' patents?
- What is a patent 'troll'?
- What alternatives to patenting are there?

Patents in context

Patents protect inventions that are a solution to some problem. A patent is a legal right granted to you by a government office. Patents are one of the most well-known forms of intellectual property rights (IPR); in fact many people only think of patents when intellectual property (IP) is mentioned. Technologies protected by IPR are the fastest-growing type of asset and the most important form of international trade. Patents can be traced back to Venice in the fifteenth century where they were used to protect the secret processes of Venetian glass-making.

The present UK legislation can be found in the Patents Act 1977, which is compatible with the 1973 European Patent Convention. Patents must be registered and a UK patent is a very strong protection that prevents others using, selling or importing an invention into the UK even if they come up with the same invention independently. The term 'invention' is not defined anywhere in the legislation but is usually regarded as the addition of a new idea to the existing stock of knowledge. An invention can result from many years of toil with a great deal of money having being spent laboriously working out the solution for a problem or it might be the result of a 'eureka' moment of insight. You can be granted a patent for a new product, a new process – and any product arising from it – or a new use for an old thing.

Patents can be used to protect inventions or a new solution to a technical problem, how a product works or how a process is used, what something is made of or how it is made. You cannot patent an idea, such as the idea of a flying machine, but you can protect the inventive technology that allows the machine to fly. Our inventor, let us call him Bert, could be granted a patent for a new type of gearbox to be fitted into a plane or a new process for making glue to stick the wings together.

However you came by your invention or whether it is for a product or a process, there are three requirements that have to be met in order to successfully file a patent application. Your product or process must be new to the public (secret use will not destroy novelty), it must involve an 'inventive step', which means that it must not be obvious to an expert in the field, and finally it must be capable of industrial application, meaning it must have some sort of use or function.[1]

As well as having these three attributes you must also be aware that some things are excluded from patenting. The list of excluded things includes, among others, methods for doing a mental act, business methods, therapies on the animal and human body and basic computer programs. A patent is not like copyright, it does not spring into life as soon as you put it into tangible form, a patent must be applied for, registered and both a fee and renewal fees paid.

Having a patent does not give you the right to use or sell your invention. It might be that by using your invention you would necessarily infringe another's patents. In addition, if you are producing a drug you will in all probability need some regulatory approval to show that it is safe before you are legally allowed to sell it. What a patent does give you is the right to stop others from using, offering for sale, making or importing the invention into the UK for up to 20 years.

This is the case even if they have independently invented the product or process themselves. The main reason people choose to patent their product or process is because this legally enforceable right gives them a monopoly. In this period they can become the market leader, building up a reputation in, for instance, gearbox production. With this high profile, employees will want to work for you and consumers will want to buy your products rather than those of a competitor. Even when the patent expires you can still be the pre-eminent player in your field. If Bert has spent time and money creating a new gearbox, unless he could keep it secret people could just copy it. Patents can aid innovation by allowing inventors such as Bert to charge a premium in this period of monopoly in order to recoup their research and development (R&D) costs. Bert, due to his patent, is the only person with a right to sell this innovative gearbox. Due to lack of any competition and assuming that people want to buy it, he will be able to price his gearbox at the maximum that customers are willing to pay before they decide that they would rather buy an inferior gearbox from another source. Although, due to the monopoly the patent gives, consumers will be disadvantaged as they will have to pay more, it is argued that they will ultimately be better off because they will have access to a better, more innovative gearbox and Bert will have the money to research into further innovative products. He can also make money by granting licences giving others permission to sell or manufacture his gearboxes. In addition, if he has a monopoly right he will find it easier to get investment from banks, shareholders or venture capitalists to fund the creation of more products. If, of course, the gearbox-producing market was extremely costly to enter a patent might not be as valuable as that high entry cost would be a sufficient barrier.

Keep in mind, just having a patent will not make you any money. An invention is something that can be patented. It is a technical solution to a problem. Innovation is making that invention into a marketable product or process. You have to translate the good idea of a new type of gearbox into a real marketable product. You not only must make a gearbox that people want to buy but you must be able to make and market it at a price they are prepared to pay. However, once the market is saturated, once every plane has Bert's gearbox, if he wants to stay in business he must innovate and create new products that people again will want to buy at a price at which he can afford to sell. Remember, patents do not just cover products. You can also obtain a patent for a

---

1 Although you do not actually have to know why it works. Conor Medsystems Inc. v Angiotech Pharmaceuticals Inc. [2008] 4 All ER 621.

process. Bert could find an improved way of manufacturing his gearbox so that production costs were cheaper or more effective. It might be that in the past Bert had to incorporate a spindle into his gearbox, using technology licensed from another. His new manufacturing process allows him to avoid that licensing cost. A patent will allow Bert not only to expand his share of the gearbox market but enter into new markets or territories. He can even use it as a bargaining tool in a cross-licensing agreement where he will be allowed to use the IP belonging to others in exchange for them using his. Finally, Bert may just decide to sell his patent outright, retiring on the profits.

We can see that a patent does not merely give you the ability to charge a premium for your product or process but ownership of a patent or patents may improve the efficiency of your business, enhance the reputation of your organisation as a source of innovative ideas and may also make it easier to borrow money or raise capital. The government encourages innovation and, as an incentive to encourage patenting, has introduced the 'Patent Box'. This allows companies to pay a lower rate of corporation tax on any products or licences of products that incorporate a granted patent. Consequently, if your product is a luxury yacht and one of the gears in the motor has a valid patent the reduced tax can be applied to the whole yacht and its worldwide sales – a worthwhile incentive.

There are disadvantages in filing for a patent. Patenting is not easy. In the UK it takes up to four years to be granted a patent, maybe a lot longer, and this time lag means that patenting is not appropriate for fast-moving areas such as computer software. The most appropriate industries for patent protection are the pharmaceutical industry and the chemical, petroleum and biotech industries where there are large R&D costs but low barriers to entry. Patenting can be very expensive and a patent must be applied for in every country where you want protection. Before you embark on the process you must ask yourself the question: will patenting enable me to make enough profit to even cover my patenting costs, let alone my time spent developing the idea? Not only must you have enough money to patent your idea but either the resources to make a viable product or a manufacturer who will take a licence to produce it. You must also ensure that people will want to buy it. Do enough people really need or want this? Is there an obvious alternative to your product or process that people will use instead? Is your product sufficiently attractive, cheaper or better than the alternative? You should consider whether lead time or secrecy would be a better option than patenting.

Eighteen months after filing your patent in the UK it will be published. Any competitors will know not only what your invention is but also how to make it. This is the bargain that you strike for your 20 years' monopoly. Others can now freely look at your good idea and see how you have cleverly made it into a product or process. Their reaction to your patent application might be to think how brilliant it is and decide not to waste time working on a similar idea themselves. Alternatively, they may decide to wait and develop your idea further after your patent has expired. However, they might decide either to oppose the grant of your patent or, rather than go to the expense of opposing, they may just use it. They will then wait for you to bring infringement proceedings against them, at which time they may claim that your patent is invalid and should be revoked. Anyone can challenge a patent at any time. Before embarking on the patenting process you must also ask yourself whether you have enough money to defend your patent. Litigation is a costly business and no one is there to help you financially, no matter how justified your case may be.

Although patent protection is regarded as a social good, encouraging innovation and the publication of knowledge, there are strong moral arguments against the system. You may file defensively to protect an existing market. Imagine you are a light-bulb manufacturer and have discovered how to produce an everlasting light bulb. You may have no intention of making the new product as its use would destroy your sustainable market in non-disposable light bulbs. You are filing a patent only so that no one else can patent or use a similar product. By defensive filing you could prevent exploitation of the new light bulb for up to 20 years, denying society the benefit of a useful product. In addition, granting a monopoly over, for instance, a drug that cures HIV/AIDS can be seen as immoral. The patent allows a premium price to be charged for these drugs, which poor countries cannot afford. It has also been claimed that patenting encourages pharmaceutical companies to concentrate their research on 'rich country' diseases where large profits can be made, while ignoring diseases found mainly in poor countries. The patent system also allows large companies to create patent thickets. Thickets are created by patenting lots of inventions in the same field that have tiny incremental improvements. With so many patents clustered around one technology they stop anyone else working in that particular field without obtaining numerous (and potentially overpriced) licences for each patent in the thicket.[2] Such use of the system is not a spur but a hindrance to innovation.

What are the requirements for protection?

In Europe a patent will not protect mere ideas, concepts or suggestions, only inventions. There must be a new product, new process or a new way of using an old thing. To be patentable the thing must be (1) new, (2) inventive and (3) capable of industrial application.

The invention must be new[3]

The standard of novelty demanded in European patent law is far more stringent than that needed when registering a design (see Chapter 7). Be aware, however, that novelty may be viewed differently in different countries. 'New' in UK and European patent law means that it has not been made available to the public whether in writing or by speech or any other form by anyone at any time, anywhere in the world. The inventive step that you are claiming must not be found in any existing patent applications, even lapsed patents, neither must it have been written about by you or anyone else in any journal article or press release. Before the date of filing no conference presentations or blog entries must have been made in a way that describes the invention sufficiently well so that people could understand what the 'inventive step' is. You must not have sold the product before you file for a patent and even one person being told about your invention, if they were not told in confidence or under a non-disclosure agreement, can destroy novelty and ruin your chances of obtaining a patent. The stringency of the test of newness is because a patent is such a strong IP right. It is a complete monopoly over a new and potentially very useful product or process. When you are looking to see if your idea is novel or if someone else has already thought of it, all sort of things that have happened in the past may be considered. In *Windsurfing International Inc. v Tabur Marine* a patent had been granted for a Windsurfer.[4] In revocation proceedings the patent was being attacked as lacking novelty. The reason for saying that it was not new was that many years before and for only a few days a 12-year-old boy who was on holiday in Hayling Island had used a sailboard. Although very roughly constructed, the boy's sailboard was similar to the Windsurfer product. It was held by the court that even fleeting use many years before will destroy novelty as long as the use was in public. But the use must be in public, that is, the public must have had the opportunity to see and understand what the invention was. That does not mean that anyone did see it, only that they would have been able to work out what the inventive concept was if they had been in the right place at the right time.[5] If the public could not have worked out from just looking at the sailboard or could not investigate further to discover what the inventive step was there will be no loss of novelty.[6]

---

2 See www.ipo.gov.uk/informatic-thickets.pdf.
3 Article 54 European Patent Convention, s 2 of the Patents Act 1977.
4 Windsurfing International Inc. v Tabur Marine Ltd [1985] RPC 59 CA.
5 Lux Traffic Controls v Pike Signals [1993] RPC 107 ChD.
6 Pall Corp v Commercial Hydraulics [1990].

The invention must involve an inventive step[7]

To obtain a patent not only must the invention be absolutely new but it must also be inventive. To be regarded as inventive your concept does not have to be startlingly clever; an incremental improvement to an existing product or process will suffice, as long as the improvement is not obvious. It is sometimes not easy to decide if something is not obvious but inventive. There are certain steps that you should go through. These steps are called the Pozzoli test. You should:

1. identify the notional person skilled in the art and the relevant common general knowledge of that person;
2. identify the inventive concept of the claim in question or, if that cannot readily be done, construe it;
3. identify what, if any, differences exist between the matter cited as forming part of the state of the art and the inventive concept of the claim (or the claim as construed); and
4. determine whether, viewed without knowledge of the alleged invention as claimed, such differences constitute steps that would have been obvious to the person skilled in the art or whether they require a degree of invention.

The notional person skilled in the art is sometimes called the 'skilled addressee'. They are someone with good practical knowledge and experience of the field in question. It has been established that if such a skilled addressee would not think that the thing was obvious then it is inventive.[8] We can go back to our little boy in Hayling Island. The surfboard that he made did not look at all like the professionally designed and manufactured Windsurfer that could be bought in the shops. There were many improvements and refinements not found in the boy's rough sailboard but the court had to decide whether the boy's sailboard 'anticipated' the Windsurfer. This means that when looking at the inventive claim in the Windsurfer patent, did the boy's sailboard do the same thing? If the patent was held to be valid would the boy be infringing the Windsurfer? Would he be prevented from doing something that was merely an obvious extension of what he had legitimately been doing before? To decide this you have to ask whether, if someone skilled in the surfing business had seen the boy's sailboard (remember, they don't have to have actually seen it), they would have decided that any improvements Windsurfer had made would have been obvious improvements on the boy's original concept. Would they or indeed anyone skilled in the business when faced with the problem of manufacturing the sailboard have come up with the same solution and made those same adjustments? If the skilled person would not have made those improvements himself, an inventive step will have been established.

A patent protects a solution to some problem. An inventive step does not have to consist only of new things. The inventive concept may be to put two or more existing things together in a way that other people would not have thought of doing. In one case textile factories were experiencing quite a problem due to a build-up of dust around their machines.[9] The solution to the problem as claimed in the patent was to create a vacuum cleaner hanging from overhead rails that ran between the rows of textile machines. Both the vacuum cleaner and the rails were existing products and not at all inventive, but the inventive step was to hang the cleaner from the rails. The fact that the dust build-up had been a long-standing problem and no one had thought of providing this type of solution before demonstrated that it was indeed inventive, even though it might seem obvious once it had been pointed out. Sometimes the popularity of a product can indicate that it must have been inventive. In the early 1990s one of the few successful female

---

7 Article 56, s 3 of the Patents Act 1977.
8 Pozzoli SpA v BDMO SA [2007] FSR 37 CA.
9 Parkes-Cramer Co v GW Thornton [1966] RPC 407.

inventors, Mandy Haberman, created the 'Anywayup Cup' – a child's feeder cup that did not spill when it was held upside down. It was a tremendous economic success, selling over £2 million worth of cups p.a. It was found that the 'Anywayup Cup', although providing a very simple solution to the problem of spillage, was technically inventive.[10] Although in this particular case large sales supported the conclusion of originality, large sales alone will not prove that there has been an inventive step. Such economic success could after all be due to fashion, a better manufacturing technique or improved marketing. Economic success without more evidence must be treated with caution.

The invention must be capable of industrial application[11]

To obtain a patent the product or process must have some use. This use should be described in the patent application. Merely identifying a DNA sequence will not be patentable unless you can show how you can use it. It is not enough to say: 'It is very clever, it must have some use; I just don't yet know what that use may be.' You must suggest a use that is plausible. In a recent case a patent was filed for a protein.[12] Because of its similarity with other proteins it was felt that this could be used to treat various diseases of the immune system. It was held by the Supreme Court that, although it could not be guaranteed that this protein would have the desired use, as long as this use was plausible, not vague or speculative, the patent would be regarded as having industrial application. In the EU this use does not have to be better or cheaper than what went before but it must be different. Depending on the country, new types of plants are protected either by the patent system or by a specific system for the protection of new varieties of plants.

The invention must not be excluded[13]

There are various things that have been excluded from patentability in Europe, some for policy reasons and some because they are protected by other IPR. Aesthetic creations such as literary, dramatic, musical or artistic works are excluded because they are protected by copyright. Granting a patent for such things would create too strong a monopoly. You may have copyright in a photograph that you have taken of Nelson's Column. Anyone else who independently creates their own photograph of the landmark would not infringe your copyright as they have not copied your photograph (see Chapter 5). A patent gives a complete monopoly even where there has been independent creation, so granting a patent for such a thing would prevent anyone else from taking such a photograph. The presentation of information – such as making products in different colours in order to distinguish them, or a scheme, rule or method for performing a mental act – are all things that could be done in a person's head and are not the sort of things that you can detect let alone prevent them from doing.[14] Although they may be protected by copyright or confidence, methods of playing a game or doing business, discoveries, scientific theories or mathematical methods are abstract ideas or information and because they have no technical effect cannot be regarded as inventions. However, if you find a practical use for a discovery or theory, that use could attract patent protection. Finding that a virus causes a disease is a discovery but creating a kit to discover whether someone has the disease is patentable.

Many of the exclusions are for reasons of policy. It is not possible to obtain a patent for an animal or plant variety[15] or a method of treatment of the human or animal body by surgery,

---

10 Haberman v Jackel International Ltd [1999] FSR 683 ChD.
11 Article 57, s 4 of the Patents Act 1977.
12 Human Genome Sciences Inc. v Eli Lilly & Co [2011] UKSC 51, SC.
13 Article 52(3)(4), s 1(1) of the Patents Act 1977.
14 Halliburton Energy Services Inc.'s Patent Application [2011] EWHC 2508.
15 There is a separate plant-breeder right to protect new varieties of plants.

therapy or diagnosis. It is felt that things such as medical treatments should be available for everyone to use and that it would not benefit society to provide a monopoly on these to one person or company. It is perfectly acceptable, however, to obtain a patent for a drug or equipment that is used in treating people or animals as the monopoly granted allows the drug-developing company to recoup the large R&D costs required to bring such drugs or technology to market. Finally, you will not be allowed to patent an invention if it would be contrary to public policy or morality, if it would be expected to encourage offensive, immoral or anti-social behaviour. This does not mean that you will be denied a patent if using the product or process would be illegal; patenting has nothing to do with legality and what is illegal may change from one country to another and over time. You may still, after all, sell a product even though you do not have a patent for it and you may get a patent even though to use it might be illegal. A patent does not give you a right to use a product; it only gives you a right to prevent others from doing so. Although biotechnological inventions are patentable, as are microbiological processes, you will not be granted a patent for cloning or modifying the genetic identity of animals or human beings. Using human embryos for industrial or commercial purposes is not patentable, neither is the process for modifying the genetic identity of animals if it is likely to cause them suffering without there being any substantial medical benefit to humans or animals.[16] The exclusions to patentability may be different in different countries. For instance, it is not possible to patent a method of doing business in the UK or in Europe under the Patent Cooperation Treaty (see later), but it is possible to do so in the USA and Japan. The same is true for computer programs, but computer programs need more explanation.

Computer programs

Source code and object code are protected by copyright but copyright just provides protection against copying. Although it is not possible to patent a computer program as such, it is possible in the UK and under the EPC to obtain a patent for the technical effect that the program has.[17] The technical effect cannot just be that it is faster to do something using a computer rather than using the human brain or doing it by hand. The program must make a technical contribution, even if that technical contribution is just making a better computer;[18] it must also, of course, be novel, non-obvious and of industrial application. You must consider, however, whether a patent is the most useful way of protecting your software. This is a fast-moving industry: will you still be using that program in four years' time when your patent is granted? Most software executives do not consider patents to be important, feeling that they benefit lawyers and 'patent trolls' rather than businesses. Being first to market is regarded as far preferable, especially if this can be backed up with secrecy and making reverse-engineering difficult. Finally, it is almost impossible to determine what is 'the state of the art' as far as computer programs are concerned. In addition, because software is often based on previous programs, novelty and inventive step would often be in doubt.

The importance of confidentiality

You must not allow your idea to become available to the public before the date of filing. If you do it will lose its novelty and will become part of the state of the art. That does not mean, however, that you may not talk to anyone about what your invention is. You need to find out whether your idea is feasible: whether a product can be made that you can sell at a price customers are prepared to pay. This means that you will have to negotiate with people who can help

---

16 SI 2000/2037 Patent Regulation 2000.
17 Aerotel/Macrossan Patent Application [2006] EWHC 705, CA.
18 Symbian Ltd v Comptroller-General of Patents [2009] RPC 1 CA.

you. Some people, like your patent agent, because of their position are automatically regarded as bound by confidence. For six months some disclosures at international exhibitions are not regarded as part of the state of the art under certain conditions,[19] but other people will need to be bound under a confidentiality or non-disclosure agreement. But even with such an agreement in place, do not talk to anyone if you do not trust them to keep your invention secret. Although there is a six-month period during which disclosures made in breach of confidence are ignored,[20] and even though you may be able to sue the discloser for breach of contract you cannot make something secret again once it is in the public domain. Also remember that to get a collaborators interest you may not have to make an 'enabling disclosure'. An enabling disclosure is explaining your invention so that it enables' someone to understand what the inventive concept is. It may be sufficient, in order to get their interest, to disclose only what it is and what its advantages are.

Patents are territorial and the laws vary in each territory

You can apply for a national patent in the UK but this will only protect you in the UK. A national patent in Germany or the USA will only protect you in Germany or the USA. You may, however, apply for a regional patent under the EPC,[21] which can be granted for a group of European countries and which may be cheaper than applying for each individual country.[22] There will soon be another European option available. A European patent with unitary effect, known as the 'unitary patent', will from January 2014 be granted by the EPO for 25 EU Member States (excluding Italy and Spain). The patent can be applied for in three official languages, English, German or French, but machine translations may be made into other European languages if needed. The 'unitary patent' will be useful for people who wish to patent in all 25 countries, but national patents may still be the preferred and cheaper route if a patent is only required in one or two Member States. Your final option is to use the Patent Cooperation Treaty (PCT) for protection in 145 countries.

It is important that you consider where you want to market, manufacture or license your invention. Patenting can be a costly business. Not only do you have to pay the initial cost of obtaining a patent but after the fifth year you will also need to pay annual renewal fees to keep it in force. Also consider whether you have the ability to monitor for infringement in each country and whether you have budgeted to defend your patent if you do find that someone has infringed. It is a waste of money to patent where you do not intend to market but it is essential to consider patenting in territories where you do.

Do a search

A patent is like a fence. It sets out the scope of your invention. Once a patent is granted no one is allowed to perform any of the acts allotted to you by the claims made in your specification, claims that come inside your fence, unless any of the permitted acts or defences apply. To file a patent application you must disclose your invention in sufficient detail to allow someone skilled in that field to make it. You must, however, first make sure that what you have is new. You can never be absolutely sure that someone has never done this before – remember the boy on Hayling Island – but you can take sensible precautions. Keep in mind that just because you have never seen a product like yours on the market does not mean that it is new. Its absence could be because, although it was marketed in the past, no one wanted to buy it.

---

19 Section 2(4)(c) of the Patents Act 1977.
20 Section 2(4)(b) of the Patents Act 1977.
21 The European Patent Convention is made up of more than just members of the EU.
22 Examples are the African Regional Intellectual Property Office (16 countries), Eurasian Patent Organisation (9 former Soviet countries), European Patent Organisation (37 European countries).

The first step to determine whether your invention is new is to look at patents that have already been granted. This is called a 'prior art search'. By looking at previous patents you may find something that 'anticipates', is the same or very similar to your 'invention'. Such a discovery will mean that your 'invention' is not new after all. If that is the case you will not be able to patent your product or process. If, however, an existing patent has expired you can make and sell the product or process without infringing, but, of course, with no legal protection. You may also be able to develop an existing valid or lapsed patent by adding to it or changing it in some non-obvious way. If you can make an adaptation in a way that a skilled person would not regard as obvious you could obtain a patent for the development that you have made. Many patent databases are available online for no charge. The UK Intellectual Property Office (UK IPO) has a free Online Patent Information and Document Inspection Service called Ipsum, which can be found at www.ipo.gov.uk/types/patent/p-os/p-find/p-ipsum.htm. In addition, Espacenet, which is run by the EPO, gives access to more than 70 million patent documents worldwide, going back as far as 1836. This database can be found at www.epo.org/searching/free/espacenet.html, or there is a UK version at http://gb.espacenet.com. You can make three sorts of searches using Espacenet. To start with, by entering keywords and phrases you can search the titles or abstracts of patents that are published in the database. Alternatively, if you know the number of a patent that you think may be relevant to your application you can search using that number. Finally, you can use the classification system to find all the patents within a technical subject heading. Patent abstracts are classified with subclassifications and indexed to make searching easier.[23] There are eight sections. These are: A – Human necessities; B – Performing operations; C – Chemistry and metallurgy; D – Textiles and paper; E – Civil engineering and building accessories; F – Mechanics, heating and lighting; G – Instrumentation; H – Electricity.

You must be aware that just because you don't find anything when you search does not mean that nothing is there. You may not be using the correct keywords to describe your product. It is sensible to use a variety of different ways to describe what your invention is. Look at other specifications for patents similar to yours and see what keywords they use. Try English and US spellings as well as common mis-spellings. After your preliminary search, if you still feel that your idea is novel you should then ask a patent agent who, for a fee, will do another search. As they are experts they will know the appropriate words to use and the patent classifications in which to search. As well as a patent search you should look at journals in the relevant areas, go to trade shows if possible and read conference papers to see if other people have already made, sold or talked about something, even many years ago, that is similar to your invention, thus destroying its novelty.

Timing your patent application

Most countries have a first to file system – so you want to get to the winning post before anyone else. But do not rush into filing for a patent. You must first ensure that you have as much information about the prior art as possible and certainly all the information that you need to successfully file. You should also ensure that you are claiming as much as you can to be included within your fence, for, although you may cut down the scope of your application after you have filed, you cannot subsequently claim more to be within your fence than was in your original claim. Make your fence encompass as much ground and be as wide as possible without infringing someone else's patent. This requires very careful wording. You may be at a very early stage of the research process, having discovered just one use for a gene.[24] With the proper choice of words you could place within your fence uses for your gene that are yet to be discovered. But there is a problem. If your claims are too broad you may find that you have put your fence posts on someone else's land and that you are infringing someone else's patent. Narrower claims are

---

23 The International Patent Classifications system consists of eight sections divided into 120 classes with 628 subclasses.
24 As in Eli Lilly & Co v Human Genome Sciences Inc. [2012] RPC 6 SC.

stronger and less open to challenge but they are much easier for people to design around. It is very difficult to get the balance right and it is strongly advised to get the help of a patent agent who will help you do this. They might be expensive but they have many years of training to ensure that your claims are as comprehensive as possible.

Priority filing

Different countries may have different procedures but in Europe your period of protection begins to run from the priority date, the date you file your patent application. Assuming you pay your renewal fees and your patent is neither revoked nor invalidated,[25] your patent will last for 20 years from that time. If, however, you have filed a patent application in another country in the previous 12 months your priory date will run from that date. If you only want protection in the UK you can apply to the national office, the UK Intellectual Property Office (www.ipo.gov.uk). You do not have to be a national of the UK to obtain a UK patent but you do need to have the right to apply for a patent. The inventor or co-inventor or the employer of the inventor or an assignee can apply for a patent, but all inventors must be named. You do not at this initial stage need to file a patent application in all the countries where you may want protection.

If you first file in your home country, say in the UK on 10 May 2012, there is normally a 12-month period, in this case up to May 2013, where you can file an application for your invention in other countries. These will all date back to the initial filing date of 10 May 2012 in the UK, the 'priority date'. You may go beyond this 12-month period and still be able to file for a patent in other countries but only if your application has not yet been published. It can take up to 18 months for publication to occur and of course in this time your invention is still regarded as secret and therefore still novel. If you do decide to use this extra time to apply in other countries you will not be able to claim priority from your filing date of 10 May 2012 in the UK, so if someone has published a similar invention in this extra six months your novelty will have been destroyed. They will have won the patenting race in those countries and you will lose your ability to patent in these territories. Some systems, but not the UK or the EPC, have a 'grace period' of up to a year where you can expose your invention to the public without losing novelty. You can use this time to do market research. You can go to trade shows or try to find people interested in licensing your invention without needing to get them to sign a non-disclosure agreement. Be very careful with this grace period, however, as it only applies to some countries. You will destroy novelty in countries that do not use this system if you make use of the grace period before filing there.

Where to make your application

The first question you must ask yourself is why you want a patent. If you want to license-out your product or sell your business outright you should file where you think licensees or purchasers will want protection. If you want to manufacture your product in China, protection must be sought there. If you decide you need protection in more than one or two territories it is not cost-effective to apply to individual countries and so you should apply under a regional system.

In Europe this is the European Patent Convention, and most of the provisions are similar to those found in the UK system. The EPC is not a European Community Patent equivalent to the Community Trade Mark where a single application gives you protection in all the European states. You can make a single application to the European Patent Office (www.epo.org) in Munich, but you then choose in which of the 36 European states you want protection. You can apply in English, French or German. The EPO will process your application and then send it to your chosen countries as if you were applying for separate national patents. The new 'unitary patent'

---

25 Supplementary Protection Certificates of up to five years are available for pharmaceutical patents to compensate for the time needed to obtain regulatory approval before they can be brought to market.

will give you protection in 25 Member States (but not Italy or Spain). If you want international rather than European protection it would be cheaper to apply via the Patent Cooperation Treaty (PCT). Using this route you only need to make one initial application in one language with one set of search fees. You can then gain protection in up to 145 countries worldwide but you must be a national or resident or have a commercial presence in one of the PCT states. A great advantage of this system is that you do not yet, though you will eventually, have to pay to have the patent translated into the languages of the countries in which you want protection. If you were applying to individual national patent offices or under the EPO system this expensive translation would need to be completed at a far earlier stage. Using the PCT route you have 30 months to study the feasibility of commercialising, producing, marketing or licensing your product or process in the countries in which you are considering registration. After you have conducted your market research you may decide not to register after all. However, if you do decide to go ahead, your application will need to be translated into the relevant language and then sent to the national offices where you want protection. You can file a PCT application either with your national office, UK IPO, or at the World Intellectual Property Organization (WIPO) (www.wipo.int/patentscope). Your patent agent will be able to tell you about the laws in the different countries and how the costs may differ. Some countries have discounts for small to medium-sized entities (SMEs) or charge more for a quicker service. Although fees are charged by the patent office, by far the greatest cost is attorney fees. The cost of a patent attorney will vary depending on how complex your claim, the number of countries in which you want to file, the translation costs and whether any objections have been raised during the application procedure. Some countries demand that local agents be used.

How to present your invention to your patent attorney to the best effect

Drafting a patent application is an extremely skilled procedure and should be performed by a properly qualified patent attorney. They are highly skilled people and they are very expensive to employ. The more you can do yourself and the more prepared you are to answer your patent attorney's questions, the less it will cost you.

Before you meet your attorney make sure that you can provide information about the technical area in which your invention belongs. You should have done some state of the art searches, looked at journals and gone to trade shows etc., so that you are aware of as much of the prior art as possible. You must know what the problem is that your invention solves. You should have found out what competition exists, what their disadvantages are and why your product is better. If there is no problem that needs to be solved or your product or process does not solve it better than existing solutions, you should be asking yourself whether you should be spending money on seeking the advice of a patent attorney in the first place. To save time you should create a clear and precise description of your invention. Try to think of as many uses and advantages for your invention as you can.

To file a patent application you need to include at least one description of how your product or process can be made. In the UK this does not have to be the best or cheapest way of making your product but it must be clear enough so that a person skilled in the art can make it. You do not always have to include drawings in your application, they are not necessary for drugs for instance, but any drawings you do include must be clear and should help your attorney understand your product and how it works. It is only once your attorney understands your invention that they can help you construct your claim. The claim is the most important part of a patent as it describes where you are positioning your fence and what, therefore, is going to be inside it. Keep in mind that your patent attorney is not there to give you business advice or to tell you whether your invention will make you rich, they are there to help you conduct a search of the prior art and construct a patent application.

WHAT ARE THE REQUIREMENTS FOR PROTECTION?

The procedure

We have now come to the point where you have decided that there is a problem to be solved and that your invention is the solution. You judge that none of the alternatives to patenting, such as secrecy or being first to market, are more appropriate and that a patent is for you. You believe that your invention is new, non-obvious and capable of industrial application and is not on the list of excluded subject matter. You know who the inventor is and that you have the right to apply for a patent. You have had your application drafted by a competent patent attorney and know where you want to market your product or process. You are now ready to file your application.

Applications whether for the UK, EPC or PCT can initially be handled by the UK IPO and so this is the procedure that will be discussed. Your application will consist of two parts. The first is the abstract, which is a brief summary of the invention with its title; the second is the specification. The specification is made up of a description of your invention, what you claim the patent will cover and any drawings. It can take quite a long time from filing your application to grant. Times vary depending on where you are filing but this time is increasing as more patents are applied for and backlogs are developing. In the UK it takes at least four years but may end up taking a lot longer. There are accelerated procedures in certain circumstances, for example for 'green patents'. You do not have a patent until it is granted. No matter how long the procedure takes the patent runs from the date of filing, your priority date. If anyone has infringed your patent during the application procedure you cannot sue them until the patent has been granted. Once granted you can backdate your claim against them to the date of publication, usually 18 months after your priority date.

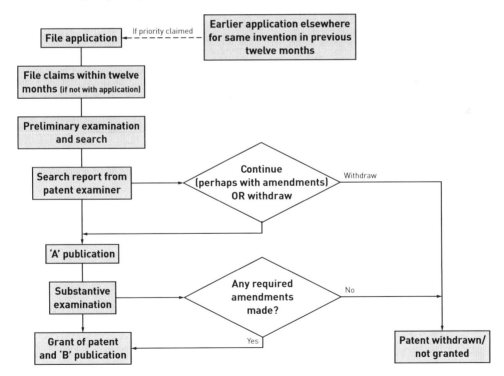

Figure 4.1 Patent filing procedure.

1 Filing

You start the patenting process by filling out the appropriate form, which can be accessed online,[26] stating who is applying and including a description of your invention and any drawings. You do not at this stage need to file your claims and abstract but you may not later add any additional information that would broaden your claim, so it is better to have it all prepared at this point. The date the intellectual property office (IPO) receives your application is your filing or priority date. Within a few days you will be given a number and the date. This is the date at which the UKIPO will consider the state of the art to decide if your invention is indeed new. You will now be able to tell people what your invention is without losing novelty, but please note that you may still decide to withdraw your application before it is published without your invention becoming part of the state of the art. It is still wise therefore to conduct any discussions as to licensing, etc., under confidentiality agreements so that novelty is not destroyed. You now have 12 months to produce a description, claims, drawings and an abstract.

Claims can vary from being quite simple with just a few claims to a very complex document with many claims. Make sure you do not waste these 12 months: you should be working very hard trying to find someone to license your invention or enter into a partnership or venture capital arrangement. If your invention needs to be manufactured it may take years to get the process just right so that the product can be made economically. You need to start as soon as possible. Any time wasted could be time when you are not profiting from your invention.

DESCRIPTION

A patent is a monopoly given to the inventor for a specific period. In exchange for this monopoly the inventor agrees to make the description of their invention available to the public. The description also allows the patent office to decide whether a patent should be granted in the first place. You should describe the problem that your invention is supposed to solve and summarise the prior art. The description should include everything you intend to claim, as new information cannot be added later. It must describe your invention sufficiently clearly so that a person skilled in the art can carry out the invention. You cannot say 'there should be a large cavity' as no one can tell what might be regarded as large. You would have to give measurements. You then explain what your invention does what its most important features are and at least one way it can be performed. It is wise, for instance, to say that it will help or be advantageous in doing X rather than that it *must* do X. It is better to say that Y *can* be used rather than Y is *necessary*. You can supply any supporting material on a CD.

DRAWINGS

Drawings can help to demonstrate your invention's technical features. If your invention is a process or a drug drawings may not be useful, but if you do include drawings they should be clear.

ABSTRACT

The abstract will appear on the front page of the patent application. It can be easily searched by others using patent databases to see if your patent anticipates or infringes theirs. The abstract is about 150 words and is a clear summary of your invention. It includes the title for the invention, the technical field in which the invention belongs and at least one use to which it can be put.

---

26 www.ipo.gov.uk/types/patent/p-os/p-apply-online/p-apply-online-uk-filingsystem/p-apply-online-uk-checklist.htm.

CLAIMS

The claims (you will usually have more than one) are the most important part of the application. They show where you have placed your fence so that other people know what they can and cannot do without infringing. It is usual to start off with a broad claim and then have 'dependent claims' that refer back to the original first claim. If the broad claim has made the fence too big you can rely on the dependent claims that restrict the areas claimed. So if we look at Figure 4.2[27] for a toy ball we see that the main broad claim would be for 'An amusement device comprising a core region and plural elastomeric filaments radiating in plural angularly offset planes from the core region'. The first dependent claim would be, 'A device according to claim 1 characterised in that it has a substantially spherical configuration', with a further dependent claim being, 'A device according to claim 1 characterised in that the outer ends of at least some of the filaments include enlargements'.

The court will look at your claims in any infringement proceedings and so they must be written very carefully. If you draft these claims narrowly you may find that your fence covers too little ground. You may not have enough territory to make your invention work efficiently without encroaching on someone else's patent. Alternatively, you may have left a gaping hole in your fence that others may sneak through or invent around. If you are claiming something, such as the cure for the common cold, you do not have to show why your invention works or that it will in fact work, you only have to show that it might work;[28] but it must be clear and precise enough to allow a skilled person to make it. Your claims must be carefully worded, precise and consistent.

Claim to protect the invention

Claim to be filed:

'An amusement device comprising a **core region** and **plural elastomeric filaments** radiating in **plural angularly offset planes** from the core region.'

Sub-module C   Understanding patent claims - (a) Toy ball   6/15

Figure 4.2 Claims.

---

27 Figure 4.2 taken from Patent Teaching Kit: www.epo.org/learning-events/materials/kit.html.
28 Conor Medsystems Inc. v Angiotech Pharmaceuticals Inc. [2008] RPC 28 HL.

2 Preliminary examination

Within one month of you making your application the UK Patent Office will conduct a preliminary examination. This merely checks that you have included all the necessary documents and that you have answered all the questions.

3 Search

Within 12 months of your priority date you must request a search and send the abstract and specification, that is the description, drawings and claims to the IPO. You must also pay the application and search fees. If you are not yet ready to commercialise your product you may decide at this stage to allow your application to lapse. As it has not yet been published, and as long as you have not told anyone about it, novelty will not have been lost. You may reapply when you are ready, at which time you will be given a new priority date.

The search is when an examiner who specialises in the technical field of your invention searches to see if your invention is new and inventive. The examiner will look at not only patents worldwide but any other relevant documents and journals and may even do an internet search. Within 18 months of your priority date the examiner will send you their report.

The report will include everything the examiner has found. It may show that your invention is not new or inventive after all. However, the report may just include information about things that have been done previously in the field of your invention but that do not anticipate your invention. If some prior art is found, you have various alternative courses of action. You may decide to allow your application to lapse and abandon the invention altogether, or you may decide to move your fence. As your application has not yet been published, if you move your fence, reducing the scope of your claim or amending it in some way, you may be able to avoid the prior art. If you do this within 12 months you can retain the same priority date. If more work is needed you can withdraw your application and reapply when you are ready and be given a new priority date. Finally, you may be convinced that you have a sound patentable invention. This is the time to consider applying for patents in other countries before the 12-month period is up. It is a good idea to keep a record of any issues that the examiner raised, just in case there might be an objection after publication concerning the points raised. It is always better to be prepared.

4 Publication

Once the patent office is happy with your application and you still wish to go ahead, the search report will be published on the UK IPO website. This will be at least 18 months from the priority date. From now on your invention is in the public domain. Other people, especially competitors, now have three months to make observations about your patent. They may, for instance, claim that it is not new or inventive, that it was anticipated in a journal article or that it is obvious and well known in the field. The UK IPO will take these objections into account when deciding whether or not to grant your patent.

5 Substantive examination

Within six months of publication you must request a substantive examination. This will cost £100. The UK IPO will make sure your application meets the legal requirements of the Patents Act 1977, is new, inventive and not excluded. They will check that the description is full enough and clear enough to allow a skilled person to make or work your invention. You may be asked to make minor amendments but you are not allowed to add any new information to your application. If you don't complete the process of dealing with any objections within four-and-half years from your priority date your application will fail. If you intend to file a PCT application you should now start the applications for the countries you have chosen. If your invention has an environmental benefit or is urgent, there is a fast-track or accelerated procedure available.[29]

6 Grant

If everything goes well your patent will be granted and you will receive a certificate. It will have taken at least four years from your priory date but unless you have used the accelerated procedure it will probably take much longer. There are patenting backlogs in most countries and the EPO can take up to ten years to grant a patent. Do not forget to start planning ahead. You may want to start thinking about filing patents on improvements to your invention as soon as possible.

RENEWAL FEES

In the UK once your patent has been granted you must pay renewal fees every year from the fourth anniversary of the filing date. Under the EPO system fees need to be paid on the second anniversary of the EPO filing date. In the UK, fees start at £70 for the fifth year increasing to £600 in the twentieth year. Renewal fees must be paid in every country in which you file a patent and this can mount up to a large sum. It is up to you to remember to pay these fees. It is essential that someone is given the specific task of keeping good records of all your patent renewal dates. You can ask your patent attorney to keep records for you for a fee. Although your invention may initially be successful, this may change. You may find that you do not wish to renew for the full 20 years. In the UK fewer than half of patents are renewed past their tenth year. Eventually most are allowed to lapse and fall into the public domain.

Who owns or is entitled to the rights in a patent?

In Europe an inventor is the person who was responsible for the inventive concept. In *IDA Ltd v University of Southampton*,[30] a university professor invented a cockroach trap that killed the insects by causing poisoned electrically charged talcum powder to stick to their legs. Mr Metcalf suggested that it would be better to use poisoned magnetic powder. The professor applied for a patent using magnetic powder. It was held that even though the professor had the original idea of the trap, the inventive step was using the magnetic powder and so Mr Metcalf and not the professor was the inventor of that aspect of the invention.

Where an invention is the joint work of two or more people, both will be named on the patent application and they will be regarded as joint inventors. In many research areas invention is a team effort and it can be difficult to pin down exactly who generated specific creations and when they did so. The questions to ask are (1) what is the inventive concept? and (2) who had the key ideas? It is for this reason that it is vital to keep a log book of all inventive activities, with entries dated, so that the development and source of all ideas can be followed. The inventor, the joint-inventor, the employer of the inventor or an assignee can apply for a patent, but all inventors must be named on the application.

If an invention is made by joint inventors, although they can each leave their share in their will and each can exploit the invention by themselves, they all need to agree if they want to sell, mortgage or license the patent. Any assignment or mortgage of a patent or patent application must be in writing and signed. The transaction must then be registered, otherwise it will not be possible to obtain costs or damages if the patent is infringed.

---

29 www.ipo.gov.uk/p-pn-fasttrack.
30 [2006] RPC 21.

If an employee created the patent, to whom does it belong?

In Europe the right to an invention created by an employee depends on the law of the country. In Germany the employee is the first owner of their invention but the employer may choose to claim ownership in return for a statutory level of remuneration.

In most countries inventions belong to the employer but inventive employees may be given fair or reasonable compensation in addition to their normal salary if the employer decides to exploit the invention. In other countries there is either no extra compensation awarded or compensation is only awarded in exceptional cases. In France inventions created during the course of employment belong to the employer but if they were created outside employment but related to the employer's business the employer can request that the ownership be transferred to them on payment of a fee.

Under the Patents Act 1977, Article 60–61 s 39, the ownership of some but not all employees' inventions are owned by the employer. In the UK, if on the face of it an employee makes an invention in the course of their employment, the employer is entitled to ownership. However, this only applies if the invention is made in the course of the employee's normal duties *and* an invention might reasonably be expected to result from the performance of those duties or if, although outside their normal duties, this task was specifically assigned to them by their employer *and* an invention might reasonably be expected to result.[31]

In addition an employer can claim ownership of an employee's invention where the employee has a special obligation to further the interests of the employer. This would be the case if, for instance, an invention was made by a senior manager or director of the company. This is because people in those more senior positions may owe the company a special obligation called a fiduciary duty. This duty goes beyond the ordinary duties owed by a normal employee. Consequently, if someone is employed as a machinist making copper pipes they would not, as would a director, owe a special obligation to the employer. Also, no one would expect a machinist to invent things as part of their job description. We can safely say that, assuming that the employer had not specifically asked them to do so, a machinist would retain ownership of a new and innovative type of golf club created by them even if they created the club in their lunch time using their employer's machine. However, remember this does depend on what you are employed to do.

To decide what an employee's normal duties are you must look at their contract of employment. If you are a research chemist employed to work on a project to find a cure for cancer your 'normal duty' is to undertake research where an invention might be expected. If you inadvertently invent a cure for arthritis this would be regarded as part of your normal duties as your job is to invent things. Here the arthritis cure would belong to your employer.

Someone else is using something that is the same or similar to my patent – can I do anything about it?

If your product or process is not commercially successful it is unlikely that anyone will bother to copy or infringe your patent: why should they? It is estimated that only about 1 in a 100 inventions will make enough money to cover their patenting costs and only 1 in 1,400 are truly successful. In all likelihood, well before the maximum 20-year period of protection you will give up

---

31 For a discussion of normal duties of an employee, see Adrian Chandler (2008), 'Ownership of Employees' Inventions: Duties, Expectations and Variable Objectivity' [EIPR] 2008 164.

paying the renewal fees, your patent will enter the public domain and stay unused and unloved forever more. However, if it is a commercial success, someone somewhere will want to copy your invention.

Infringement, however, is not restricted to mere copying, it is also an infringement to manufacture, use, sell or import a patented product or process without the owner's consent. As the owner of the patent it is up to you and you alone to bring proceedings against infringers who are performing any of these prohibited acts. It is wise to have a strategy for what you will do if you discover infringement (see Chapter 8). Litigation is expensive and time-consuming and should not be entered into lightly. However, infringers will not have the expense of recouping any R&D costs and could make your product cheaper than you can and you will lose your market if you don't do something.

If you suspect infringement you should contact a lawyer immediately. Most people will want an injunction to stop infringers using their product or process, followed by an award of damages for any sales that have been lost due to the infringement. The first thing that the lawyer will do is check that you do have the right to bring proceedings. You will not be able to bring infringement proceedings unless your patent is valid, that it is still in force and all the fees have been paid. They will need to establish that you are the proprietor or joint proprietor of the patent or that, if it has been assigned to you, the assignment has been registered at the IPO.[32] If the assignment has not been registered you will not be entitled to recover your costs until registration has been completed. It is wise to make sure that some identified body is responsible for ensuring that all your IPR are used and maintained, with all renewal fees being paid on time.

Availability of 'watching services'

Many specialist companies offer patent watching services. A patent watch, as the name suggests, is a monitoring and tracking system. You can use such a service to monitor your own patents, competitors' patents or all patents in a particular technical field. This information not only can help you identify your competitors but can make sure you avoid infringing other people's patents while making you aware if others are infringing your patent. Such a service can also help you discover potential collaborators or licensing opportunities. You will need a watching service for each country in which you trade. But remember, it is no use detecting infringers if you don't have an infringement budget enabling you to do something about them if you find them.

What amounts to infringement?

If your patent is for a product, infringement occurs where without your consent someone makes, disposes of, offers to dispose of, uses or imports the product or keeps it, whether for disposal or otherwise.[33] However, if your patent is for a process, infringement occurs if someone uses or offers the process or a product obtained from means of the process[34] for use in the UK when they know, or where it would be obvious to a reasonable person, that the proprietor has not consented.[35] It is also an infringement if someone supplies the means for making the product (e.g. a kit of the product). So you can see here that use of a *product* can be an infringement even if you don't realise that you are infringing, whereas with a *process* you must not know or have a reasonable suspicion that you are infringing.

Remember, if you have a UK patent one of these infringing acts must be done in the UK; if it is done in another country you cannot complain unless you have a patent there or the product

---

32 www.ipo.gov.uk/p-buying.htm.
33 Section 60(1)(a) of the Patents Act 1977.
34 Section 60(1)(c) of the Patents Act 1977.
35 Section 60(1)(b) of the Patents Act 1977.

is imported into this country (which is one of the infringing acts). This can cause a problem if the patented product, such as a gaming system,[36] is being used on the internet. In such a situation the infringement does not take place where the host computer is but where the person using the gaming system is situated. If the users are in the UK they would be infringing in the UK, if the users are in France they would be infringing in France.

If you do detect infringement you need to have as much information as you can muster as evidence to support your case. It would be helpful to know if the infringer is intentionally copying your patent or if they have done so accidentally. This will be relevant when assessing any remedies awarded against them. Although remedies such as an injunction should be available, neither damages nor an account of profits will be granted if the defendant can prove that they had no reason to believe that a patent existed. Some people put the word 'patented' plus the number of the patent on their product to prevent infringers claiming ignorance of the patent. The one positive side to having your patent attacked for invalidity is that if you win, your patent is proved to be valid; the court can then order a certificate of contested validity. This is proof that yours is a strong patent. It not only may deter future infringers but you are now in a very strong position and may be able to negotiate greater licensing fees when exploiting your invention.

The claim

If you allege that someone is infringing your patent the first thing that will happen is that your specification will be studied to see what it is that you have claimed to be inside your fence. The claims are crucial as they determine the scope of your monopoly. Is the 'infringing' product or process really inside the fence that you have created by your claims backed up by your description and any drawings? If your patent has been copied exactly it is reasonably straightforward to demonstrate that the infringer is sitting fully inside your fence and, unless he has any defence, your rights will have been infringed. It is more difficult, however, if the basic idea has been used but changes or variations made. If there has been a variation, how do you decide if they are really inside your fence or are hovering outside it?

To determine whether or not a patent has been infringed you do not look at whether a substantial part has been taken, as is the case with copyright law. You ask instead where a skilled person in the field in question, when looking at the precise wording of what you have claimed, would think you intended your boundary to lie. The court then decides whether or not the defendant is within that boundary. This is why it is so important to get an experienced patent attorney to draft your specification. The words used are critical. It is often difficult to describe completely new things accurately but an experienced patent attorney knows the pitfalls.

In one case the claim was for two 'U-shaped bows'.[37] The defendant had used a 'C-shaped bow'. Had the words used in the claim put a 'C' shape inside the fence? It was held that it had not. If the patentee had wanted to claim both U- and C-shaped bows they should have said so. The most important case in this area is that of *Catnic Components Ltd v Hill & Smith Ltd*.[38] The invention was for a new type of door lintel that had a vertical or 90-degree support. The defendants made a similar lintel but their support was about 6 degrees off-vertical and it worked just as efficiently and in exactly the same manner as the patented lintel.

To decide whether there was infringement the question was whether the wording of the claim had included a slightly off-90-degree angle within its fence. The main problem was, should the claim be taken literally as meaning that only a 90-degree angle was claimed or would a slightly off-vertical angle be included inside the fence? The court said that one should ask the question:

---

36 Menashe Business Mercantile Ltd v William Hill Organisation Ltd [2003] RPC 31 CA.
37 Rodi & Wienenberger AG v Henry Showell Ltd [1969] RPC 367 HL.
38 [1982] RPC 183.

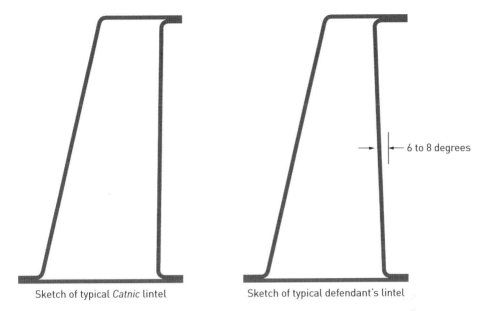

Sketch of typical *Catnic* lintel   Sketch of typical defendant's lintel

Figure 4.3 Infringement.

> Was strict compliance with a particular descriptive word or phrase appearing in a claim intended by the patentee to be an essential requirement of the invention so that any variant would fall outside the monopoly claimed, even though it could have no material effect upon the way the invention worked?

What would a reasonable person skilled in the art reading the claim think the patentee was intending to claim? Was being vertical an essential part of the lintel? It was held here that being vertical would not have been regarded by the patentee as being essential (unlike a product like a guillotine where it would not work unless it was vertical) and that a skilled person would assume that the claim was meant to cover slightly off-vertical also.

Keep in mind that the patentee has the choice of what to claim. They might deliberately restrict their fence to a smaller area to avoid prior art. They may, however, just be finding it very difficult to be completely precise, but if they do not choose the correct words they have only themselves to blame. What makes the whole way of interpreting the claims more confusing is that different EU countries interpret the claims in slightly different ways.

In *Improver Corp v Raymond Industries Ltd*,[39] the patent was for a device called the 'Epilady'. It used helical springs to remove hair from arms and legs. The defendant produced a similar product, 'Smooth & Silky', but that product used a rubber rod to remove the hair rather than a spring. The question was whether this variant, being a rubber rod rather than a spring, fell within the fence of the claims. The UK courts' view is that if the change or variant is doing the same thing in the same way (as in *Catnic*) or performs the same function but in a different way (as in *Improver*) then you must ask if the patentee intended that the language should be strictly complied with.

It was held in the UK that the variation would have no material effect on how the invention worked, as both rod and spring pulled out the hairs in a similar way. It was decided that an expert would think that it was obvious that the rubber rod would work in the same way as the spring. Looking at the language used the patentee was claiming only a spring, not anything else,

---

39 [1991] FSR 223.

and so a rubber rod could not be included within the fence because if they had wanted to include a rubber rod they would have known that it was obvious to say so. As they did not mention a rubber rod, they obviously did not want to include it. Unfortunately, the same case was fought in the German courts, patents being territorial and needing to be litigated in any country where infringement occurs, and the court there took a less literal approach to the claims. They found that the purpose of both the spring and the rod was to pull out hairs and that the patent was therefore infringed.

Even if found to be infringing are there any defences available to the defendant?

The best form of defence is attack. If accused of infringement most defendants will try very hard to find a way to revoke the 'infringed' patent or have it declared invalid so that there is nothing left that they can be accused of infringing. They may use a number of strategies. They may claim that the patent lacks novelty, is obvious, that the patent was not granted to the person entitled to it or that the specification does not include a description that is clear enough for a skilled person to make it.

There are, in addition, defences to claims of infringement. It is not an infringement to do any of the prohibited acts if you are doing them both privately and for non-commercial purposes.[40] You do not infringe if you are using the patent for experimental purposes, for instance to use it to discover something new, to test a hypothesis[41] or to check that the instructions on how to make it included in the specification are adequate. It is also a defence to show that you were already using the invention before the priority date of the patent. This use would of course have been in secret or it would have become part of the prior art and novelty would have been destroyed.

There is also a common law right to repair a patented product but you must be careful not to go so far as to actually remake the product as this would amount to infringement. The purpose of this defence is to allow a consumer to use non-patented parts in repairing a patented product that they have bought.

One Supreme Court case concerned the boundary between repair, which is permissible, and making a patented product, which is not allowed.[42] It involved a wire-sifting screen used to recycle mud and drilling fluid used by offshore oil drills. The sifting screens consisted of wire mesh in metal frames. The wire regularly wore out. The defendant, Screen Repair Services, took the used metal frames and refurbished them by replacing the wire mesh and then sold them on. United Wire Ltd claimed that Screen Repair was infringing their patent by making replacement spare parts. Screen Repair claimed that they were merely making a permissible repair. The court held that the product had ceased to exist when the wire mesh was removed and what Screen Repair did was then to remake the screen, which infringed the patent. In a Supreme Court case it was held that the difference between 'make' and 'repair' is all a matter of 'fact and degree' depending on the circumstances of each case.[43]

Groundless threats of infringement[44]

You may have found a product that looks very like your patented product in a shop or online. Whatever you do, on finding out that someone has, in your opinion, infringed your patent, do not under any circumstances contact them and say that you are going to sue them or anything

---

40 Section 60 of the Patents Act 1977.
41 Auchincloss v Agricultural & Veterinary Supplies Ltd [1997] RPC 649 CA.
42 United Wire Ltd v Screen Repair Services (Scotland) Ltd [2001] RPC 439 HL.
43 Schutz (UK) Ltd v Werit UK Ltd [2013] 2 All ER 177.
44 Section 70 of the Patents Act 1977.

that could be construed as a threat to sue. As with Trade Marks and Design Right if you do make such a threat and if your threat turns out to be unjustified, an 'aggrieved party' may bring proceedings against you. This highly criticised provision[45] is almost unique to UK law and is intended to protect innocent retailers whose businesses could be ruined as a result of an unjustified threat to bring infringement proceedings.

Threats do not have to be made in a letter, they can be conveyed by email or any means whatsoever. To determine if there was a threat, you ask if an ordinary reader of the letter (or other communication) would interpret what is written or communicated as a threat. The 'aggrieved party' will usually want damages, if they suffered any, and a declaration that the threats are unjustified combined with an injunction to stop you making any further threats.

Not only may you find yourself in trouble by rushing in and accusing someone of infringement but this might not be the best strategy when dealing with infringers. It is possible for a lawyer to write a carefully worded 'cease and desist letter'. This formally claims that you own the patent and if properly worded will not be regarded as a threat to bring proceedings. If infringement was accidental or the infringer just thought that you would not bother to sue them this might be the better course. You can then come to an amicable arrangement about a licence fee and avoid any further legal costs. However, such a letter may just put the infringer on warning that they have been discovered. If the infringer is a real rogue having infringed intentionally such a letter will give them sufficient time to destroy any evidence of infringing goods that they have in their possession.

With such deliberate infringement you will probably want your lawyer to act swiftly and rather than write a letter it would be better to obtain an 'interim injunction'. This will order the infringer to stop infringing your goods. You may be able to get an order to seize any infringing goods that they have on their premises; these goods can then be used as evidence against them. You may also, if you have sufficient evidence of infringement, apply for an order to prevent the importation of infringing goods. In some circumstances you may be able to enlist the help of your local Trading Standards Office to help you.

How to avoid infringing third-party patents and recognise how easy it is to invent around a patent

You must ensure that you do not infringe other patents. If you want to use a product or process that you think is covered by a patent the first thing that you should do is a patent search to establish whether the patent is still in force.[46] It may have come to the end of its 20-year time limit or the owner may have failed to pay renewal fees, allowing it to lapse.

If the patent is still in force, study the claims and see if what you want to do really is likely to infringe. It might be that the specification is so broadly worded that it would be easy to claim that it should be revoked as obvious or lacking in novelty. It might be so narrowly worded that you could easily invent around it. If their patent is for a cup hook you could claim that your patent is a hook for all crockery apart from cups. If the patent still looks like an obstacle you could ask the owner if you may take a licence or have the patent assigned to you.

The risk from unauthorised acts by employees

Companies can be held to be vicariously liable for acts of their employees. This means that even though you have not authorised it you can get into trouble for acts that your employees have committed. You must also ensure that you have appropriate licences or agreements in place for all the IP that your employees use. It is your responsibility to ensure that your employees work within the terms and conditions of these licences. You should have policies and procedures in

---

45 There is a move to have this section repealed.
46 www.epo.org/searching/free/espacenet.html.

place so that staff and contractors know how to avoid infringing the IP of others and what to do if they discover IP infringement. You should have regular checks or audits to ensure that they are complying with these procedures.

If someone sues you

If someone does sue, you must go to your lawyer and get his or her advice. At once! Their first step will be to establish the validity of the patent that you have allegedly infringed. If you feel that you might have infringed, the best form of defence is attack. You could try to claim that their patent is invalid. This can, however, be expensive. If you win, as there will be no patent you will not have infringed, but if you lose you may have to pay not only damages for infringing but both your and the claimant's legal costs. If the case is small and heard in the Intellectual Property Enterprise Court there is a damages cap of £500,000 but nevertheless costs can still be high. So beware, it might be cheaper to enter into alternative dispute resolution (ADR) and negotiate a settlement.

Patent trolls

A phenomenon that has emerged in the last few years is that of the 'patent troll'. A troll is a firm whose business is to buy up patents or patent licences, often from the assets of companies that have gone insolvent. The troll conducts no R&D, produces no products and does not try to commercialise their assets. They just own the rights to patents. They then wait, like the fabled troll under the bridge, hoping that someone, the smaller and less able to defend themselves the better, infringes one of their patents. The troll then sues the infringer, having them over a barrel. Trolls usually demand an excessively expensive licence. If this is not paid the infringing product would have to be removed from sale. If the patented product has been incorporated into even an insignificant part of a product an injunction could destroy the whole of a business.

Trolls make their greatest profits in software or telecommunications where there are many overlapping patents. A smartphone, for instance, might incorporate up to 250,000 patent claims. Trolls are a particular problem in the USA where there is no offence of 'groundless threats' and where the cost of litigation is much higher than in the UK. In the USA even if you win a court case you have to pay your own costs. Larger firms may be able to fight the validity of the patent or replace the infringing part with a non-infringing variant but smaller firms usually just give in and pay. The power of the trolls may, however, be reduced by the practice of American courts to refuse an injunction unless the patent holder can show that they will suffer irreparable harm unless the injunction is granted.[47] Patent trolls, due to their lack of commercial activity, would find it hard to establish such irreparable injury but they can of course still demand an award of damages.

Need for an infringement budget

Being involved in a patent dispute can have a catastrophic impact on a business. It is wise to have a risk assessment and a budget for dealing with such events. It is possible to get insurance to cover some of these costs but it is difficult to find and is very expensive.

Alternatives to obtaining a patent

Secrecy

Secrecy is cheap and quick with no registration costs or renewal fees and can start immediately. Secrecy can last indefinitely, not just the 20 years of patent protection. A good example of a

---

47 eBay Inc. v MercExchange LLC 547 US. 388 (2006).

successful secret is the Coca-Cola recipe. Secrecy will not always be a possibility, however. To be regarded as confidential reasonable steps must have been taken to keep the information secret (see Chapter 3). It is a feasible option if your invention is a process where the invention is not revealed but if it is a product there may be nothing to stop people reverse-engineering it. Once the secret is out your invention can be used by all. Finally, secrecy does not give you a monopoly against someone independently inventing and then patenting the same thing.

Getting to market first and creating a monopoly

The lead time gained before others can catch up is always going to be an advantage if used effectively. However, the strength of the advantage depends on the market. If the market is easy to enter any advantage will be lost very quickly. Competitors will learn the details of your invention and, as no monopoly exists, can compete on cost and quality with no R&D costs to recoup.

Utility models

Although not available in the UK many countries such as France, Germany, China and Brazil have what may be called utility models, petty patents or innovation patents. They are similar to patents but are easier, quicker and cheaper to obtain. The level of invention necessary to obtain utility model protection is usually lower than that of a patent but the term of protection is shorter, usually between six and ten years.

Other IP rights

Design rights protect the shape of products and in some countries are called design patents. But design will only cover non-functional aspects of the shape or design of the article while patents protect technical solutions. Copyright is appropriate to protect computer programs, drawings and written descriptions of inventions. Copyright only protects the individual expression of an idea, while a patent can protect a new article or the idea of a new way of making something.

Summary

Patents protect inventions and can cover new products or processes. To get a patent the invention must be new to the public (secret use will not destroy novelty), it must involve an 'inventive step', which means that it must not be obvious to an expert in the field, it must be capable of industrial application, meaning it must have some sort of use or function, and finally it must not be excluded. A patent does not give you the right to make or sell a product or process but it does give you the right to stop others from using, offering for sale, making or importing the invention into the territory for up to 20 years. This is the case even if they have independently invented the product or process themselves. Patents may not be appropriate for fast-moving areas. Patenting can be very expensive and a patent must be applied for and renewal fees paid in every country where you want protection. In return for the monopoly right the details of your invention will be published. Consider when and where to file. Do not file too early but remember that it is a race. You can file in national patent offices for national patents or under the EPC for countries in Europe or under PCT in signatory countries throughout the world. Consult a lawyer immediately if you either commit or detect infringement and consider including ADR clauses in any licence or collaboration agreements.

Management tips

He who has the technology wins.

- Spend a great deal of time considering if you really want a patent. A PatVal-Eu survey found that only 7.2 per cent of patents were worth more than €10 million, 68 per cent were worth less than €1 million and 8 per cent less than €30,000.
- Most patents are filed to prevent competitors copying, to improve the chances of funding, to enhance a company's reputation or to act as a bargaining chip with others.
- If you have applied for a patent it might be a good idea to put patent pending on your product. This is not a legal requirement and has no legal force but it does warn people that they may be infringing. Beware, however, it is a criminal offence to indicate that patent has been applied for or granted if it has not.
- Employ a monitoring service to detect infringement.

Exercise

Mary worked in a small office with Brian, her boss. She found that after a few hours sitting at her computer her arms began to ache. Brian suggested that she try his resistance band: a latex band used to provide tension when exercising. He attached the band to the back of her chair so she could exercise her arms. To Mary's delight the band did the trick and after a few weeks her arms became stronger and more toned. She then noticed that Brian had a Wobble cushion on his office chair. This is an exercise cushion designed to improve 'core strength' by requiring the sitter to balance when using the cushion. Mary then had a great idea. She decided to create an office chair that doubled as a gym. One morning she attached small exercise balls to the arms, resistance bands to the back and exercise tubes with loops, in which to insert feet, to the legs of her office chair. Finally, she bought a Wobble cushion to sit upon. When Brian saw the chair he suggested that Mary should get a patent for the chair as he thought she could make a fortune selling it. He also reminded her that he had been the one to attach the band to the chair in the first place and that she had created the chair while at work.

Discuss the patentability of the chair and who the inventor and owner of any invention might be

Novelty

To be granted a patent an invention must be new. That means it must not be part of the state of the art. We can see that Mary has combined an existing chair with existing exercise equipment. But the fact that these things already exist may not matter. If a combination of things are put together in a novel way it is the combination that can be regarded as novel. We may have a problem about people seeing it, however. We have to ask whether the chair had been disclosed to the public. Would it have been possible for a skilled person to have seen the chair even if they had not? See the Lux case above (note 5). As this is a private office you could assume that the public do not have access. There was no feeling of confidentiality around the chair, however, and this might prove to be a ground for invalidity if a patent were granted and it was discovered that someone had been into the office and seen it.

Inventive step

Is what Mary did inventive? We look at the Pozzoli test. First, we have to ask a person skilled in the field; in this case the field would be the exercise industry. Second, identify what is inventive about Mary's chair. That would be adding exercise equipment to an office chair. Third, we must identify how Mary's chair differs from existing exercise equipment and then finally determine whether the skilled person would have thought that it was obvious looking at previous exercise equipment to attach these items to a chair in this way.

Industrial application and exclusions

Finally, the chair must be capable of industrial application, meaning that it has some sort of use. It does not have to be better, just different. It does not seem to fall into any of the excluded categories.

Who is the inventor?

Although Mary had the idea of creating this chair, Brian attached the band to the chair in the first place. We must therefore ask who had the inventive idea of making an office chair gym – the core of the invention. See *IDA Ltd v University of Southampton*. Brian and Mary could be regarded as co-inventors.

Invented at work

Mary did invent her chair at work and she did use her employer's equipment to do so. However, we must ask whether she invented this chair as part of her normal duties, whether she was specifically asked by her employer to invent this chair or whether she was employed in a job where an invention would be expected to result. It would seem that the answer to all these questions would be 'no', and so her employer would not be entitled to claim ownership.[48]

Conclusion

We should be aware that Mary is using products that might be subject to IP rights that belong to other people. Even if she was granted a patent this would not give her the right to use other people's IP without their consent. Finally, we must ask whether Mary should patent her chair and if so in what territories? Is she in the position to manufacture and market such a product? Does she have the resources to pay for patent attorney fees both to obtain the patent and to defend it?

---

48 S 39 PA 1977.

Chapter 5

Copyright and Rights in Performances

In this chapter we will explore the nature, acquisition, entitlement and scope of copyright. By the end of the chapter you should be able to answer the following questions:

- What is copyright?
- What are the requirements for copyright protection?
- How long does copyright last for?
- Who owns or is entitled to copyright in a work?
- An employee created the work – to whom does copyright belong?
- I have engaged a consultant to create a work – who owns or is entitled to copyright in the work?
- Someone else is using a work that is similar to mine – can I do anything about it?

Copyright in context

Long, long ago, before the digital age, people rarely thought about copyright unless they were playwrights, authors or musicians. To discover whether an 'autobiography' had been written by an acclaimed star or an unknown ghost writer you might have turned to the front page of the book to look for the name attached to the copyright notice, but few would have bothered or even known to do so. Today, however, in our digital environment we see copyright notices every time we view a film, whether it is in the cinema or on a rented DVD. We are all well aware of the legal and moral issues surrounding piracy, file-to-file music sharing, unauthorised copying of films, counterfeit luxury goods and even counterfeit engines, spare parts and medicines. Some people feel that copyright should not prevent them from freely downloading films and music from the internet but most feel that authors should be able to profit from their creations.

    We live in the digital age where the internet is a prime business tool. Every business or professional person creates, owns or deals with copyright matter during the course of their daily lives. Most businesses have a website that is their global shop-front. The internet is where customers go to find out about the organisation, the products and the people involved in the operation in which they are interested. From the time you search on the web for the supplier of the goods or services you seek you are in the area of copyright, whether it is in the form of the written word, photographs of products or podcasts extolling the benefits of the goods of the enterprise. In any business there is likely not only to be a website full of copyright material but large amounts of computer software, both off the shelf and bespoke, being used, all protected by copyright. There may be marketing literature, instruction manuals and even tweets about the business and its products. In the digital age copyright works can be copied and multiple copies can be transmitted as never before. Not only can they be reproduced but they are easily adapted and stored on a tiny memory stick. Whether you are selling electronic products, financial services, computer programs or games, whether you are a university, a museum or a health spa, you need to know about copyright. You need to know what you own and what is owned by others that you or your employees may infringe.

History

Until the introduction of the printing press into England by William Caxton in the fifteenth century books needed to be copied by hand. This was a highly skilled art in an era when the majority of people were illiterate. Most books were created by monks and were very valuable, often being chained to prevent theft. Chained libraries, such as the one in Hereford Cathedral, can still be found. The advent of the printing press allowed multiple copies of books to be made. The entrepreneurs who had invested in this new technology then wanted a right to prevent others copying the works. This economic right to copy, or more accurately to prevent others from copying, was intended to protect printers, the entrepreneurs, not authors, the creators of the works. In the UK the first true copyright act was the Statute of Anne, of 1709. This gave authors of books a 14-year fixed term of protection but allowed them to transfer their rights to the printers. Gradually, over the years, in order to reflect new technologies, other works such as engravings, sculptures, computer programs and databases were added to the protection of copyright.

The UK's current copyright Act is the Copyright, Designs and Patent Act 1988 (CDPA). There have been rapid technological changes since 1988, including the renting and lending of DVDs and the growth of the internet. To reflect these changes the CDPA has been amended by EC Directives and other legislation, but is overdue for reform. There is also the Trade-Related Aspects of Intellectual Property Rights (TRIPS) agreement, which requires Member States to provide effective copyright enforcement for works that have been recorded digitally; not an easy task!

Today copyright protects literary, dramatic, musical and artistic works, sound recordings, films, broadcasts or cable programmes and the typographical arrangement of published editions. It gives the owner of the copyright control over how a work is used. An owner can prevent others from copying their work, making it available to the public or dealing with it without their consent. The author can license their work to an entrepreneur such as a publishing house or a recording studio and receive royalties; alternatively they can sell or assign copyright outright. After sale the author may retain their moral right to be acknowledged as the author and not to have their work treated in a derogatory way. If someone infringes a copyright work the owner can sue them and obtain damages or an injunction to prevent them infringing again.

Justification

The creative industries are regarded as a benefit to society as a whole. Not only is the entrepreneur publishing a book or producing a film seen as creating jobs and contributing to the economy of the country, but the author creating art and literature is seen as improving the quality of the lives of people on a personal level. Copyright can be explained as an incentive for both the economic rights of those bringing copyright works to market but also the moral rights of authors of the initial creation.

There are three main approaches to justifying giving copyright protection. If poets receive no compensation for the time they spend creating a poem, they may have no choice but to spend their time earning money in another way in order to feed their families. If the producer of a film cannot recoup their expenditure they cannot continue losing money indefinitely and will eventually stop producing films. Copyright can also be justified as a reward. The more a book is valued, the greater the number of people who will buy it and the larger the reward made by both the author via royalties and the publisher from the sales of the book will be. A further justification is that a work of creation actually belongs to the person who created it; that it is their property. If I grow an apple it is my property. I have the right to eat it, give it away or sell it. In the same way, if I compose a piece of music I should have control over what happens to it and should be able to prevent others from using it without my permission. The final justification for copyright is also about fairness. It is seen as unfair for others to gain an advantage from what they did not create, 'to reap where they did not sow'.

What are the requirements for protection?

Originality

To obtain copyright in a work, the work must be original. There is no precise legal definition of originality, which allows for flexibility. Because of this freedom all sorts of creations can be accommodated that had not been thought about at the time the legislation was enacted in 1988. For copyright, unlike patents, originality does not mean that the creation must be inventive or innovative; it just means that it must have originated from the author and that they used their skill and labour to create it. The work must be the author's own intellectual creation and it must not have been copied.[1] Consequently if two people stand side by side in Pall Mall and each take a photograph of Buckingham Palace, even though the photographs may look exactly the same, each photographer has copyright in their own photograph.

For example, the two photographs below were taken completely independently. Neither photographer was aware that the other had taken their own photograph, yet the photographs are very similar though not identical. Each photographer has his or her own copyright in their respective photographs (one of the co-authors of this book took the better photograph!).

We can see that the standard of originality required for copyright is quite low. In the old case of *University of London Press Ltd v University Tutorial Press Ltd* a maths exam paper that had been created by the University of London had been copied without permission.[2] The questions were being sold along with the answers. The university wanted to stop the sale and claimed that they had copyright in the exam questions that the defendant was infringing. In order to establish copyright the university had to show that the maths exam was an original literary work. However, the maths in the exam paper was not new or novel and copyright does not protect ideas or facts. For originality, as far as copyright is concerned, you do not need new or original thought, you just need to have expressed the thought in an original way. The Court held that the exam questions were original literary works. The maths might not have been new but the way the questions were expressed was new. This case is the source of the expression 'What is worth copying is worth protecting', but that statement cannot be taken at face value as some things that people may want to copy may not be eligible for copyright protection.

It has been accepted by the courts that you need the input of an author to create a copyright work and that the author must have expended a minimum amount of skill and effort in creating it. Although the standard of originality is not very high the right type of skill and effort must have been employed.

In the case *Exxon v Exxon Insurance* an oil company had decided to change its trading name from Esso to Exxon.[3] The marketing team had spent a great deal of time and money inventing the new name and a substantial amount of market research had been undertaken to establish that this was

---

[1] Infopaq International A/S v Danske Dagblades Forening [2009] ECR 1–6569.
[2] [1916] 2 Ch 601.
[3] [1982] 1 Ch 19.

Figure 5.1 Originality and copyright.

the best name for the new brand. The defendant used the name Exxon. The oil company claimed that the word Exxon was an original literary work and that the defendant had infringed their copyright in it. It was held that one word cannot be a work of literature, no matter how original and no matter how much effort had gone into creating it. It follows from this case that you may not use copyright to monopolise words such as titles of books or names of characters. Neither is there copyright in command names in a computer program as they also are too insubstantial to be a literary work.

There will be no copyright in parts of sentences and probably not in short advertising slogans, although they may be able to be protected as trade marks in the right circumstances. One case has, however, held that a sentence consisting of 11 words is a literary work.[4] Although hypertext links on a website would probably not be substantial enough to be regarded as a copyright work, some headlines, if sufficiently original, are capable of being independent literary works. There is a question mark over tweets. Twitter is a blogging website that allows users to make posts, or 'tweets', limited to 140 characters. Like some short poems they contain a very small amount of text but surely if a significant amount of literary skill and effort has been invested by the author in the Tweet, copyright should arise.

Although it is not difficult for works to be considered as original there have been exceptions. Lego is a very famous and popular interlocking toy brick for children. There had been original design drawings for the brick that had initially been protected as a registered design but this right had expired (see Chapter 7). Later the company decided to make a larger brick for younger children. The later brick looked for all purposes identical to the original smaller brick but a great deal of work had gone into making the larger brick function effectively, so there were quite a few important technical changes to the design. Tyco copied the larger brick and Lego claimed copyright infringement.[5] The issue was whether, as the new drawings for the larger brick looked almost identical to the earlier drawings for the smaller brick, could the new drawings be said to be original for copyright purposes? Had the small technical modifications made to the existing drawings of Lego bricks give rise to a fresh copyright? The Court concluded that the new drawings lacked originality. The modifications to the dimensions were technically significant but as they were not 'visually' significant they would not give rise to a new artistic copyright. To hold otherwise, the Court said, would result in potential permanent copyright. Again, although the engineers had used skill and effort in their drawings, that was not enough; it was the wrong sort of effort to be regarded as creating an original creation.

Fixation

Copyright springs into life the moment an original work is expressed in 'tangible' form. That means as soon as it is put into writing, notation or recorded in digital form or in any other way whatsoever so that others can see, hear or reproduce it. Recording a piece of music electronically would be sufficient, as would putting software code into machine-readable form. I am writing this passage on a laptop computer and the moment it goes into my RAM and hard drive it has been recorded and has been fixed. The work does not need to have been published for copyright to arise. Although you would assume that the author would record their own work, this is not necessary for copyright to exist.

It is difficult to envisage anyone other than the artist putting a picture into tangible form but easy to imagine a person creating a new song by strumming on a guitar but not recording it. If some other person records the song this will 'fix' the work, allowing copyright to spring into

---

4 Newspaper Licensing Agency Ltd v Meltwater Holding BV [2012] RPC 1.
5 In Interlego AG v Tyco Industries Inc. [1989] 1 AC 217.

existence. Fixation would occur even though the guitar player had not consented or even been aware that the recording was taking place.

An old example of fixation by another is *Walter v Lane*.[6] The Earl of Rosebury made an impromptu speech at a political meeting. A reporter from *The Times* newspaper was in the crowd and took down the speech in shorthand. The reporter wrote up the speech, adding appropriate punctuation, and it was published in *The Times*. The speech was copied by the defendant and the issue was whether copyright existed and whether *The Times* had a right to sue for infringement. The Court held that copyright did indeed exist. The Earl of Rosebury was the author of the speech; however, the reporter, having used skill and judgment in recording the speech, adding structure and punctuation, was the author of the report of the speech. This situation must be distinguished from a secretary taking dictation for a letter verbatim. In that case, although the work will have been put into tangible form by being recorded by the secretary, they will be regarded more as a tool as they have not employed the right sort of skill and labour or intellectual creation to be the author of the letter. Although copyright will exist, the author will be the speaker, not the secretary.

What does copyright protect?

For copyright protection the author must have created a 'work', as defined by the CDPA. The first or primary works that copyright protects are literary, dramatic, musical and artistic works. However, copyright also covers derivative or secondary works such as sound recordings, films, broadcast and typographical arrangements (how the words and pictures are laid out on the page) that do not require the same level of originality as the primary works. One work can be protected by more than one type of copyright. For example, a recording of a song will have copyright in the music itself plus copyright in the sound recording.

You cannot have copyright in mere ideas, facts, algorithms or general information but you can protect the way you have expressed the idea or facts. You may watch the film *The Lord of the Rings*, a story about a young hobbit named Frodo from a small village in the Shire, entrusted with an ancient ring. If you then write your own story based on that idea you are not infringing copyright in the film, providing you do not copy the script-writers' and film-makers' expression of the story. Once fixed you will gain your own copyright for your original work because it is your expression of the story of Frodo.

Copyright will not cover common things like a name or circle, which should be available for all to use. In a past case a substantial amount of a year diary had been copied by a competitor.[7] It was held that what had been copied was merely information such as conversion tables of weights and measures and postal information, which is normally found in diaries. Although the information in the diary had been selected and arranged by the publisher it was so commonplace there had been no creative judgement involved in the selection and so no copyright. It seems that to protect yourself against others copying such general information, you would need to add additional material such as headings or a classification system.

Although copyright does not protect facts or historical events, it may protect the structure or the order in which they are expressed. *The Holy Blood and the Holy Grail* was a non-fiction book first published in 1982. The book offered the theory that Jesus Christ had been married to Mary Magdalene and that they had had children whose descendants still live in the South of France. Much later the defendants wrote *The Da Vinci Code* (published in 2003), a mystery novel with a similar theme. The authors of *The Holy Blood and the Holy Grail* claimed that *The Da Vinci Code* infringed

---

6 [1900] AC 539.
7 Cramp (GA) & Sons Ltd v Frank Smythson Ltd [1944] AC 329.

the copyright in their book.[8] It was held that although the selection and arrangement of the raw material could be protected under copyright, you cannot use copyright to monopolise historical knowledge or theories. Although the authors of *The Da Vinci Code* obtained facts, theories and ideas from the original book they did not take the expression of these ideas. Copyright only extends to the way facts and ideas are expressed, not the ideas and facts themselves.

Literary works

The CDPA specifically states that no merit is required to gain copyright in a literary work. Not only is this because the Courts would not be willing or even necessarily able to establish what is good or bad literature but because literary copyright is used to protect more than merely creative writing. Literary works include not only books, poems and lyrics for songs, but all sorts of functional works: technical reports, manuals, promotional literature, advertising, business letters, company balance sheets (but not mathematical theories or algorithms as they are facts), software and websites.

All these can be protected as long as they are written, spoken or sung. Consequently, instructions on how to use a product or even patent specifications (see Chapter 4) will be protected by copyright. In addition, writing does not just refer to words. Syllables, numerals and code also come under the heading of literary works and can be found in any type of storage media such as computer discs, word processors, etc. There is literary copyright not only in the source code and object code of computer programs but also the flow charts or preparatory design material for computer programs as well as computer-generated works – if there is no human author of the work. We have already seen that there is literary copyright in maths exam papers, and in the past the *Yellow Pages* directory has been held to be eligible for copyright protection as skill and judgement had been deployed in selecting the classification system and adverts. A listing of TV programmes to be broadcast, a racing information service (but not a formula for calculating the racing forecast) and knitting patterns have also been categorised as literary works, as have numerals, compilations and tables (but not the facts included in the tables). If you create a selection of Shakespearean poems there will be no copyright in the poems themselves as copyright lasts for the life of the author plus 70 years and Shakespeare died 400 years ago. You would, however, gain copyright protection in your original selection of which poems to include and the order in which they are to appear. Those decisions demonstrate your intellectual creation, skill and effort. If an English book is translated into French there will be a separate copyright in the French-language version and if an adaptation is made, a book made into a play, there will be a separate copyright in the adaptation.

Artistic works

As with literary works, copyright covers not only the traditional aspects of art such as original pictures and sculptures, but also functional visual work and would include multimedia works. Most of these artistic works don't have to have any particular artistic merit, and much modern art, although regarded by many as lacking charm, will still attract copyright protection. Some types of craft are also included as artistic works for copyright purposes but these are an exception and do have a quality requirement in order to attract protection.

Artistic works include graphic works such as paintings, drawings and diagrams, as well as maps, charts or plans. An item such as a circuit diagram will include diagrams, letters and numerals and so are both literary and artistic works. Photographs, sculptures (which includes a cast or model made for the purposes of sculpture), engravings, etchings, lithographs, woodcuts and

---

8 Baigent v Random House Group Ltd [2007] FSR 24.

collage (where items are placed together and glued to a surface) are also artistic works. Architects have copyright protection in the drawings or plans for a building (graphic works), in the models made to show what the building will look like when completed and the building itself. We can see that engineering or technical plans are artistic works (the way the information is presented, not in the facts themselves). A screen layout of a website would be a graphic work.

The last category of artistic work is a work of artistic craftsmanship. This covers products like handmade jewellery, handmade chairs or designer cutlery. There is a problem with this category as merit is required, and this can pose a problem especially if items are mass-produced. There is an overlap with artistic works and some aspects of design law; see Chapter 7.

Photographs

Photographs are a very important part of marketing a business. They may be used in advertising, on websites and in magazines, brochures, letterheads and email signatures. Although protected by artistic copyright, one could ask, in these days of the digital camera, whether the skill and effort required of the author of a photograph is sufficient to give rise to copyright protection. In the past when there was substantial skill involved in taking a photograph – choosing the lighting, aperture, etc. – the justification for protection was obvious, but can just taking a snapshot with a digital camera be sufficient? The photographer still makes free and creative choices in the arrangement of the scene, the background and the angle at which the shot is taken. This can amount to the minimum amount of creative effort required, as long as the photograph was created independently and not copied. It has been held that a photographer can have copyright in their photograph of a painting and indeed many art galleries and museums make a substantial profit from photographing paintings in their collections and selling the photographs as postcards. In one case there was even copyright in a photograph of an engraving taken from a painting.

Sculpture

One would not expect sculptures to be of great significance in most businesses, unless involved in the arts, but that might be a mistaken assumption. It is difficult to say exactly what a sculpture is apart from being three-dimensional. The legal definition of sculpture has been very widely drawn to include casts, moulds or models made for the purpose of a sculpture. Again, as with literary works, sculptures are not required to display any artistic merit. In 1974 the Tate art gallery displayed 120 firebricks arranged in a rectangular formation. This was regarded as an important minimalist sculpture. You can be sure, however, that such acclaim would not be given to a pile of bricks found in a building site, even if they looked very similar to the Tate bricks.

In the past a totally functional item, the wooden model from which a mould was made to manufacture plastic Frisbees, was held to be a sculpture. Although being able to protect their moulds and casts as sculptures might be advantageous for an engineering business, the expansion of the meaning of sculpture was curbed in the 2009 case of *Lucasfilm v Ainsworth*.[9] The issue here was whether the helmets made as part of the costume for the Storm Troopers in the *Star Wars* films were sculptures. It was held that they were not. The CDPA states that quality or merit is irrelevant, so a work of sculpture does not have to be something that would appear in an art gallery.[10] In the *Star Wars* case, however, it was decided that we must actually take into account the normal meaning of the word 'sculpture'. We must consider whether the creator thought they were producing something with visual impact, as was the case with the firebricks in the Tate, or if their aim was only to create something that was functional. So we now know that although when making a sculpture artistic merit is not required, the creator must have intended there to be some visual appeal, even if there were also functional aspects to the work.

---

9 [2009] FSR 103.
10 Section 4 CDPA 1988.

Artistic craftsmanship

The most challenging aspect of artistic copyright is artistic craftsmanship. The problem can be demonstrated in the case of *George Hensher Ltd v Restawhile Upholstery Ltd*.[11] The claimant designed a new suite of furniture. The defendant copied the furniture and the claimant unsuccessfully sued them for copyright infringement. If the claimant had made a design drawing in order to show how the furniture was going to look when produced this would have been protected as a graphic work or unregistered design (see Chapter 7). They did not do this, however, but instead made a rough prototype. With no drawings there was no graphic work and the suite was certainly not a sculpture or an engraving, so the only option left was to claim that the prototype gained copyright protection as being a work of artistic craftsmanship.

The category of artistic craftsmanship is the only one that has a quality criteria,[12] 'artistic' indicating some visual attractiveness and 'craftsmanship' suggesting a level of quality. The prototype was, however, roughly made, with no intention to create a work of craft, and its function was to serve as a demonstration rather than an attractive piece of furniture. Unhelpfully, the Court could not decide what a work of artistic craftsmanship should be. They confusingly offered various criteria that it should possess or approaches to how the decision should be made as to whether it was artistic or a work of craft. The suggestions were that a work of artistic craftsmanship should give pleasure and be valued for its appearance. A prototype could not be regarded as having aesthetic appeal. Or the creator must have consciously tried to create a work of art; this was not the case with regard to a rough mock-up. Or there must be genuine craftsmanship involved, which again was not applicable to a purely functional prototype of this kind. Finally, it was suggested that it is up to the court to decide after talking to expert witnesses – people experienced in the furniture design trade. As the prototype did not fit into the category of artistic craftsmanship it was not a 'work' for the purposes of the CDPA. Consequently, although there was no doubt that the suite of furniture had been copied, there was no copyright and so no infringement.

This area of artistic craftsmanship is of growing importance. There is a great overlap with design law, and today we would hope that the claimant would have registered their design to obtain protection under the design legislation (see Chapter 7).

Musical works

A musical work consists of music but not any words or action intended to be sung, spoken or performed with the music. Consequently there will be music copyright in the song and a separate literary copyright in the lyrics. These can be, and often are, created by different people. Again there is no quality requirement for musical copyright and just a few notes will attract protection, even though they may be regarded by many as lacking in musical appeal. Music copyright will cover ringtones, so if you take a piece of music that is still in copyright and download it onto your mobile phone you are copying and therefore need the permission of the copyright owner. A business may use sound in their advertising and on their website and may have a jingle as a trade mark. All these could be protected by music copyright. There is today a large industry in music sampling. This can be done by taking part of a song and using it as an instrument to create a different tune. It is also common for an adaptation of music to be made, such as taking an existing ballad and changing it into drum and bass. The new song in both cases may attract their own copyright but may be infringing the original if done without authority.

---

11 [1974] AC 64, HL.
12 Section 4(1)(c) CDPA 1988.

Dramatic works

A dramatic work includes a work of dance or mime. It does not include a literary work but could cover a script for a play or film. Films, videos, cable or radio broadcasts can all be dramatic works; however, the copyright in the film etc. would be separate as they are not original but derivative works. To be categorised as a dramatic work it must be capable of being performed before an audience and should include some motion.

This definition of dramatic work will exclude some things that you would have thought should be included. In the case *Norowzian v Arks* an actor had been filmed dancing when making the art film, Joy.[13] Mr Norowzian, the creator, had the idea of using 'jump cutting' (removing bits of film) and 'flash framing'. These innovative editing techniques gave the surreal effect of abruptly jumping the dancer from one position to another, creating an effect of discontinuity. The defendant remade the film for use in their advertising campaign, copying the idea of the dancing man and using the same editing techniques. Mr Norowzian sued them for copyright infringement. It was held that as Joy had been remade there had been no actual copying of the film. To infringe the defendant would have had to copy the underlying dramatic work. Joy was not, however, a dramatic work for the purposes of the CPDA. Although Joy certainly contained motion, as no person could move in this way it could not be performed before an audience. Mr Norowzian could not prevent his idea being copied.

The definition of dramatic work as being a work of motion capable of being performed before an audience would cover cartoons (which would also be regarded as film), as would synchronised swimming, but not TV formats. In the past TV formats have been held not to have been fixed in tangible form as they vary from episode to episode depending on what the people involved say or do at the time of recording. Unless there is some sort of script being followed or the action is sufficiently recreated in each programme, these shows, although dramatic, will have no copyright as they are mere ideas. This will also be the case with computer games. Although they may contain audio, video and text images and include movement, how they perform will depend on the person playing the game and so will change on each playing.

Secondary or derivative works

Secondary or derivative works typically protect the entrepreneur, the film, or recording studio rather than the author of a work. Derivative works are usually, but do not have to be, based on original musical, dramatic, artistic or literary works that will have their own separate copyright. It is the entrepreneur who will take any infringement proceedings if a derivative work is copied. There is no requirement that these works be original but they must be recorded. The definition of recording is broad to allow for the development of new technologies. There is, however, copyright only in the master copy of the film or sound recording. This prevents a potential everlasting copyright that would otherwise result if a new copyright arose every time a CD or videotape is reproduced.

Sound recordings

A sound recording is a recording of sounds from which sounds may be reproduced.[14] There will usually be more than one copyright associated with a song. The author of the song will have their musical copyright, the author of the lyrics will have literary copyright and the creator of the sound recording will have copyright in that recording. The sound recording does not have to be of an original work. A recording of, for example, birdsong is not a 'work' as defined under the

---

13 [2000] FSR 363.
14 Section 5A CDPA 1988.

Act but would nevertheless gain protection. Of course in that case the only copyright would be in the recording itself as we do not grant copyright to birds. If two people recorded the same bird singing they would each have their own separate copyright in their sound recording. There is no quality requirement for recording and although a sound recording does not have to be original it will not attract copyright if it has been copied from another sound recording. Sound recordings may also involve issues relating to performers' rights (see Chapter 5).

Film

Film means a recording on any medium from which a moving image may be produced.[15] The inclusion of the word 'medium' ensures that any new technology is covered. Films will contain numerous copyrights and these will probably be owned by different people. The soundtrack accompanying a film is regarded as part of the film, as is the medium, the videotape or celluloid. A film can be a recording of a dramatic work but also a dramatic work itself, as it can be performed before an audience (see *Norowzian v Arks* above), or it could be a recording of something that is not a dramatic work, such as a swimming race. A film may include computer games, but a computer game will not be a dramatic work as the game varies depending on how it is played. Making a copy of an existing film will not give rise to a new copyright; however, remaking it will probably do so.

Broadcasts

Broadcast means an electronic transmission of visual images (pictures), sound or other information.[16] A broadcast is something that is either transmitted for simultaneous reception by members of the public (and is capable of being lawfully received by them) or transmitted to members of the public at a time determined solely by the person making the transmission. It is transmission by one to many (the broadcaster/author to the public). So a broadcast covers radio and television. Most forms of internet transmission, unless they consist of streaming or are live events, are not regarded as broadcasts as they are one-to-one (broadcaster/author to listener). A podcast is probably not a broadcast if it can be accessed on a website at any time. No fixation is required for a broadcast. Satellite broadcasts by their very nature can reach other countries. They may be re-broadcast to further countries before being finally broadcast to the public. The law governing the broadcast is that of the country from where the original broadcast was made, the up-leg. Broadcasts are regarded as broadcast to the public even if they are encrypted, as long as the public has had the decoding equipment lawfully made available to them.

Typographical arrangements of published editions

This right is intended to protect publishers.[17] It protects the image on the page from exact copying by photocopying, scanning or other means. It covers the type and size of letters used, the number of words on a page and the visual appearance of the page of published editions. The literary work itself can be out of copyright, as would be the case with the Shakespeare play *Hamlet*, as the playwright died more than 70 years ago, but the publisher would have copyright in the new typography or layout of the book. The whole book or dramatic or musical work is protected. This means the entire 'between the covers' work. So taking parts of an article from a newspaper is not an infringement of the typographical arrangement as it is not sufficiently substantial (see infringement).

---

15 Section 5B CDPA 1988.
16 Section 6 CDPA 1988.
17 Section 8 CDPA 1988.

Who owns or is entitled to copyright in a work?

Original works

In most countries the author, the person who created a work, is the first owner of the work. As we have already acknowledged, people may get ideas and inspiration from seeing the work of other authors. It is, however, their own interpretation of the idea, fact or event as they expressed it that they may claim as their own. The author does not need to be the person who recorded a work. A secretary will not own the copyright in a letter dictated by their boss; the author of the letter would be the boss, the person who is directly responsible for what actually appears on the paper (or screen if the secretary is using a computer).

If Tom asks Ben to make a technical drawing or write a report and merely makes suggestions as to what might be included. Remember, copyright protects expression not ideas, so Tom will not be the author. But if Tom gives Ben very detailed instructions and Ben merely records Tom's expression exactly, making no creative contribution of his own, Tom is clearly responsible for the end result and Tom will be the author of the report. If a work is created by more than one person but you can tell which person created which bit, for example, one person wrote the lyrics to a song while another wrote the music, they will own their copyright separately in the part they created. If, however, their contributions cannot be separated they would be regarded as joint authors. If Ben had added some facts or information to the report, he would still not be regarded as a joint author as these are not protected by copyright, but if Ben, as would be probable in this sort of situation, added some creativity of his own in writing the report, Tom and Ben would be regarded as joint authors and would both be entitled to a share of any benefits derived from the exploitation of the report.

If the right to use the work was going to be licensed both authors would have to agree to the terms of the licence. To be regarded as joint authors the contributions of each do not have to be equal. You do not need to have intended to create a work of joint authorship but you do need to have intended to create a work. A famous case is that of *Fisher v Brooker*, which concerned the popular 1960s song 'A Whiter Shade of Pale', recorded by the band Procul Harum.[18] This is apparently the most-played song in radio broadcasts in the last 70 years. The song had originally been written by Gary Brooker but Matt Fisher rewrote the piano part and introduced a highly distinctive organ introduction, which was then used in other parts of the song (the organ part is in effect what made the song so appealing). Even though the song had already been written before Mr Fisher reworked the piano part, it was held by the court that his was an original contribution and that he was a joint author. Even though he had not contributed to the other aspect of the song, his organ part was sufficient to entitle him to a 40 per cent share in the copyright. This case demonstrates how important, indeed how essential it is that authorship should be agreed before any work is created. In the music industry session musicians are often employed. They are expected to devise their own interpretation of a piece of music, so there should always be a written agreement about the authorship of any work before anyone is asked to contribute.

Secondary works

It would seem to be more difficult to work out who are the authors of secondary works such as films and broadcasts. There are likely to be quite a few people contributing to the creation of such works and they might all be working for a company or even different companies. It has, however, been stipulated by the CDPA who the author of such works should be.[19] In a nutshell, it

---

18 [2009] FSR 25.
19 Section 11 CDPA 1988.

will be the person responsible, or the person who makes the necessary arrangements, for the work to be made.

In respect of films, the producer and director are joint authors. In one case, a film about sky-diving over Mount Everest was made.[20] Both the skydiving cameraman who had shot the film and the financier who had paid for the entire expedition claimed to own copyright in the film. They each claimed that the other was infringing their right. It was held that as the cameraman had decided what to film and how to film it he was the principle director, but the financier who made all the necessary arrangements for making the film was the producer.[21] Consequently copyright was jointly owned and as they each needed the consent of the other to exploit the work they were infringing each other's copyright. If the film had been based on a book the author of the book would have a separate copyright, as would the authors of any music included in but not specifically written for the film.

An employee created the work – to whom does it belong?

Usually the author is the first owner of the copyright in the work they have created. However, in many countries if a work is created during the course of employment, as part of the job the author was employed to do, the work will belong to the employer. The employer alone will be entitled to use, sell or license the work to another. They will not need the consent of the employee and the employee will not be entitled to any further benefit from its use or sale. But if someone who is employed to sweep floors creates a poem when at work they would not lose their right to be regarded as first owner of the copyright in the poem. As a cleaner they could not be regarded as being employed to create poems. The author, not the employer, would own the copyright in the poem.

To decide ownership it is therefore necessary to establish if someone is in fact an employee and what they are employed to do. In most cases this will not be a problem. Normally people know what they are employed to do and you can just look at the person's job description and contract of employment to establish what their duties are. But there can sometimes be problems. Contractors may work for many months or even years for the same firm and this may give rise to ambiguity about their employment status. An employee may do work that is not related to their normal duties as stated in their employment contract. In the case of *Stevenson, Jordan & Harrison v Macdonald and Evans*, an accountant, using his employer's facilities, wrote a book about accountancy.[22] He included a report in the book that he had prepared for one of his firm's clients. A question arose as to the ownership of the copyright in the book. It was held that he had been employed to be an accountant advising the clients of his firm. He had not been employed to write books and neither had he specifically been asked by his employer to write a book. He had used the help of his firm's secretary when writing the book but this did not change his employment status. Note, however, there were two separate issues here: the book and the report. It was held that as he had created the report for a client of the firm and as this was part of the job he was employed to do copyright in the report belonged to the employer. However, copyright in the rest of the book belonged to him. It should be noted that if the employer had specifically asked the accountant to write the book, even though it was not part of his normal duties, copyright would in all likelihood belong to them. The fact that his name appeared as the author on the front of the book added weight to the conclusion that he was indeed the author. If he had written the book as part of his employment it would probably have had the name of the firm on the cover.

---

20 Slater v Wimmer [2012] EWPCC 7.
21 Section 178 CDPA 1988.
22 [1952] RPC 10 CA.

Although the employer usually owns work created by an employee during the course of their employment it is wise to have clauses in the employment contract that deal explicitly with IP issues. It is also essential to deal with the ownership of IP in any contract made with commissioned workers or if workers are based overseas.

I have engaged a consultant to create a work – who owns or is entitled to the copyright?

Please be aware that there is a trap here that many people fall into. Someone who is commissioned to create a work is not treated in the same way as an employee. In the UK, although not in all countries, if you commission a work, paying an artist to paint a portrait of your dog Fido, although you may own the physical painting of Fido you do not own the copyright in the painting unless there has been a signed agreement in writing. If you make a photocopy of the painting you will be infringing the rights of the author. This means that if you ask a contractor to work for you, whether it is to write software or a report or to create some artwork, you should always, as part of the written contractual agreement, ask them to assign the copyright to you. This may affect how much they charge for their services but if you fail to have copyright assigned in this way it may cost a great deal more in the long run. By not owning the copyright you will have no right to use the commissioned work in the way that you would like.

It is true that the courts many come to your rescue by implying a licence, as was the case in *Blair v Osborne & Tomkins*, but it is by no means certain that they will.[23] Here an architect had been contracted by builder A to create drawings so that two houses could be built on a particular piece of land. Builder A then sold the land to builder B who built the houses. The architect claimed that he owned the copyright in the drawings and that he had not given permission to builder B to use the drawings to build the houses. It was held that, although the architect did own the copyright in the drawings, it was implied as part of the agreement with builder A that the drawings were to be used to build houses on this particular piece of land, otherwise there would be no point in having the drawings. Builder B as the owner of the land was held to have an implied licence to build the two houses on the land. The court would not go further than to imply a licence to fulfil the intended purpose of the original contract. Builder B could build on the original piece of land but would not be able to use the plans to build similar houses on any other piece of land.

In another case the owners of the company that markets Dr Martens shoes asked a freelance designer, Ross Evans, to create a logo to be used as a new trade mark for their business.[24] As he had been commissioned Mr Evans was the author and owner of the work. The company failed to ask Mr Evans to assign the copyright in the logo to them. After the company had registered the logo as a trade mark they realised what they had done but Mr Evans had them over a barrel. Eventually the case came to court where it was said that Mr Evans must have known that the artwork was to be used as a trade mark. However, to grant Dr Martens a mere licence to use the design as in *Blair* was not sufficient for their needs, so Mr Evans was ordered to assign the work to Dr Martens. Dr Martens was lucky; they should have known better. Going to court should be avoided.

Remember, copyright should be assigned in writing and it is better to have an agreement in place before any work is started rather than to wait until a problem has occurred. Litigation is expensive and time-consuming and creates bad feeling between people who may otherwise have happily worked together for many years. It is much better and cheaper to prevent problems than to try to patch them up after the event.

---

23 [1971] 2 WLR 503.
24 Griggs Group Ltd v Evans [2005] FSR 31.

How long does copyright last for?

One of the reasons that it is important to know the identity of the author of a work is that for literary, dramatic, musical and artistic works copyright lasts for the life of the author plus 70 years. You need to know who the author is and when they died in order to work out when copyright will expire. Once a work has entered the public domain you will be free to use the work without gaining the author's permission. You also need to know who the author is to establish that there is copyright in the first place.

To be entitled to UK copyright the author must either be British or live in Britain or the work must have been first published in Britain. In addition, authors may claim reciprocal protection in other countries that have signed the Berne Convention (over 164 countries) or the Universal Copyright Convention. That means that authors from each country are entitled to receive the same protection as authors in another signatory country. Although it is not a legal requirement it is wise to place the © sign, your name and the date of creation on your work. This makes it clear that copyright exists and it is easier to find the author to ask permission to use their work. In a work of joint authorship or co-authored works (e.g. music and lyrics of a song where the two works are created to be used together) copyright protection lasts 70 years from the death of the last author to die. A work of joint authorship must not be confused with a compilation, say a book of poetry. In such a compilation each individual poem will have an author and copyright will last for 70 years after their death but the person who chooses the poems and decides on the order in which they appear in the compilation will be the author of the compilation itself.

The duration of copyright in secondary works is shorter than that for the primary literary, artistic, musical and dramatic works. It is usually 70 years from the end of the year in which the work was released. The exception is for typographical arrangements where copyright lasts 25 years from the end of the year of first publication. A film, however, is treated the same way as a primary work and its copyright will last until 70 years from the death of the last author to die. If it is impossible after a diligent search to find the author of the work it is called an anonymous or orphan work. There is a presumption that the publisher of an anonymous work is the owner of the copyright and that the author died more than 70 years ago. There are proposals to make it easier to use orphan works without fear of infringement if copyright in the work is found to exist after all. A scheme of collective licensing is to be introduced but at the time of writing details had not yet been announced.[25]

Moral rights

Copyright is in essence an economic right, the right to make money from a creative work. Copyright can be bought and sold (even after the death of the author). Many authors are not capable of exploiting their own works. Ben may be excellent at writing film scripts but cannot afford or does not have the skills needed to make a film. To get his script made into a film he would need to assign the copyright to a film production company. Once assigned he will no longer own the copyright. On the other hand, there is an increasing capacity to reach an audience via the internet, with many songwriters now choosing to put their music online themselves rather than attempting to get a recording contract.

Entrepreneurs are, however, still a powerful and necessary part of the creative industries, an industry that amounts to 7.3 per cent of the UK economy, employing two-and-a-quarter million people. It would be unwise for a record company to spend large amounts of money recording

---

25 Sections 116A and B CDPA 1988.

and marketing a piece of music if they did not have exclusive rights in it. Invariably the author will be asked to assign the copyright in their work before any exploitation will be undertaken. This leaves the author vulnerable, for if they no longer own their copyright they have no further rights over their work. In order to protect authors, not exploiters, moral rights have been introduced. These rights are intended to create a balance between the economically powerful exploiters of the work and the economically weaker authors.

Unfortunately, in the UK moral rights can be waived. As most authors are very keen to have their work exploited they usually agree to waive their moral rights if asked to do so by the entrepreneur. This reduces their strength substantially. There are four moral rights, although only the first two truly arise from the original work of the author.[26] These are the right to be acknowledged as the author and the right to object to modification and derogatory treatment of your work. In addition there is a right not to have another's work falsely attributed to you and a right to privacy in certain domestic photographs and films. There is, in addition, the *droit de suite*, which gives authors of works of art and manuscripts a royalty when the work is resold on the open market. To claim a moral right the work must still be in copyright.

Right to be identified as the author or director of a work

The first moral right, the right to be identified as the author of the work, is called the 'paternity right'. This right, unlike copyright, does not arise automatically; it must be asserted by the author. If you look at the front of this book you will see that David Bainbridge and Claire Howell have asserted their right to be identified as authors in accordance with the Copyright, Designs and Patents Act 1988. This means that, unless we have waived the right (which we have not), even if the publishers have bought the copyright in the book they must still acknowledge us as the authors. The paternity rights lasts for 70 years after the death of the author (or last to die of joint authors) and, once asserted, the name of the author, or their pseudonym, must be attached to every copy of the work.

The best time to assert your right is at the time of transfer of the copyright: for example, when you are selling the copyright in your music to a music recording company. You may assert your paternity right at a later time but this can cause problems if the copyright is sold on to third parties who are not aware that you asserted the right. Rather than binding everyone, including future purchasers of the copyright in your music, later assertion will only bind people who know that you have asserted your right. An author can also assert their right by signing a picture or including their name (or a pseudonym if used) on a CD cover.

There are some exceptions to the right of paternity. It does not apply to employees as it would be too burdensome on employers to have to name all the employees who created works of copyright while working for them. For the same reason it does not apply, among other things, to creators of computer software. Software can take a long time to produce and is usually written by teams of people who may change over its development. It would be unreasonable to expect them all to be named. There are similar exceptions relating to newspapers, dictionaries, encyclopaedias and disc jockeys; they do not have to name all the authors of the music they play on their music shows. Be careful, however. A myth has grown up that if you acknowledge the author then it is perfectly acceptable to copy a work. This is not the case. Acknowledging the author just means you are not infringing the moral right, but the owner of the copyright, who may or may not be the author, can still sue you for infringement of the copyright itself.

---

26 Sections 77–79 CDPA 1988.

Right to object to derogatory treatment of the work

The second right is the 'integrity right'.[27] This right is aimed at preserving the reputation of an author. As with the paternity right it applies to works that are still in copyright, benefiting the same people with the same exceptions applying. The integrity right prevents the new copyright owner from changing the work in a way that would distort or mutilate it in a way that would affect the author's reputation or honour. This right need not be asserted but it only applies to works where the author has been named and that can be seen by the public.

Let us imagine that Tracey, an artist, has painted a picture of her daughter. She assigns the copyright to Fred, who then daubs a moustache on the painting in an amateur fashion. Can Tracey, who no longer owns the copyright in the painting, do anything? In the case *Confetti Records v Warner Music* a rap version of a song was made that contained references to violence and drugs. The author of the original song failed in his claim that his integrity right was abused as the judge held that it was impossible to decipher what the rap lyrics were.[28] Although the song had indeed been distorted, the author's reputation could not have been damaged by the alteration if no one could work out what was being said.

However, in *Emma Delves-Broughton v House of Harlot*, no prejudice to the author's honour or reputation was required for infringement to occur as long as there had been distortion amounting to derogatory treatment of the work.[29] Here a photographer, E, had taken a photograph of a model with a beautiful forest background. E had agreed that the model could use the photograph in her portfolio for her own personal, non-commercial use. D was given the photograph by the model to use on a website. Without realising that E owned the copyright, D reversed and cropped the image, removing the beautiful forest background. It was held that even though he did not know he was doing anything wrong, D was infringing E's copyright by putting the image on the website. In addition, by manipulating the photograph in this way he was distorting the work and the distortion amounted to derogatory treatment, hence infringing E's moral right of integrity. I think that, following this case, Tracey could claim that her painting has been altered in such a way as to amount to derogatory treatment. But remember, she will only have a case if Fred allows the public to see the painting. If Fred keeps it in his private study, Tracey cannot complain that her moral rights have been affected.

False attribution of a work[30]

This is a right to stop someone pretending to be you. Consequently, you would infringe the moral right of J.K. Rowling, the author of the Harry Potter books, if you wrote a book and pretended that it was written by her. However, as Rowling has no copyright at all in your work the right does not last for your life plus 70 years but only 20 years after her death. This right is only concerned with commercial not private communications. Rowling is able not only to stop you falsely attributing a work to her but may also stop a business, such as a bookshop, possessing or dealing with copies of the work if they knew or should have known of the false attribution. There are no exceptions to this right, so it applies to employees, computer programs, disc jockeys, etc.

Right to privacy in photographs and films[31]

The final moral right concerns photographs and video films. It infringes the moral rights of the commissioner to use photographs or videos that have been commissioned for domestic purposes.

---

27 Sections 80–83 CDPA 1988.
28 [2003] EWHC 1724.
29 [2012] EWPCC 29
30 Section 84 CDPA 1988.
31 Section 85 CDPA 1988.

It is perfectly acceptable for you to go to a famous person's wedding (or in fact anyone's wedding) and take a photographs of the occasion. You would be the author of the photograph and you would own the copyright in it. You are free to sell the photograph to the newspapers and, if it were of a famous person, make a nice profit. However, if you are asked or commissioned, whether for payment or not, to take photographs of the wedding or other domestic event, although you are still the owner of the copyright, unless you have agreed to the contrary you can be prevented from selling the photograph to the newspapers or commercially exploiting the images. This right lasts for the life of the photographer plus 70 years.

Although, on the face of it, moral rights seem to be of great benefit to the authors of original works, the main drawback is that they can be waived. Many authors need to assign their rights to publishing houses or record companies as they cannot afford to exploit the work themselves. These companies may put great pressure on the authors to waive their moral rights so that they do not have to worry about limitations on changing the work or having to acknowledge the author. In addition, some authors may not know that they have to assert their paternity right in order to obtain it or even that such a right exists in the first place.

You think there has been copying – what can be done about it?

It is important to know what copyright material you can protect but it is probably just as important, if not more so, to know how not to infringe somebody else's copyright. Many myths have arisen about what you can and can't do with respect to another's work, but these are myths and should not be relied upon. You really don't want to be on the receiving end of a solicitor's letter or even end up in an expensive court dispute because of something you didn't realise you were doing wrong. To avoid this happening read on.

Despite the word 'copyright' sounding as if it gives the owner only the right to stop others copying their work without their permission, it covers more than this. The term 'copyright infringement' does include the making of unauthorised copies of a work without any defence being available (see later), but the copyright owner also has the exclusive right to issue copies of the work to the public; rent, lend, perform, play or communicate the work to the public; or make an adaptation of the work. If someone does any of these things with a copyright work without the copyright owner's consent they will be infringing. Copying may be assessed differently depending upon which type of work you are dealing with.

Copying software is different from copying a piece of art and a different interpretation of the rules will be applied. There are some things called the 'permitted acts' that you are allowed to do with regard to copyright works. There are some things that are regarded as so serious that if done they amount to a criminal offence, so it is worth knowing what they are. One important myth that has grown up is that if something is on the internet everyone has the right to copy it. This is *not* true. The internet is no different from any other form of communication; it is just much easier to download something from the internet than to photocopy a book or picture. The same applies to copying a CD or downloading a film from the internet. The fact that you are using a computer to copy rather than a photocopier is irrelevant as the legislation stipulates that copying includes copying in electronic form and extends to transient or temporary copies. We can see that just accessing a file on a computer can constitute copying, as would storing a photograph the copyright of which belongs to another. So storing any work in a computer amounts to copying the work. If it is still in copyright, you have not got the permission of the owner and none of the defences apply, you will be infringing.

When you buy a CD or a book or even a painting you are buying the physical object. You are not, unless you specifically agree to do so, buying the copyright in the work and therefore have no right to reproduce the work. There is, however, something called the 'Private copying' exception. If you are an individual who has lawfully acquired, say, a CD, you are allowed to copy the content onto another medium, for example by storing it online or on a device that you own such as your mobile phone or MP3 player, but this must be *only* for your personal use. You are not allowed to share these copies with others.

Copying

Remember that if you stand next to Ann and, using a common source, say Nelson's Column, you each take what looks like identical photographs, you have each independently created your photograph and are not copying each other's work. However, you can be held to have copied something and therefore be infringing even if the end result does not look the same. This is because copying can include indirect copying, or copying in different dimensions.

An example of this can be found in the case LB (*Plastics*) v *Swish Products Ltd*.[32] LB (Plastics) made design drawings for a set of interchangeable drawers. These drawings were artistic works and LB (Plastics) owned the copyright in them. The company then made drawers according to the drawings, so they had made a 3D version of the 2D drawing. Swish Products never saw the original drawings but they did see the drawers and decided to copy them. LB sued for copyright infringement and the question was, had Swish Products infringed the copyright in the 2D drawings? It was held that yes, the copyright was traced back from the 3D drawers into the 2D drawing and Swish Products had infringed the drawing indirectly.

You can see that by taking a photograph of a sculpture you could be infringing the artistic copyright in the sculpture (although there is a defence available if the sculpture is in a public place) and by making a book into a film you could be infringing copyright in the book. If an issue does come to court there may, however, be a problem of actually proving that something has been copied and not independently created. The claimant owner would have to prove that they created their work before the defendant's work; one good reason for putting the date of creation along with your name and copyright notice on the work. The claimant also has to prove that the defendant had the opportunity to see or hear their work. The defendant does not need to remember that they saw or heard the work as infringement can occur subconsciously.

Take, for example, the case of Fred and Ann. Fred is an aspiring music writer who sends his latest composition to a famous pop musician, Ann, in the hope that she will agree to record the song and make his fortune. A year later Fred hears Ann sing a song that is very similar to the one he sent her. When it becomes a bestseller Fred brings an action against Ann claiming that she has copied his song. In order to refute the suggestion Ann could show that she had created the song before Fred had sent his tune to her. If she had sensibly sealed a copy of the song in an envelope and deposited it with her solicitor who had never opened the envelope to tamper with its contents this would be good evidence that she had created the tune independently. Ann could claim that the reason the tunes sound similar is that they had a common source: she had copied a work of Mozart, which is now out of copyright, and obviously the reason the tunes sound similar is that Fred had copied Mozart too. If neither of these courses or any other sensible reason for the similarity are open to her, claiming that she can't remember listening to the song will not be sufficient to disprove infringement. It would be too easy for people to get away with infringement by just saying 'I can't remember ever having heard it'.

---

32 [1979] RPC 551.

Altered copying

Ann's song, even if she did copy Fred's, is unlikely to be an exact copy of his music; there are bound to be differences. What, therefore, is the copyright situation if there has been altered copying? It is here that there are an abundance of myths in circulation. Some people think that if they copy only a few bars of a piece of music or take only 10 per cent of a book, this means they are not infringing. Others believe that if they make five or six changes to a graph, that is sufficient to get them off the hook. These are myths. What you must ask is, has there been 'substantial' copying? So what is substantial?

This concept has been left vague so that it is flexible and will cover many situations. It does not necessarily refer to the quantity of copying, although if you have copied a complete work that would indeed be regarded as substantial.[33] It really refers to the quality of what you have taken. You may have used only a small amount of the work, for example, the smile of Leonardo da Vinci's *Mona Lisa* (assuming it was still in copyright), but if that is a very important part and a part that people would recognise, like the hook in a piece of music or the organ introduction in Procul Harum's song 'A Whiter Shade of Pale', it will be regarded as a 'substantial' part of the author's creation, skill and labour, and you will be infringing. The question is whether, after very commonplace things have been ignored, the similarities in the works can be recognised by other people. In addition, have you, instead of putting in the hard work of creating something yourself, taken advantage of the author's creative work?

There has been a recent and controversial case in the Patents County Court that seems to widen the boundary of what constitutes copyright infringement.[34] Mr Fielder, on behalf of Temple Island Collections Ltd, created a photograph of a London Routemaster bus going over Westminster Bridge with the Houses of Parliament in the background. The photograph had been taken and then digitally manipulated by Mr Fielder. He enhanced the red colour of the bus, made the sky white and the background monochrome. He then digitally removed all the people who were in the photograph. The striking image was used by the company on souvenirs of London. The defendant, New English Teas Ltd, on seeing this iconic image, themselves produced a photograph of a red Routemaster bus on Westminster Bridge with the Houses of Parliament in the background with a monochrome background and a white sky. They used the image on souvenir tins for tea. The photographs were not identical but Temple Island claimed that New English Teas had infringed the copyright in their image. New English Teas claimed that Temple Island did not have a monopoly of photographs of red buses on Westminster Bridge and that as they had not actually duplicated the original photograph they had not infringed. It was held, however, that if a photograph was the photographer's own intellectual creation, reflecting the photographer's personality and expressing their creative choice in style, composition and selection, then this expression can be protected by copyright.

If the defendant creates a new photograph that is influenced by the first and, although containing differences, takes a substantial part of the original image, infringement will occur.[35] Here the judge held that the defendant's photograph did indeed take the key visual features chosen by Mr Fielder. The red bus, the monochrome colouring of the bridge and the Houses of Parliament and a white sky all combined to make the image visually interesting. As the defendant could not give an alternative reason for the similarities they were held to have infringed. However, this does not mean that every image of a red bus going over the bridge with the Houses of Parliament in the background would infringe, only those that looked substantially similar to Temple Island's photograph. We wait to see if this case will be followed by future courts.

---

33 Designers Guild Ltd v Russell Williams (Textiles) Ltd [2000] 1 WLR 2416 HL.
34 Temple Island Collections Ltd v New English Teas Ltd [2012] EWPCC.
35 Designer Guild Ltd v Russell Williams (Textiles) Ltd [2000] 1 WLR 2416.

Remember, you may still be infringing if you make an adaptation of the work, reproducing it in a completely different form. When writing a film script, if you take a substantial amount of the plot, characters or incidents or events that happened in a book you could be infringing. In one case the defendants had made a film that the claimants maintained breached copyright in their book.[36] Many of the dramatic events in the book had not been copied but the theme was the same: it was based on the claimant's life story and some important incidents, such as starting the film with a football chant, had been taken directly from the book. Because of these similarities the court concluded that there had been copying and the amount taken did amount to a substantial part of the book.

If you copy lots of little bits of different stories in a newspaper, would this be regarded as substantial? The answer for copyright purposes, but not for databases (see Chapter 6), is no. It is not regarded as taking a substantial amount because 'the work' is regarded as the newspaper as a whole, not the individual stories within it.

Issuing copies of the work and renting and lending to the public

The copyright owner has the right to be the person to first release their work into the European Economic Area (EEA) or license another to do so.[37] This is often referred to as the right to distribute. A record company has the right to put into circulation in the EEA *each* individual CD they record, but once put on the market the owner cannot prevent resale of each CD within the EEA. In addition, only the copyright owner has the right to rent or lend the CDs to the public (the owner then has a right to royalties). This right applies only to the EEA so if the owner marketed the CDs only in the USA they can be resold by anyone but only to other non-EEA countries such as Canada. Only the owner has the right to import them into the EEA. In one case a website in Hong Kong was selling DVDs to people in the UK.[38] The DVDs had never been sold by the owner in the EEA. It was held that the website was infringing the owner's copyright as by sending the DVDs to people in the UK it was putting the DVDs into circulation in the UK for the first time.

Performance and showing of the work to the public

Copyright covers plays and films, lectures, speeches and broadcasts. To protect the rights of the owners of these works and to allow them to make money from their work, only the owner has the right to perform or show these works to the public. If someone wants to perform a play, they should apply to the copyright owner for a licence to do so. The right, however, relates only to public performance; no one will try to stop you humming a song to yourself (unless you are tone deaf and that will not be for copyright purposes) or a child re-enacting in front of their grandparents a play they have seen. These actions do not affect the economic rights of the owner so you would not be expected to buy a licence for these private acts. However, if you own a pub, a shop or a factory and you play music on your premises, you will be expected to pay for the use of the music by purchasing a licence.

There have been questions about whether a TV in a hotel bedroom, surely a private area, would be regarded as providing a copyright service to the public.[39] To decide the issue you should ask whether the economic exploitation of the owner would be affected. Should the hotel have paid for a licence to show the programmes in these circumstances? The answer is yes, as it is part of the service provided by the hotel. However, it has been decided that a dentist playing

---

36 Hodgson v Isaac [2012] ECC 4.
37 Section 18 CDPA 1988.
38 Independiente Ltd v Music Trading Online [2007] FSR 525.
39 Sociedad General de Autores y Editores de España (SGAE) v Rafael Hoteles SA [2006] ECR I-11519.

music to his patents is not providing a service and is not expected to obtain a music licence. If some audio-visual apparatus is used to perform the work it is the person in charge of the equipment who will be infringing if no licence has been obtained, not the person who performs the work.

Communication of the work to the public

The copyright owner has the right to communicate the work to the public. This right refers to electronic transmission and is aimed at internet use and file-to-file sharing. However, the right would include any communication that would prejudicially affect the owner of the copyright and includes providing a hyperlink, no matter in which country the server on which the website is hosted is located. An exception would be if there has been a broadcast of a football match (e.g. in a pub) to which the public has not paid for admission.

An example of communication to the public can be found in *Dramatico Entertainment Limited and others v British Sky Broadcasting Limited and others*.[40] The Pirate Bay was a Swedish file-sharing website with over 30 million users. The claimants were a group of record companies. The record companies wanted to stop The Pirate Bay encouraging unauthorised sharing of their sound recordings. The claimants knew that it was not practical to sue the individual private users of the service. Rather than sue The Pirate Bay the claimants successfully sought an injunction against the internet service providers (ISPs) who hosted The Pirate Bay service in the UK. Although ISPs are not required to monitor their sites for copyright infringement,[41] section 97A(1) of the CDPA states that an injunction can be obtained against an ISP 'where that service provider has *actual* knowledge of another person using their service to infringe copyright'. The record companies therefore had to show that some infringement was taking place and that the ISPs knew about it.[42] The claimants showed that the users of The Pirate Bay were infringing in two ways. First, they were infringing by downloading sound recordings and copying them onto their own computer.[43] They were then communicating the sound recordings to the public by uploading them for other users to download.[44] It was also claimed that as The Pirate Bay were doing far more than merely enabling or assisting users to infringe they were authorising copyright infringement by their users.[45] The record companies could prove that they had informed the ISP about this infringement by The Pirate Bay; consequently, the ISP had actual knowledge and an injunction could be awarded.

Adaptation of the work

The owner of the copyright has the right of adaptation. This right would include making a book into a film or translating a book from English into French. If enough skill and care was put into the adaptation it is likely that there would be a fresh copyright arising in the film or the translation, but it would still be infringing the original if done without consent of the copyright owner.

---

40 [2012] EWHC 1152 (Ch).
41 Article 15 of the E-Commerce Directive 2000/31/EC of the European Parliament and Council of 8 June 2000 on certain legal aspects of information society services, in particular electronic commerce, in the Internal Market (OJ 2000 L 178, p. 1).
42 Twentieth Century Fox v British Telecommunications plc [2011] EWHC 1981 (Ch).
43 Section 17 CDPA 1988.
44 Section 20(1)(b) CDPA 1988 and Article 3(1) of the Information Society Directive.
45 Section 16(2) CDPA 1988.

Authorising infringement

You will be infringing copyright if you authorise another to do infringing acts.[46] Think back to the Swish Products case and imagine that you have asked a carpenter to make you a set of drawers, giving them the exact dimensions of the LB (Plastics) drawers. The carpenter has seen neither the drawers nor the original drawings but they will be infringing copyright in the drawers via your instructions and you will be authorising the infringement. To authorise infringement you must do more than just stand back and see people infringe. You have either to ask them to infringe or in effect be giving them permission to do so.

In the 1980s Amstrad created the first twin-deck tape-copying machine, which could be used to copy music. The recording industry tried to prevent the machines being sold. They claimed that Amstrad was authorising copyright infringement by selling the means by which music could be copied.[47] It was held that, yes, the machines could be used to facilitate infringement, but Amstrad was only giving the power to copy; they were not actually authorising the copying. In addition, the machines could be used for legitimate purposes such as recording birdsong (birds do not have copyright in their chirps and trills). It is common, however, to see signs above photocopying machines including a warning not to make illegitimate copies. This is because the person in charge of the machine wants to make it very clear that they are not authorising copyright infringement.

What about people who deal with infringing works?

In all likelihood the person dealing with or selling infringing copies will not be the same person who actually copied them. In addition, the copying may well have been performed in another country and the person who copied may not only be difficult to find but may not be infringing any laws in their own territory. Legislation that prevents the copying of works only in the UK would be pretty useless if people were still allowed to import infringing copies and then sell or deal with them freely. To make the system work it is necessary to make the person who knowingly deals with infringing works an infringer also. By importing, selling, possessing for business purposes or facilitating primary infringement you are committing secondary infringement. However, there are some differences between primary and secondary infringement.

Primary infringement, as we saw with Ann and Fred, is when you copy an original work such as a song. You can infringe subconsciously, having forgotten that you ever heard or saw the original work. With secondary infringement you either must have known or ought to have known that you were dealing with an infringing work. If you just shut your eyes to the obvious you will still be infringing. Imagine that your business intends to import 'Best Trainers' from China. You have been sent a letter by a UK firm, Fit Ltd, saying that they have copyright in the shoes and what you intend to import are counterfeit goods made in China. A 'reasonable man' would most certainly think that these could be infringing copies and so you would be guilty of secondary copyright infringement if you imported or sold the shoes. It is always worthwhile when dealing with goods provided by others to put a clause into any contract whereby they guarantee or warrant that they have the right to supply the goods. It is also wise to ensure that they indemnify you if it turns out that they do not have such a right. Then they will have to reimburse any damages that you may have to pay the true owners, assuming that they are still in business and have not gone insolvent in the meantime, of course.

---

46 Section 16(2) CDPA 1988.
47 CBS Songs Ltd v Amstrad [1988] 1 AC 1013.

Software copyright

Computer programs are literary works and the term 'software' can include computer programs and games for games consoles. The software industry is estimated to be worth £100 billion to the UK economy – almost as much as the financial services sector. Although computer software is regarded as a literary work, there has been an attempt to harmonise the rules in the EU. Slightly different rules apply to software than to other literary works. Copyright in a computer program lasts for 50 years from when produced and belongs to the persons who made the necessary arrangements to have it made. The term 'software' includes the instructions given to the computer, the source code, which could be written in a computer language such as BASIC or FORTRAN, as well as the object code which comprises a series of zeroes and ones. This is machine-readable code and tells the computer what to do. The term also covers design materials, flow charts and manuals used by the programmer in creating the software. Computer programs are usually written by a team of people and may take a great deal of time to produce. This could give rise to the problem of team members changing and issues concerning whether some members of the team are employed or commissioned. It is common for new versions of a program to be made that may or may not be sufficiently different from the original to have their own new copyright. Detailed records of who worked on what and when should be kept when software is being produced.

Literal copying

Running a computer program involves copying and unless you have a valid licence to run the software on that particular computer you will be infringing copyright in the software. As with other copyright infringement, computer software can be either copied exactly or changed: there can be literal or non-literal copying. Literal copying of a program would arise if a copy of the program – disk-to-disk – was made without the licence of the copyright owner. This literal copying is very easy to do and although the legislation states that you are allowed to make a necessary back-up copy, many people simply copy a disk and then give it to another to use rather than, as the legislation envisages, saving it for their own use if it becomes necessary.

Due to this copying, many businesses have unlicensed disks in the possession of their employees. It is estimated that in Britain 27 per cent of personal computers use illegal software, but the global figure is closer to 57 per cent. Piracy costs the software industry hundreds of thousands of jobs and hampers economic growth. In 2011 the commercial value of illegal software globally was US$63.4 billion.[48] Much software is sold under contracts such as click or shrink-wrap licences where you agree to the terms of the licence by opening the wrapping or clicking on an icon. Due to the ease of copying, technological locks or copy-protection measures such as encryption or scrambling are commonly used in an attempt to prevent infringement. If such technological copy-protection measures or locks have been applied to a copyright work it is an infringement to knowingly do something to circumvent them that will prejudicially affect the rights of the copyright holder.

In a company, the directors and officers are responsible for ensuring that their organisation complies with the law. Ignorance is no excuse, so even if an officer of a company is unaware that illegal software is being used or that employees of the company are abusing its licence terms, the directors may still be exposed to the threat of legal proceedings. Not only does having pirated software within a business leave employers exposed to litigation but the business will not have access to necessary technical support or information regarding upgrades. In addition, such software may contain viruses or trojans. These can read your keystrokes and not only uncover personal facts but give access to financial information such as bank details. In addition, technical

---

48 Business Software Alliance 9th Global Software Piracy Study.

support that you will need if anything goes wrong will not be available and you can be sure that software companies will not help you rid yourself of these self-inflicted wounds without charging quite a high fee.

Non-literal copying

There is more of a problem associated with non-literal copying of software. When writing code, programmers often insert deliberate mistakes, such as the names of their children or the recipe for their favourite pudding, into the software as a trap. It would be too much of a coincidence for these additions to occur in an independent creation so their replication will act as evidence of copying. Making an adaptation or translation of a program by putting it into a different programming language is infringement, but remember, an idea cannot be protected and neither can the principles underlying computer programs.

There have been cases where the 'look and feel', for example, the screen displays or menus of software, has been taken, and the answer to whether there has been infringement may well rest on whether or not there has been access by the defendant to the source code. If there has been access to the source code you must first identify the features of the claimant's computer program that are present in the defendant's computer program. Second, decide whether these are ideas or principles that cannot be protected. Finally, ask whether what is left amounts to a substantial part of the claimant's program.

What if there has been no access to the source code but the defendant has rewritten the program to look and feel the same as the claimant's? In one case, E, an airline, commissioned N to create a ticket-less online booking system for their flights.[49] Later E no longer wanted to use N but the customers had got used to using the site so E wanted to keep it functioning in exactly the same way, using the same business logic behind it. E asked another company to emulate the 'look and feel' of the site. N claimed that their software had been copied. However, the defendants had not had access to the source code, only copying the idea of how the site worked, and as there is no copyright in ideas there could be no infringement. In another case, the defendant's computer game for playing pool emulated that of the claimant but again as the source code had not been copied there was no infringement.[50] All you had were two different programs that ended up producing a similar result, just as if two separate photographers took two separate photographs of Nelson's Column.

Remember, infringement occurs if you do one of the restricted acts – copying, communicating to the public, etc. – without the permission of the owner. If you want to use another person's photograph in your advertising or another person's music in your jingle, just contact them or their agent and ask if you may use it. They might give you permission for free or just charge a small licence fee.

There are some things you are allowed to do even though it looks like infringement

Despite wanting to give authors control over their works it is felt that some things should be available for all to use, not just because it is fair but also in order to encourage innovation. Because of this wish to create a balance between the rights of society and those of the owners of copyright, some acts are categorised as permitted acts, although they are also sometimes called defences. In order for these defences to apply there will always have been an infringement in the

---

49 Navitaire Inc. v easyJet [2006] RPC 3.
50 Nova Productions Ltd v Mazooma Games Ltd [2006] RPC 14.

first place. A substantial amount of the claimant's work will have been used without permission. Apart from the private copying exception, which has already been discussed, for a defence to succeed the infringing use made of the work must be fair and so would rarely cover a situation where the whole of a work has been taken. It will not apply in most cases if there has been commercial use made of the work or if people would end up buying the defendant's work in place of the claimant's.

It is acceptable to parody a work as long as the amount taken is fair and any moral rights are respected. You are allowed to make some use of copyright works in the course of research and private study. The use must be for non-commercial purposes only and you must make sufficient acknowledgement of the owner or authors and the title of the work. This would mean that you could not use this defence when writing a report for a client as they would be paying you for your services. It is also permitted to use a work for the purposes of criticism or review. This defence is needed so that people cannot prevent reviews of their work by anyone who is likely to be critical. The work must have been published by the author so if the work is leaked or stolen this defence will not apply. Remember, an acknowledgement must always be made. Only a fair amount of the work may be taken but if the work itself is very small, such as a three-line poem, taking the whole work may still be regarded as fair. Be aware, it is the amount taken that must be fair; the criticism itself can be unfair. It is allowed to use a work in order to report current news events as long as the use is fair, such as a short quotation, and sufficient acknowledgment is made.

This defence is very important for the media but would not cover fashion advice, personal finance or lifestyle articles as they are not current news. It will apply, however, to events that, although having occurred in the past, are of current interest. So if an expensive piece of jewellery that had been owned by a member of the Royal family 70 years ago was being auctioned, it would be acceptable to use an old article concerning its provenance written at the time the jewellery was bought. The news defence does not apply to photographs. You must always obtain the photographer's permission to reproduce these, and of course the defence will not apply to works obtained in breach of confidence.

There is also a defence allowing you to use a work if it is in the public interest to do so. Such a defence will usually succeed if a work is regarded as immoral. However, it is sometimes difficult to prove that it is necessary to take a substantial amount of a work. We can see this if we look at the case of *Hyde Park Residence Ltd v Yelland*.[51] The day before Diana, Princess of Wales and Dodi Fayed were killed in a car crash, they had been recorded on videotape visiting a house owned by Mr Al-Fayed, Dodi's father. The time of their arrival and departure were displayed on the film. Mr Al-Fayed later claimed that the couple had spent more time visiting the house than was evidenced in the video. Stills from the video were published in the *Sun* newspaper to show that Mr Al-Fayed had lied about the duration of the visit. The *Sun* claimed, when sued for copyright infringement of the film, that they should be permitted to use the work as it was in the public interest that Mr Al-Fayed should be exposed as a liar. The court held, however, that the information about the times of the couple arriving and departing the house could have been made available without infringing copyright in the film.

It is almost impossible in this day and age not to accidentally infringe copyright. If I go to London and take some photographs or a video of my family, it is almost certain that a building, sculpture or some sort of copyright work will be included in the shot. There is therefore a defence of incidental inclusion of works, such as a piece of music being played in the background, as long as it has not been included intentionally. There is also no infringement if you make images of, for example, sculptures that are on public display. There are some defences for

---

51 [2000] RPC 604, CA.

educational use made at educational establishments and libraries, as long as the use is fair and for non-commercial purposes. These defences are quite limited and most institutions pay for licences so that they can use copyright material with greater freedom. There are also exceptions for copies of works to be made for the visually impaired; archiving and preservation purposes in museums, galleries and libraries for public administration; and data-analysis for non-commercial research.

Computers

There are separate permitted acts relating to computers.[52] As it causes no economic harm to the copyright owner, it is permitted to make temporary copies that are transient or incidental. This allows 'browsing' and 'caching' on the internet. A web browser such as Google allows a user to access information from the internet. Once found it may take some time to download. 'Caching' allows your browser to save the webpage so that it does not have to be downloaded each time you wish to access the information. The rest of the exceptions relate to the use of computer software.

To take advantage of these permitted acts, the rights to make necessary back-up copies, decompilation, study and testing, you must be a 'Lawful User'; that is, a person who has a right to use the program under a licence agreement. It should be noted that the right to make necessary back-up copies will not apply if the copyright owner makes replacements available. The right is not to enable you to give a copy to someone else but to have a spare copy in case your original disk is damaged in some way. Decompilation or reverse-engineering is also permitted but only in order to achieve interoperability. This means that you may reverse-engineer a program you have licensed in order to work out how to make it interface with another program so that they can work together. It is also permitted to observe, study and test a computer program in order to work out the underlying ideas and principles. The lawful user is also allowed to copy or adapt software but only in order to correct errors.

Remedies

There are both civil and criminal remedies available for copyright infringement but on the whole it is up to the owner or exclusive licensee of the copyright to enforce their rights. But remember, all litigation is both expensive and time-consuming. It might, depending on who the infringer is, be better to try to negotiate a settlement or enter into mediation or some other alternative dispute resolution (ADR) rather than embark upon a lengthy court battle. A well-qualified IP solicitor will be essential if you do find yourself embroiled in a legal action.

Civil

Remedies applicable to civil infringement include injunctions, damages or an account of profits, delivery up and destruction orders. Quick action may need to be taken when a copyright owner discovers that their work is being infringed or that infringing items are being sold, but all this needs to be proved to a high standard. A search order will allow the copyright owner to seize infringing goods that are being sold in such places as car boot sales, streets or markets. However, what most owners want is the infringement to stop. They will therefore apply for an injunction to stop further infringing use; however, if damages for lost sales would adequately compensate the claimant, if successful, an injunction will be refused. But if copies of a film that has yet to be

---

52 Sections 50A–C CDPA 1988.

released are being sold at a car boot sale and this would destroy the market for the film, an injunction will probably be granted. It is often the case that any dispute stops at the injunction stage and never actually comes to trial.

Although a defendant who copies a work will be guilty of infringing, even if he didn't realise that he was infringing copyright, damages will not be awarded if they did not know, and had no reason to believe, that copyright existed in the work. Thinking that you have permission to use the work when you do not is no defence. In one case a charity, although knowing that copyright in photographs existed, mistakenly thought that they were entitled to put images taken from a government website on their site.[53] They had to pay the copyright owner £10,000 in damages for their mistake. This was an assessment of the sum that a willing photographer would have charged them for the use of the photographs. If they had genuinely thought that copyright did not exist in the photographs, as might be the case if the images were very old and it was reasonable to assume that copyright had expired, damages would not be awarded but an account of profits may be available. An account of profits is the profit made by the defendant due to the infringement, not the retail value of the infringing articles. Such a remedy is intended to prevent unjust enrichment.

Criminal sanctions

Any type of good can be faked: pharmaceuticals, spare parts for cars, tobacco and even UGG boots.[54] There is no guarantee of quality in counterfeit goods and no one to be held accountable if these goods turn out to be faulty or even dangerous. In 2009 the Organisation for Economic Co-operation and Development (OECD) calculated that the global trade in counterfeit goods was worth around US$250 billion per year.[55] It is thought that in 2010 the UK lost at least £2.2 billion in tax revenue purely due to smuggled alcohol and tobacco,[56] while it is estimated that cyber crime cost the UK economy £27 billion in 2011.[57] The main businesses targeted by cyber crime are software, computer and financial services, the pharmaceutical and biotech industry and electronic and electrical equipment suppliers. Criminal sanctions may apply when copyright is infringed on a large scale but only if the person performing the infringing acts of making, selling, importing or distributing the work knew or had reason to believe that the works were infringing. Such commercial infringement is usually called copyright piracy and often also involves trade mark infringement. No one will help the owner or the exclusive licensee to bring a civil action against a trader in pirated goods and such actions can be very difficult and expensive. A criminal prosecution, however, is a far more attractive proposition for the copyright owner as it will be taken and paid for by either the police or the local Trading Standards Office.[58] Trading Standards will require good evidence of infringement and will only get involved in a criminal prosecution if it is both in the public interest to do so and there is a strong likelihood of success. They have the power to investigate offences after obtaining an order to seize infringing goods. An unlimited fine and/or a maximum term of ten years' imprisonment are available for criminal offences. European customs authorities seized over €1 billion-worth of counterfeit goods in 2010. It is also a criminal offence if a person makes, imports, sells or possesses in business devices or provides services (such as file-sharing) that are designed to allow circumvention of technological locks or copy-protection measures. A person found guilty could face imprisonment of up to two years.

---

53 Hoffman v Drug Abuse Resistance Education (UK) [2012] EWPCC 2.
54 Fashionable fur-lined boots. The writer herself saw such counterfeit boots that had been seized by Customs and Excise officers.
55 www.oecd.org/dataoecd/11/11/2090589.pdf.
56 IP Crime annual report 2010–2011: www.ipo.gov.uk/ipcreport10.pdf.
57 'The Cost of Cyber Crime', Report for the Cabinet Office by Detica.
58 Section 107A CDPA 1988.

Crime in the workplace

Many counterfeit[59] and pirated[60] goods are found in the workplace. This could be due to employees copying legitimately licensed software or by counterfeit or pirated goods being sold to colleagues. If infringing activities are uncovered in your workplace it could cause your business extreme reputational damage as well as a possible civil action or even a criminal penalty (the penalty can be up to ten years in prison, a fine or both). It is therefore important that you educate your employees into what is and is not acceptable and make them aware of the penalties. They should know how you will deal with any IP infringement and that you have policies and procedures in place that you will enforce.

A structure to reward employees who report IP misdemeanours could encourage them to take IP protection seriously. You must ensure that employees using your facilities do not deal with counterfeit or pirated goods. You must check that all your licences are in order and that you have the right to use any software, databases, designs or patents etc. that you use in the running of your business. It could be catastrophic if you incorporated substandard, fake parts into your own products. Not only might they be unreliable or dangerous but you could have an injunction brought against you so that you could no longer trade in any of the products that contained the counterfeit elements.[61] To minimise this risk make sure that you know all your suppliers and check that they are genuine. Keep records of both your suppliers and your customers and ensure that if any of your employees suspect that goods are not legitimate, there is a designated person to whom they can turn.

You should also make sure that your employees do not tarnish the reputation of your business or abuse the privacy of their colleagues when using email or social networking sites such as Facebook (www.facebook.com) and Myspace (www.myspace.com). There should be disciplinary procedures in place for employees who comment inappropriately about their employer or divulge confidential information via such networking sites.

How do I get protection outside the EU?

Originally, copyright only applied in the territory in which it was created. You would be protected in the UK if you wrote your book in England but would have no protection in France. In the nineteenth century there was a huge expansion of international trade. A group of European authors led by Victor Hugo (author of *The Hunchback of Notre-Dame*) recognised that an international agreement regarding copyright was needed. This led to the Berne Convention of 1886, which has been added to and amended over the years. Although there is no international copyright, the Berne Convention gives the citizens of each of the countries that sign the treaty the same minimum standard of protection as citizens of other signatory countries. There are now 164 signatory countries, including China. For members of the Berne Convention there is no registration or payment needed; copyright just springs into existence once a work is put into tangible form.

Rights in performances

Copyright protects certain types of work, which include literary, dramatic and musical works. These works in particular may be subject to a live performance. But what protection do the performers have if the work they are performing is out of copyright or does not qualify for copyright protection?

---

59 Fake trade marks.
60 Unauthorised copy of copyright works.
61 See Supply Chain Toolkit, UK IPO: www.ipo.gov.uk/ipctoolkit.pdf.

Think of actors on stage performing a Shakespeare play, or a mime artist who performs on an impromptu basis. What if someone in the audience makes a recording of their performances?

Performers, and recording companies having exclusive recording contracts with performers, now have rights in respect of those performances and recordings. These rights are of fairly recent vintage and can be described as rights related to copyright. They are of the same genus and bear some similarities to copyright law.

Performers have three sorts of rights:

- non-property rights;
- property rights; and
- moral rights.

The first form of rights, non-property rights, are those that were first available to performers, after some doubt as to whether they had any rights at all, even though it was a criminal offence to make an illicit recording of a performance. The second form, property rights, are not dissimilar to copyright and they are true rights in property. The performance is treated as a form of property. The final and most recent, moral rights, are equivalent to the rights to be identified and to object to a derogatory treatment.

Recording companies also have a recording right if they have the exclusive right to make a recording of the performance concerned.

For the provisions on rights in performances to apply, the performance must be a live performance made by a qualifying person (for example, a citizen of the EU) or made in a qualifying country, being a Member State of the EU.[62]

An important definition for some of the rights and infringements is that of an 'illicit recording'. That is, one made

- without the performer's consent (for the performer's rights);
- without the consent of either the performer or person entitled to the recording rights (for the recording rights); or
- under the permitted acts that apply to performances but has been used subsequently outside the scope of the relevant permitted act.

Each of the rights is now considered in a little more detail.

Performers' non-property rights

These rights are set out in a negative way by specifying the acts that will infringe these rights. Basically, the rights are infringed by a person carrying out the following acts in relation to the whole or a substantial part of a qualifying live performance without the performer's consent. They are:

- making a recording directly from a performance;
- making a live broadcast of the performance;
- making a recording directly from such a broadcast;
- playing in public or communicating to the public a recording (a direct recording or made directly from a live broadcast), knowing or having reason to believe that it was made without consent;

---

62 The provisions are extended to other countries offering reciprocal protection, for example under the Agreement on the Trade Related Aspects of Intellectual Property or the Rome Convention for the Protection of Performers, Producers of Phonograms and Broadcasting Organisations 1961.

- importing into the UK such a recording other than for his own private and domestic purposes, or in the course of a business possessing, selling hiring, exposing for sale or distributing an illicit recording, knowing or having reason to believe that it is an illicit recording.

Note that the last two forms of infringement require a form of knowledge. Whether a person has reason to believe is based on whether a reasonable person would believe the recording was an illicit one.

As opposed to performers' property rights, the non-property rights may not be assigned. They will, however, pass under his will or intestacy to the person entitled on the death of the performer.

Performers' property rights

Performers' property rights are analogous to rights under copyright and include a reproduction right, distribution right, rental and lending rights and making available to the public right, such as by online transmission.

Performers also have a right to an equitable remuneration where sound recordings of their performance are exploited commercially.

Where a performer has assigned his rental and lending rights to a collecting society, as is usually the case, he or she has a further right to an equitable remuneration in respect of the right.

Performers' property rights may be assigned and licensed as with copyright works. The formalities are the same, so an assignment of a performer's property rights, or any of them, must be in writing and signed by the person making the assignment (in the first instance this will be the performer).

Performers' moral rights

Performers' moral rights include the right to identified as the performer. In the case of the live performance itself, the method of identification must be such as to bring the performer's identity to the attention of any person hearing or seeing the performance. In the case of sound recordings of the performance it may be placing the performer's name on copies. Where a group of performers are involved, it may be acceptable to use their group name rather than name them individually.

There are some similarities to the equivalent right under copyright in that the right must be asserted. But there are differences: in particular, the exceptions to the right follow the permitted acts under rights in performances (see below) rather than the special exceptions under copyright law, such as excepting the right in relation to authorship of computer programs.

The other right is the right to object to a derogatory treatment of a performance. This applies to a treatment that is any distortion, mutilation or other modification that is detrimental to the reputation of the performer.

There are exceptions in relation to reporting current events, modification consistent with normal editorial and production practices and for the purpose of avoiding the commission of any offence, complying with statutory duties or, in respect of the BBC, avoiding anything likely to offend public decency or would incite crime, etc.

Recording rights

A person to whom the performer has granted an exclusive recording contract is given rights that are infringed by making a recording of the performance without the permission of the person having recording rights. The recording right is similar to the performers' non-property right. Subsequent use of that recording by showing or playing it in public or communicating to the public also infringes. Importing, possessing and dealing with illicit recordings infringes the recording right as well as the performer's right.

Duration

The duration of rights in performances was 50 years from the end of the calendar year during which the performance took place or, if released to the public during that period, the rights endure for 50 years from the end of the calendar year in which it was released.

Some performers, such as Cliff Richard, lobbied for an increase in the duration of rights in performances to that application to the original works of copyright, that is, life plus 70 years. In a partial victory, an EU Directive modified the term of protection for copyright for sound recordings to 70 years, from the present 50 years, to be complied with by Member States by 1 November 2013. It also modifies the position of music by considering musical compositions as a form of copyright. Previously, copyright protected the music and the lyrics as two separate forms of copyright.

Permitted acts

There are a number of permitted acts for rights in performances. These are acts that can be done without consent and without infringing the relevant right. Many of these are similar to those applicable to copyright, though are usually less extensive. The permitted acts include fair dealing for criticism or review and reporting current events, educational uses, certain forms of lending, etc.

Offences

There are a number of offences that mostly apply to dealing with illicit recordings. As with copyright, some of the offences carry a maximum term of imprisonment not exceeding ten years and/or a fine. Where tried in a magistrates' court, the maximum is six months' imprisonment and/or a fine not exceeding £50,000.

Summary

Copyright protects original literary, dramatic, musical and artistic works and also derivative works such as sound recordings, films, broadcasts or cable programmes and the typographical arrangement of published editions. The work must be original, meaning that it must have originated from the author. It must be the author's own intellectual creation and not copied from another. Copyright protects the *expression* of ideas, not ideas, facts or information, and for copyright to exist the work must be fixed in tangible form. Fixation can be via new technologies. Once fixed copyright arises automatically, so you do not have to fill in any forms or pay any fees. Copyright in the primary works lasts for the life of the author plus 70 years (or, if a joint work, the last author to die) but the duration is shorter for derivative works. The author or authors are usually the first owners of the copyright, but employers own copyright in works created during the course of employment. Unless agreed otherwise, authors own the copyright in commissioned works but exceptionally the court will imply a licence or assignment. Authors retain moral rights even if they have sold the copyright in their works, but these moral rights can be waived. Infringement is not just copying (even for private use) but includes issuing the work to the public, performing and playing in public, communicating to the public, renting or lending the work and making an adaptation.

To infringe, a substantial amount of the work must be taken. What is substantial depends on the quality or importance of what has been used. It is an infringement to authorise another to do an infringing act. It is possible to infringe copyright in the primary works subconsciously but for secondary infringement dealing with the works must be done intentionally or carelessly. Some defences are available and there are separate permitted acts in relation to software copyright. Remedies for copyright infringement are mainly civil but if there has been counterfeiting or piracy on a large scale there could be a criminal conviction. Directors of companies or employers can be personally responsible if it is found that their employees have been infringing copyright.

Management tips

- If you claim that your copyright has been infringed you need to have accurate records identifying your copyright, who created it, their status (employee or contractor) and when it was created, showing not only that you have copyright but providing sufficient evidence to work out the level of damages that you are entitled to.
- If you discover that someone has infringed your copyright the best action may be to ask a solicitor to write them a letter. It might be that this is all that is needed in order to stop them in their tracks. If a letter doesn't work you may need to go to court to ask for a seizure order and an injunction. It is worth trying to negotiate a licence agreement before entering litigation.
- Even though an employer owns the copyright in works created by an employee, if an employee has been identified as the author of a work they may have moral rights that the company must respect.
- When commissioning works you should include a copyright ownership clause in the contract. This could be accompanied by a non-disclosure agreement if the work needs to be kept confidential.
- It is wise to put the name of the business or author, the date of creation and the copyright symbol on any website, stating that the copyright is yours.
- It is just as much an infringement to put copyright material on your website as it is to print it in hard copy.
- If you have a licence to use copyright material in hard copy this agreement will not necessarily cover use on a website as it is regarded as a different type of use. You should always check.
- Always credit other people's material but if you want to use a work and can't identify the author try contacting bodies such as the Society of Authors or the copyright hub www.copyrighthub.co.uk/.
- If you want to use copyright material check to see if what you want to do is covered as a permitted act. Be careful, however, because the defences are very limited if you intend to use the work for any commercial purpose, whether direct or indirect.
- Do not add material to a report written by another without making it clear that you have done so. It is false attribution and an infringement of the author's moral rights.
- Do not use photographs of weddings or other domestic events in your marketing unless you have checked that no moral rights are involved.

Exercise: copyright

Sid and Mike started up a business manufacturing sensors. They wanted to market and sell their sensors online and in September last year asked Mary to design a website. Mary wrote some software especially for the job, charging them £5,000.

Mike translated a poem, 'About Sensors', by the modern French poet Hugo and asked Mary to post the translation on the site. She did this, illustrating the poem with various images of sensors she had made during her lunch break. The site went online in January and has been very successful. Sid and Mike now want to update it, putting up some photographs of sensors they have taken from a competitor's website. They also want to post a cat-training video they saw on YouTube. The video depicts a device that was made of a sensor attached to a liquidiser. When a cat leaps onto a kitchen counter the sensor detects its presence and the liquidiser whizzes into action, making the cat jump back onto the floor. Sid and Mike asked Mary to arrange for the updating of the website but she said that she wanted another £5,000 to do the work. They then asked her for the source code so that they could change the site themselves. She refused to give to it to them, saying that they had no right to it. They have now approached Janet to recreate the website and add the updates that they want.

What copyright issues arise in this scenario?

Mary

Mary was the author of the website. Copyright subsists in the software, which is a literary work. As Mary was commissioned to do the work and as there was no agreement to the contrary she has retained copyright. Mary cannot prevent Janet recreating the look and feel of the website as these are, in effect, ideas.

There is artistic copyright in the images she made. Although she made them at work, this was not part of her job description, and as she had not specifically been asked to make the images, the copyright will belong to her.

If Sid and Mike went to court a licence to use the software might be implied or even an assignment ordered but this is uncertain and expensive and should have been avoided by having a written assignment.

The poem

Unless he had obtained Hugo's permission, in translating the poem from French Mike will have infringed Hugo's copyright but may still have his own copyright in the translation. He has also authorised copyright infringement by asking Mary to put the infringing translation on the site.

Competitors' photographs and YouTube

By downloading photographs from another's website without authority the artistic copyright will have been infringed. Likewise, the video of the cat will be infringed. It is not the cat that has the right to its image but the person who took the video who has copyright in the film.

Exercise: rights in performances

Alice and Betty are songwriters. Alice wrote the music for a new romantic ballad, called 'Devotion'. Betty wrote the lyrics, largely based on a poem she found in a book of poetry.

The poem was written by Duncan, who died 60 years ago. Before he died, Duncan granted Pitville Publishing an exclusive contract to publish his poems for the remainder of the term of the copyright. Duncan's son George inherited his copyright under Duncan's will.

The song was performed live by Cilla, who was accompanied by the Edwin Blues Quartet. A recording was made by Gecko Records Ltd, which had an exclusive recording contract with Cilla and the Edwin Blues Quartet.

Copies of the record were sold to the public. The record was included in a radio broadcast by Southwold Broadcasting Corporation.

Identify all the people that have rights in relation to the song and the broadcast and what their various rights are under copyright and rights in performances.

Chapter 6

Databases

Databases are a key and valuable tool in business. They are created and used for many different purposes, from keeping track of customers' accounts, stock control and use in direct marketing to keeping and maintaining patient healthcare records. The functions served by databases are almost endless and they are used in every sort of business in the private and public sectors and every profession.

Databases range from the very simple, such as a handwritten shopping list or directory of friends' and relatives' addresses and telephone numbers, to the extremely large and complex, such as those operated by airlines, the DVLA and HM Revenue and Customs.

Databases can be very expensive to create and maintain. It was reckoned that the database of racehorses, jockeys, trainers and horserace meetings costs the British Horseracing Board around £4 million per annum to maintain and to generate lists of runners and riders, handicaps, etc. for each horserace.[1] It is fitting, therefore, that databases are afforded sound and effective protection against unauthorised use and copying.

Databases used to be protected as compilations, a form of literary work under copyright law. However, there were worrying signs that database protection was limited and many valuable databases that were the result of a substantial investment might not be protected under copyright law. The concerns were reinforced by a decision of the Supreme Court of the United States that confirmed that there was no place for the 'sweat of the brow' doctrine in copyright.

'Sweat of the brow'

In *Feist*, the US Supreme Court held that the 'white pages' section of a telephone directory was not protected by copyright as it did not require skill, judgement or intellectual creativity in its making.[2] It was the result of effort only. Creating a work by the sweat of the brow only was not sufficient to endow a work with copyright subsistence. According to O'Connor J, delivering the judgment of the court: 'there is nothing remotely creative about arranging names alphabetically in a white pages directory'. Denying copyright protection to works that lack creativity could leave many databases without protection, and noting that protection of databases varied between Member States, the EU decided to act by providing a twin-track approach to database protection. This was introduced by means of the Directive on the legal protection of databases. This Directive now applies to database protection in all the EU Member States, the remaining States of the European Economic Area (EEA) (Iceland, Liechtenstein and Norway) and the Isle of Man.

---
1 British Horseracing Board Ltd v William Hill Organisation Ltd [2001] RPC 31 at para 6.
2 Feist Publications Inc. v Rural Telephone Service Co Inc. 499 US 340 (1991).

Twin-track approach

Put briefly:

- Databases are protected by copyright provided that they are the *author's own intellectual creation*.
- Where the making of a database required a *substantial investment*, they are protected by the database right, referred to in the Directive as a *sui generis* right (meaning a right of its own kind or unique right).

What type of intellectual creativity and what type of substantial investment are explained more fully later. At this stage, it must be pointed out that the two rights are not mutually exclusive and some databases will have both forms of protection where the requirements for the subsistence of both rights are present.

While the database right can be described as a right related to copyright (or a neighbouring right), it is important to stress that it is unlike copyright in a number of ways. In particular, the requirements for subsistence and infringement are quite different and the term of protection is much less than for copyright.

Before looking at copyright in databases and the database right in more detail, there are some common provisions to be set out. For example, the definition of database is the same for both rights and there are the same limitations on the scope of each right.

Common provisions

'Database' is defined as 'a collection of independent works, data or other materials arranged in a systematic or methodical way and individually accessible by electronic or other means'.[3] This covers electronic databases but, because of the term 'or other means', also extends to manual databases, such as a card index. Note that the collection of works, data or other materials must be *independent*. Furthermore, the contents of a protected database are not limited to works of copyright but may include data, such as a collection of numbers or names, and 'other materials', such as recordings of live performances.

Protection, whether under copyright or the database right, does not extend to computer programs used in the making or operation of databases accessible by electronic means. Computer programs have their own regime of protection under copyright law and the Directive on the legal protection of computer programs is without prejudice to EU provisions on the protection of computer programs, rental and lending right, the term of copyright, etc.

An important proviso, which applies to both forms of protection, is that the protection of the contents is unaffected. For example, a database may contain a selection of poems, each of which has its own copyright. A newspaper archive may contain many news stories, again with their own copyright. Information in a database may be confidential or a trade secret or include representations of trade marks. Whatever the rights in the contents of a database, those rights are unaffected by the protection of a database as a database. Of course, the contents of some databases may not be subject to any rights individually but this is not relevant in determining whether the database itself has protection.

The Directive makes it clear that a collection of several recordings of musical performances on a CD does not fall within the scope of the Directive. It will not meet the requirements for copyright 'as a compilation' (that is, it is unlikely to be considered as an intellectual creation in

---

3 Article 1(2) of Directive 96/9/EC of the European Parliament and of the Council of 11 March 2006 on the legal protection of databases, OJ L 77, 27 March 1996, p. 20.

terms of the selection or arrangement of the individual recordings). Nor does such a collection meet the requirements for the *sui generis* database right as it does not represent a substantial enough investment. Note that the Directive is referring to protection under the Directive, notwithstanding the use of the word 'compilation'. It is possible that such a collection of recordings could be protected under copyright as a compilation per se, provided it is original in a copyright sense. This could be the case where putting together the compilation required skill or judgement on the part of its author, the compiler.

Copyright

The Copyright, Designs and Patents Act 1988 was modified to comply with the copyright provisions in the Directive on the legal protection of databases. Databases are classified as a form of literary work separate from compilations, which are now stated to exclude databases.

Apart from the following material on copyright in databases, the copyright provisions that apply generally to literary works also apply to databases. For example, the generous rules on the duration of protection of the life of the author plus 70 years also apply to copyright databases.

Subsistence

The test for subsistence of copyright in a database is whether, by reason of the selection or arrangement of its contents, it constitutes the author's own intellectual creation. No other criteria may be used to determine the eligibility of a database for protection.

The intellectual creativity is in relation to the selection or arrangement of the contents of the database. It may be that the contents already exist and are in the public domain. But this is not fatal to copyright subsistence. The question is whether the work of selecting the contents or arranging them can be considered to be the author's own intellectual creation. Typically, this will be so if the author has used skill and judgement in either or both of the acts of selection or arrangement. Clearly, this would not be so in the case of a database of names, addresses and telephone numbers arranged alphabetically by name.

Scope of protection

The scope of protection of a copyright database is measured by the restricted acts in relation to the database. Any person who carries out a restricted act, directly or indirectly, in relation to a substantial part of the database without the licence of the copyright owner infringes that copyright. As has already been mentioned, the protection of a database as a database is unaffected by any rights in the contents of the database, such as copyright, trade marks rights, etc. Where the contents are subject to separate rights, infringement of the copyright subsisting in a database may also involve infringement of the rights in the contents of the database.

The Directive sets out the restricted acts as:

a   temporary or permanent reproduction by any means and in any form, in whole or in part;
b   translation, adaptation, arrangement and any other alteration;
c   any form of distribution to the public of the database or of copies thereof. The first sale in the Community of a copy of the database by the rightholder or with his consent shall exhaust the right to control resale of that copy within the Community;
d   any communication, display or performance to the public;
e   any reproduction, distribution, communication, display or performance to the public of the results of the acts referred to in (b).

In respect of (c), the doctrine of exhaustion of rights applies and the first sale of a database or copies of it within the EEA and the Isle of Man by the copyright owner or with his consent exhausts the right to control the resale of that copy within the EEA and Isle of Man. For example, if the owner of the copyright in a database sells copies of the database on DVD in the UK, he cannot prevent persons buying those copies from reselling those copies within the EEA and Isle of Man.

Temporary reproduction covers the situation where the database or part of it is copied into a computer's RAM or downloaded online. An example of a translation would be where the database is converted or reformatted so that it can be used with a different computer program and an arrangement would include a case where the contents of the database are reordered. As 'any other alteration' is mentioned, it is hard to see what additional acts could be covered by 'adaptation'.

Communication to the public will apply where the database is made available online whether for consultation or downloading. The other restricted acts are self-explanatory.

The recitals to the Directive make it clear that the protection of a database by copyright extends to its structure. To some extent the work of selecting and arranging the contents of a database is reflected in its structure. For example, Figure 6.1 shows a simple single database structure consisting of names, addresses, phone numbers and email addresses. Figure 6.2 shows a very simple database system consisting of a number of related databases that are used to record and generate income and expenditure reports.

It is not suggested that this database meets the requirement of being the author's own intellectual creation but it serves to illustrate what is meant by database structure. The database has a modular structure comprising four separate databases. These are linked in pairs. Each database has its own internal structure, represented by the fields that denote particular types of data, such as 'Invoice No.'. A set of data for a specific entry, such as details of a particular client, is called a

Last name	First name	Address					Phone	email
		House No or name	Street	Town	County	Postcode		
Atkins	John	13	Hope Crescent	Seatown	Cumbria	CA3 9HG	01231-532109	jatkins@cnet.com
Tracey	Brains	Dunroamin	Thunder Road	Newport	Hampshire	BN8 6TG	01543-787821	BT69561@ukol.co.uk

Figure 6.1 Database of names and addresses.

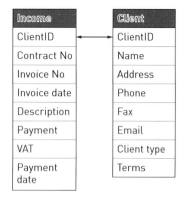

Figure 6.2 Simple relational database structure.

record. The layout of the fields is part of the database structure while another structural aspect is the links between databases. In more complex database structures, these links, or relationships, will be more numerous and potentially more complex. Database structure can thus operate on two levels: the internal structure and the relational structure.

It is submitted that taking both or either of these structures, without taking any of the database contents, could constitute infringement of the copyright subsisting in the database. Indeed, it could be argued that what is really being protected in a copyright database as a database is its structure.

Author and owner of copyright in a database

The usual rules apply to authorship and ownership of copyright in a database. Thus, the author is the person who created the database, that is, the person whose intellectual creation the database is. Where two or more persons jointly create a database such that the contribution of each is not distinct from that of the others, they will be the joint authors. The first owner of the copyright will be the author, with the usual exceptions for employee authors creating databases in the course of their employment and in respect of Crown copyright, parliamentary copyright, etc.

Permitted acts for databases

Generally, the permitted acts that apply to literary works also apply in relation to databases, with a couple of exceptions.

A person having a right to use a database, for example, under a licence agreement, can carry out acts necessary for the exercise of his right, such as access and use of the contents of the database consistent with his right. This permitted act cannot be prohibited or restricted by any term or condition that purports to constrain it.

Making a temporary copy of most forms of works does not infringe copyright where the copy is transient or incidental, and which is an integral and essential part of a technological process and the sole purpose of which is to enable a transmission of the work in a network between third parties by an intermediary; or a lawful use of the work where this act has no independent economic significance. This means, for example, that an intermediary such as an internet service provider does not infringe copyright in, say, an artistic work simply because the work is transmitted via his service. However, this permitted act does not apply in relation to databases (nor computer programs).

In practice, this apparent limitation should have no real consequences as a person who makes his database available for online consultation must be taken to have impliedly authorised the transmission through a service provider's network.

Database right

The database right is intended to afford protection to databases that might fail to reach the standard for copyright protection but that may nonetheless be the result of a substantial investment and be commercially valuable. As mentioned previously, copyright and the database right are not mutually exclusive and both rights will apply to some databases where the rules for the subsistence of both rights are present. Another important point is that the two rights are quite different in many respects.

Subsistence of database right

The Directive on the legal protection of databases provides that the database right subsists in a database where its maker shows that there has been 'qualitatively and/or quantitatively a substantial investment in either [sic] the obtaining, verification or presentation of the contents'. The recitals to the Directive speak in terms of investment being in human, technical or financial resources but this is not necessarily exhaustive, although it is no easy matter to think of another type of resource that could be used in the making of a database. An important factor is that it is for the maker to show that there has been a relevant substantial investment. In other words, it is he who bears the burden of proof should this be a live issue in any legal action.

Note that quality and/or quantity may suffice in terms of the investment. In human resources, this could mean that a skilled professional has been involved (quality) or a number of lower-skilled persons (quantity). The combination of quality and quantity could be useful where neither separately would meet the threshold but taken together they might exceed it.

A serious limitation on the database right is that the Court of Justice of the EU (CJEU) has ruled, on more than one occasion, that 'obtaining' means seeking out and collecting together existing materials. It does not cover the situation where the maker of the database creates the contents himself. For example, in *British Horseracing Board*,[4] the database in question contained information about horses, trainers, jockeys, race meetings, handicaps and associated data. The CJEU confirmed that this creating the contents of a database was not an act of obtaining and, furthermore, verification in relation to contents created by the maker of the database was not a relevant form of verification for the subsistence of the right. The same must apply to presentation.

Maker of a database

The identity of the maker of a database is important as the maker will be the first owner of the database right. There are some exceptions to this basic rule similar to copyright: for example, where the maker was an employee who made the database in the course of his employment. However, as we will see, the identification of who is the maker seems to make the exceptions redundant.

The recitals to the Directive define the maker of a database as the person who takes the initiative and the risk of investing but goes on to expressly exclude 'subcontractors in particular'. It is unlikely that an employee could be viewed as taking the initiative and the risk of investing. However, the rule for employees could cover the situation where the relevant investment is in terms of human resources only.

There are some qualification requirements for database right. They are that, at the time the database was made (or a substantial part of the period during which it was made if made over a period of time), the maker was:

- an individual who was a national of an EEA state (the EU countries plus Iceland, Liechtenstein, Norway) or the Isle of Man (IoM), or was habitually resident in an EEA state or the IoM;
- a body incorporated in an EEA state or the IoM, having its central administration or principal place of business in an EEA state or the IoM or registered office in the EEA or IoM and the body's operations linked on an ongoing basis with the economy of an EEA state or the IoM; or
- a partnership or other unincorporated body formed under the law of an EEA state or the IoM, having at that time its central administration or principal place of business within the EEA or the IoM.

---

4 Case C-203/02 British Horseracing Board Ltd v William Hill Organisation Ltd [2004] ECR I-10415.

Although the qualification requirements will pose no serious issues in many cases, where the maker is, for example, a US company, the database in question will not be subject to the database right. However, if the database is a copyright database, protection will be available throughout the Contracting States of the Berne Convention for the Protection of Literary and Artistic Works.

Term of protection

The duration of the database right is 15 years from the end of the calendar year during which the making of the database was completed. If it was made available to the public before the end of that period, the right will continue to endure for 15 years from the end of the calendar year during which it was first so made available.

Once initially created, many databases are subject to ongoing modification, by expansion, erasure of records, corrections, etc. A new period of protection accrues if subsequent changes are substantial and, including any substantial change resulting from an accumulation of successive additions, deletions or alterations, which result in the database being considered to be a substantial new investment. The substantial investment might come about in a number of ways, including by a wholesale verification process or by presenting the contents in a new way. Whether a change is substantial is to be evaluated qualitatively and/or quantitatively.

Rights and infringement of database right

The owner of the database right has the right to prevent the unauthorised extraction and/or re-utilisation of the whole or a substantial part of the contents of the database, evaluated qualitatively and/or quantitatively. Thus, anyone who performs any of these acts without the authorisation of the owner will infringe the database right. There is also a form of infringement by the repeated and systematic extraction and/or re-utilisation of insubstantial parts of the database.

To get a fuller understanding of the scope of protection, some of the above terms require further examination.

Extraction and re-utilisation

'Extraction' means the permanent or temporary transfer of all or a substantial part of the contents of a database to another medium by any means or in any form.

'Re-utilisation' means any form of making available to the public all or a substantial part of the contents of a database by the distribution of copies, by renting, by online or other forms of transmission.

In British Horseracing Board, the CJEU ruled that extraction and re-utilisation covered both direct and indirect acts. To take an example, say that a newspaper prints details of race meetings with lists of horses, jockeys, trainers, form and handicaps for each race at a forthcoming meeting. The newspaper obtained these details from the owner of the database. If a third party copies those details and publishes them he will have extracted and re-utilised the relevant contents of the database even though he did not have direct access to the database.

In Directmedia, the CJEU also confirmed that an online consultation of a database could fall within the meaning of extraction.[5] In that case, the defendant consulted the claimant's database of titles of famous German poems and, using many of the titles, compiled its own database of poems (obtaining the text of the poems from its own sources). Nonetheless, the original online consultation could constitute an unauthorised extraction of the contents of the claimant's

---

5 Case C-304/07 Directmedia Publishing GmbH v Albert-Ludwigs-Universitat Freinburg [2008] ECR I-7565.

databases. The act of extraction did not require that the contents were actually removed from the original database nor was it limited to a 'cut and paste' operation. Furthermore, the purpose was of little importance. It was largely immaterial whether the purpose was to create a commercial, competing database or whether it was to create a database of the same or different size.

In *Apis-Hristovich*,[6] a case involving claims of infringement of a database of Bulgarian legislation and case law, some of the contents, though not all, were available from public sources. The CJEU also confirmed in that case that the purpose of transferring the contents was irrelevant. On the issue of extraction, the CJEU further ruled that the nature of the computer program used to manage the two databases was not a relevant factor in determining whether an extraction had taken place.

Substantiality

In *British Horseracing Board* the CJEU ruled that substantiality, evaluated quantitatively, referred to the volume of data extracted or re-utilised assessed in relation to the total volume of the contents of the database.

Evaluated qualitatively, a substantial part of the contents of a database referred to the scale of investment of obtaining, verifying or presenting the contents extracted or re-utilised regardless of whether it was a substantial part of the general contents of the database.

Finally, the court came to the axiomatic conclusion that any part that did not fulfil the definition of a substantial part, evaluated either quantitatively or qualitatively, was an insubstantial part.

In *Apis-Hristovich*, the CJEU added further guidance to the meaning of 'substantial' in relation to extraction and/or re-utilisation of the contents of a database in particular circumstances. In relation to a database made up of several modules:

- where a module is itself subject to the database right, the question of whether the contents represent a substantial part evaluated quantitatively requires a comparison between those contents from that module and the total contents of that module;
- otherwise, the comparison must be between the total contents extracted and/or re-utilised from the various modules and the entire contents of the database.

Where the materials extracted and/or re-utilised come from sources not accessible to the public, depending on the human, technical or financial resources used to collect those materials, this may affect the classification of whether they represent a substantial part of the database evaluated qualitatively.

On the other hand, where the materials in question come from official sources accessible to the public, this does not preclude the national court from assessing whether the materials extracted and/or re-utilised represent a substantial part of the contents of the database, evaluated quantitatively and/or qualitatively. The assessment must be whether those materials represent, in terms of their obtaining, verification and presentation, a substantial human, technical or financial investment.

Repeated and systematic extraction or re-utilisation of insubstantial parts

Because of the damage that may be done to the owner's economic interests by a repeated and systematic course of unauthorised extraction and/or re-utilisation of small parts of the contents of a database, a further form of infringement is provided for. The repeated and systematic

---

6 Case C-545/07 Apis-Hristovich EOOD v Lakorda AD [2009] ECR I-1627.

extraction or re-utilisation of insubstantial parts of the contents of a database may infringe. This may amount to the extraction or re-utilisation of a substantial part of those contents. Guidance is found in the Directive on the legal protection of databases, which states that:

> the repeated and systematic extraction and/or re-utilization of insubstantial parts of the contents of the database implying acts which conflict with a normal exploitation of that database or which unreasonably prejudice the legitimate interests of the maker of the database shall not be permitted.

This is intended to catch situations prejudicial to the owner that might otherwise escape. Acts of repeated and systematic extraction and/or re-utilisation of insubstantial parts that are cumulatively equivalent to taking a substantial part infringe. It is implied that such acts do indeed conflict with the normal exploitation of the database or unreasonably prejudice the legitimate interests of the owner of the database.

Permitted acts in relation to the database right

Permitted acts include the use of a substantial part of a database for the purposes of teaching or research providing the person doing so is a lawful user and the source is indicated. Other permitted acts relate to parliamentary and judicial proceedings, Royal Commissions and statutory inquiries, material open to public inspection or on a public register, communication to the Crown in the course of public business, public records and acts under statutory authority. These broadly mirror equivalent acts under copyright law. A further permitted act applies in relation to Legal Deposit Libraries so that libraries such as the British Library may add works including databases to their archives.

There are no permitted acts such as the fair dealing provisions under copyright.

Presumptions

Presumptions are similar as for copyright. For example, where copies of a database bear a person's name as the maker of the database, that is presumed to be true unless shown otherwise. The burden of proof will be, therefore, upon a person claiming that the person so named was not the maker of the database.

Summary

Many databases will be protected by copyright and by the database right. The purpose of introducing the latter right was to protect databases that might have been commercially significant but that failed to be classed as their author's own intellectual creation. While being the result of a substantial investment, such databases would have been deprived of protection independent of their contents.

Some important points to note about database protection are as follows.

- Databases are collections of independent works, data or other materials arranged in a systematic or methodical way and that are individually accessible by electronic or other means.
- Database protection is separate from protection for the contents of the database, if any, and does not prejudice protection of the contents.
- Copyright databases are subject to the usual rules that apply to copyright with some special permitted acts that apply only to databases.

- Thus, copyright databases are infringed by copying, etc., a substantial part of the contents of the database, including its structure.
- The database right comes into existence if there is a substantial investment in the obtaining, presentation or verification of the contents of the database.
- The maker of a database is the person who bears the risk of that investment.
- Database right only lasts for 15 years but if made available to the public before the end of that period, it lasts for 15 years from the end of the year in which that happens; a new database right will come into existence following substantial changes to the database equivalent to a new substantial investment.
- database right gives protection against extraction and/or re-utilisation of a substantial part of the contents; this can apply to repeated and systematic acts involving insubstantial parts if this is equivalent to taking a substantial part.

Management tips

- Provide expressly for ownership where contractors, subcontractors, consultants or self-employed persons are involved in the creation of a database or where there is any doubt as to an employee's status as such or whether the work is in the course of employment.
- Ensure that licences are acquired in relation to the rights, if any, in the contents of a database where those rights belong to others.
- Keep adequate records of the work done and resources used in the creation and maintenance of databases. This is particularly important in relation to the database right where the maker must show that there has been a relevant substantial investment in obtaining, verifying or presenting the contents of the database. This should be an ongoing exercise as the maker also has the burden of proof if, because of subsequent changes, a new term of protection is claimed.
- Bear in mind that 'obtaining' for the purposes of the database right does not extend to creating the contents. If the maker of the database creates all or most of the contents, the database may still qualify if he can show a substantial investment in verifying or presenting the contents.
- Don't forget that the author of a copyright database will have moral rights. This can be important where the author writes software that includes databases and is easy to overlook as moral rights do not generally apply in relation to computer programs. If you publish a database make sure all moral rights are dealt with, either by identifying the authors of the database and works in the contents or by seeking waivers from the right of identification.

Exercise

Consider all the databases you use or have access to, whether paper databases or electronic databases, including online databases. Apply the basic rules of subsistence for copyright and the database right to them and decide which of the rights apply to the database in question. Bear in mind the definition of database and whether the database was the result of intellectual creation or a substantial investment.

Can you think of any databases that contain contents that are themselves protected by intellectual property rights?

Chapter 7

Design Rights

In this chapter, we will explore the nature, acquisition, entitlement and scope of design rights. By the end of the chapter, you should be able to answer the following questions.

> What are design rights?
> What is a design?
> What are the requirements for protection?
> How long do the rights last for?
> Who owns or is entitled to the rights in a design?
> An employee created the design – to whom does it belong?
> I have engaged a consultant to create a new design – who owns or is entitled to the rights in the design?
> What are the rights in a design?
> How do I go about registering a design?
> What should I do to maximise protection?
> How do I get protection outside the EU?

What are design rights?

Imagine that you have created a new design for an article or product such as a chair, a television stand, a webpage, a children's toy, a locking device for a window, an earring, a car body, a wall-clock, a wheelbarrow, a set of cutlery or a garden statue. A number of rights might exist in or be obtained for the designs. For example, the webpage may be protected by copyright as an artistic work; patent protection may be sought for the window lock if it is new and inventive.

This chapter is, however, concerned with design rights, a mixed bunch of rights that can protect designs, as such. Design rights are much underused and misunderstood. Yet some provide inexpensive monopoly protection (by far the cheapest monopoly you can get) and others are automatic and free.

What are the forms of design right protection?

There are four specific forms of design right protection. Three are very similar in a number of respects, but the fourth is quite unlike the others. The rights are:

- unregistered Community design;
- registered Community design;

- registered UK design;
- UK unregistered design right.

The unregistered Community design is intended to give short-term protection to new designs that are unlike the existing corpus of designs. *Novelty* and *individual character* are the two requirements for protection. The key meaning of design, briefly put, is the *appearance of the whole or part of a product*. These terms will be described in more detail later. There is a grace period during which an owner may decide to register a design, which he has already put on the market, gaining the benefit of stronger protection that may last for up to 25 years.

With virtually the same basic requirements for protection as the unregistered Community design, the two forms of registered design (Community and UK) are, to all intents and purposes, the same, except that the first (and, of course, the unregistered Community design) applies throughout the EU while the latter applies in the territory of the UK only. However, there are some important differences. In particular, the rules for entitlement are different. In the UK, where a design is created by a designer, not being an employee, working under a commission, the person commissioning the creation of the design is automatically entitled to be the proprietor of the registered design. This does not apply to a Community design created under a commission and it is vital that express provision is made for entitlement.

The benefits of registration are that this provides stronger protection and can last for longer. Registration of a design is relatively straightforward and inexpensive. If a design is registrable, it ought to be registered.

The UK unregistered design right is unlike the other forms of design right protection. Protected designs must be *original and not commonplace in the relevant design field*. A design in this context is the *shape or configuration of the whole or part, external or internal, of an article*.

It should be noted that, in some cases, a design may be subject to the UK unregistered design right as well as some or all of the others. Some designs may only be protectable as UK unregistered designs and some may be protectable under the Community design and UK registered designs regime. But there is an overlap that students should be aware of.

To summarise the different forms of protection, Table C may be useful.

It should already be clear that the UK unregistered design right is nothing like the other design rights. It can best be described as a maverick right and it is arguable that it ought to be scrapped. It is, however, a most useful right in practice. It costs nothing to acquire and maintain and is free from any formal requirements. That does not mean that steps should not be taken to maximise the protection it provides, as will be seen later in this chapter.

This chapter is structured to look first at unregistered Community design. Next follows the registered Community design. The UK registered design is then discussed, though only to the extent that it differs from or has specific provisions for the UK. Some of the matters dealt with here are the rules as to entitlement to commissioned designs and some of the practical aspects such as the registration procedure.

Table C

	Community design		UK registered design	UK unregistered design right
	Unregistered	*Registered*		
Protects a design, being:	The appearance of whole or part of a product			The shape or configuration of whole or part of an article
To be protected, the design must be:	New and have individual character			Original and not commonplace in the relevant design field
Lasts for:	3 years	up to 25 years		15 years maximum

The UK unregistered design right is described last of all. This right can be described as an accident of history. It was brought about long before the Community design rights and was an attempt to reduce the extremely generous, and probably unintended, protection afforded to industrial designs through the medium of copyright in the drawings representing the design created during the design process. Bear in mind that, despite the possibility of overlaps in protection in some cases, this right is quite unlike the others.

Before continuing, it is worth pointing out that the registered forms of design protection give monopoly rights while the unregistered forms, despite their differences, are really a right to prevent copying.

The unregistered Community design

What is a design?

A 'design' in lay terms can mean the visual appearance of a product or article; its shape, ornamentation, or structure; the way in which it is assembled; or materials from which it is made (this is by no means intended to be exhaustive). A design may relate to the whole or part of the article or product. For example, it could be a design applied to a new range of crockery or the knob on top of a teapot lid. A design might be the shape or arrangement of internal components of a complex article such as a washing machine or car engine. A particular product may be subject to numerous designs: for example, where they are applied to parts of a vacuum cleaner (the cylinder, handle, brush heads, etc.).

Given the wide views on what a design can be, it is no surprise that legal definitions are broad, while attempting to be as specific as possible. For example, Article 3(a) of the Community Design Regulation states that a design is:

> the appearance of the whole or a part of a product resulting from the features of, in particular, the lines, contours, colours, shape, texture and/or materials of the product and/or its ornamentation.

The Regulation goes on to define 'product', which is, by Article 3(b):

> any industrial or handicraft item, including inter alia parts intended to be assembled into a complex product, packaging, get-up, graphic symbols and typographic typefaces, but excluding computer programs.

For completeness, a 'complex product' is, by Article 3(c):

> a product which is composed of multiple components which can be replaced permitting disassembly and re-assembly of the product.

Students should reflect on the width of these definitions, noting, in particular, that:

- the definitions apply to three of the four forms of design right protection, being the Community design (unregistered and registered) and the UK registered design;
- although appearance is key, there is no distinction between attractive designs and functional designs – the design in question does not need to be aesthetic;
- computer programs are excluded (but this does not prevent other items of software being protected as designs, such as screen displays, software fonts, computer icons, etc.);
- machine-made products are included and the definition of product is not limited to hand-made items or articles made by craftsmen;

- designs applied to parts of complex products may be protected if they can be replaced, permitting disassembly and reassembly of a complex product – this could include, for example, the wand handle of a Dyson vacuum cleaner.

What are the requirements for protection as an unregistered Community design?

Bear in mind that the requirements also apply to the registered Community design, though the meaning of 'new' is slightly different.

First of all the design must comply with the definition of design above, that is, that it relates to the appearance of the whole or a part of a product resulting from the features of, in particular, the lines, contours, colours, shape, texture and/or materials of the product and/or its ornamentation.

The meaning of product, and where applicable, complex product, must also be satisfied. Thus, for example, the design must be applied to the whole or part of an industrial or handicraft item, which can be packaging, get-up, graphic symbols or typographic typefaces. It cannot be a computer program (these are protected as works of copyright and may, in some circumstances, be protected indirectly by way of patents).

The design must be *new* and have *individual character* (Article 4(1) of the Community Design Regulation).[1] Novelty and individual character have their own specific meanings, described below. But, just to recap, the design must:

- be a 'design' (that is, fall within the meaning of 'design' above);
- be new;
- have individual character; and
- finally, the design must not be excluded from protection.

We have already seen what a design is for the purposes of the right and it is now time to look at the requirements of novelty and individual character. Before doing so, it is important to note that because the right is one that applies throughout the EU, the requirements of novelty and individual character are judged according to whether persons specialising in the relevant sector operating within the EU would reasonably be expected to know of the design. As we will see, the test for novelty is not as straightforward as one might expect.

Novelty

Under Article 5 of the Community Design Regulation, a design is new if no identical design has been made available to the public, including any design differing only in immaterial details. Thus, a design is not new if it differs only in respect of minor aspects that are not readily noticeable. An example might be where an average consumer sees a product one day and then sees another product a few days later and, if asked, would think they were both to the same design. In other words, the differences are too insignificant to be noticeable. That is not to say that if the two products were examined side by side, the differences would not be discerned.

Whether a design has been made available to the public is rather more complicated. Article 7 of the Community Design Regulation contains the fine detail.

---

1 In this and other parts of the chapter on the Community design and the UK registered design, references are made to the Community Design Regulation only, unless the UK Registered Designs Act 1949 differs or covers aspects not within the scope of the Community Design Regulation.

A design is made available to the public if it has been published, following registration or otherwise, or exhibited, or used in trade or otherwise disclosed. But there are two provisos to this:

- a design is not made available to the public if any of the events described above could not reasonably have become known in the normal course of business to the circles specialising in the sector concerned operating within the EU;
- disclosures by persons under an obligation of confidence are ignored.

The reference to a design being published following registration applies specifically where an application has been made to register the design. Normally, designs are published after being accepted for registration, whether as a registered Community design or registered national design.

The first of the provisos introduces a test of whether those likely to be familiar with designs in that field, operating within the EU, would already know of such a design or one very similar to it. This could apply, for example, where an EU-based importer of products from the Far East is familiar with the design because he is aware that products to that design are being marketed in China.

The second proviso could apply where an employee discloses details of the design to a competitor of his employer before it has been put on the market by his employer.

The time when novelty is judged is, for the unregistered Community design, the date when the design is first made available to the public.

Note that there is no limitation as to the territory where the relevant event occurred. Thus, for example, if an EU-based manufacturer of cameras would be likely to know of a new camera design registered and published in Japan, that would be sufficient to destroy novelty of a later similar design created in the EU even before any of the cameras to the Japanese design have been exported to the EU or publicised in any other way in the EU.

Individual character

A design has individual character if the overall impression it produces on the informed user differs from the overall impression produced on such a user by any design that has been made available to the public (Article 6 of the Community Design Regulation). The amount of design freedom of the designer in developing the design is taken into account. Design freedom may be limited because the shape of the relevant product is to a greater or lesser extent constrained by the product's function. For example, electric kettles tend to have a lid at the top and a spout on the side.

The informed user is a person who is familiar with the features of the product concerned and, when assessing the overall impression created by the design, will take account of any limitations on the freedom of the designer and will weigh the various features consequently.

In *Procter & Gamble Co v Reckitt Benkiser (UK) Ltd*,[2] the Court of Appeal distinguished the informed user from the 'average consumer' in trade mark law. The informed user would be more discriminating and what mattered was what stuck in his mind when looking at the design, not what stuck in his mind after he had looked at it. The concept of imperfect recollection played a limited role. The informed user would also know that some designs were the way they were because of limitations on design freedom. Where this was the case, smaller differences might be sufficient to create a different overall impression.

---

2 [2008] FSR 8.

The Court of Justice of the European Union ruled that the qualifier 'informed' suggests that, without being a designer or technical expert, the user knows the various designs that exist in the sector concerned. He has a certain degree of knowledge of the features that those designs normally include and, as a result of his interest in the products concerned, pays a relatively high degree of attention when he uses them.[3]

Whether a design has been made available to the public has the same meaning as for the test of novelty. The time novelty and individual character are assessed are the time products to the design are first made available to the public. Bear in mind the meaning of making a design available to the public.

Excluded design

Even though they may comply with the meaning of 'design', be new and have individual character, some types of designs are excluded from protection. The exclusions are set out in Articles 8 and 9 and are:

- features of appearance of a product solely dictated by its technical function;
- features of appearance of a product that must necessarily be reproduced in their exact form and dimensions in order to permit the product in which the design is incorporated or to which it is applied to be mechanically connected to or placed in, around or against another product so that either product may perform its function (this does not apply to designs serving the purpose of allowing the multiple assembly or connection of mutually interchangeable products within a modular system);
- a design that is contrary to public policy or accepted principles of morality.

The first and second exclusions do not prevent the protection of a design if other features of its appearance are outside the scope of the exclusion. For example, a wheel for a vehicle must be circular – this is dictated by the wheel's function. Other features of the design of the wheel may not be so dictated, such as certain aspects of the design of the sides of the wheel. Just look at the enormous range of designs of alloy car wheels for confirmation of this.

The second exclusion applies to prevent the protection of interconnections, such as the holes in a wheel permitting it to be fixed to the hub of the vehicle. The design of components in a modular system are not caught by this exception, an example being the design of modular furniture.

The third exclusion needs no further discussion except to note it is the whole design that is excluded. The fact that some features may escape the exclusion does not mean that they are protectable separately. The question is whether the design as such is contrary to public policy (for example, the design of a handgun) or accepted principles of morality (for example, the design of a sign advertising prostitution).

How long does the right to an unregistered Community design last?

The duration of protection is relatively brief, standing at three years from the date on which the design was first made available to the public (Article 11 of the Community Design Regulation). The meaning of making available to the public is as before. That is, whether persons specialising in the relevant sector operating in the EU would be reasonably taken to know of the design through its publication, use in trade or otherwise, etc.

---

3 Case C-281/10P Pepsico Inc. v Gruper Promer Mon Graphic SA, 20 October 2011.

The rationale behind giving such short protection is that:

- it allows informal protection against copying to short-lived designs, such as fashion clothing or accessories, without the need and expense of registering the design;
- because of the period of grace (the owner of the design may market products to the design for up to one year before registering the design without prejudicing novelty or individual character, as will be seen), if the design turns out to be successful and protection is likely to be wanted for more than three years, he or she may apply for registration within that first year.

Of course, the owner of a design may choose to register the design immediately so as to take advantage of the stronger protection registration brings. If a third party uses a registered design without permission, he will be liable for infringement even if he did not know of the existence of the protected design. In the case of the unregistered Community design, the owner must prove that his design has been copied by the defendant.

As is usual with intellectual property rights (IPR), it is important to keep proper records, for example, of the acts of creation and when and where the design was first made available to the public.

Who is the first owner of the unregistered Community design?

By 'first owner' we mean the person who is initially entitled to the right in the design. He or she may subsequently transfer ownership of the right or grant licences under it, as will be seen in Chapter 8.

The basic rule is that the designer is the owner of the right to a Community design (Article 14). If, during the life of the right in the design, the owner dies, his successor in title will become the owner.

If a design is created by two or more designers, the right belongs to them jointly.

The only exception recognised by the Community Design Regulation is where the designer creates the design in the execution of his duties or following instructions given by his employer; the employer will be the first owner of the right. The only exceptions to this are:

- where there is an agreement providing otherwise, for example, the employer and employee might agree (expressly or by implication) that the employee should be entitled to the right in the design; or
- where national law provides otherwise.

There is no provision in the Regulation covering the situation where a design is created under a commission: for example, where a self-employed designer has been contracted to create the design.

In a case involving the creation of a design for cuckoo clocks under a commission, the Court of Justice of the European Union confirmed that, in the absence of an assignment of the right by way of contract, the right to a Community design created under a commission vests in the designer, not the person commissioning its creation.[4]

---

4 Case C-32/08 Fundación Española para la Innovación de la Artesanía (FEIA) v Cul de Sac Espacio Creativo SL [2009] ECR I-5611.

What are the rights in an unregistered Community design?

The owner of the right has the exclusive right to use it and can prevent its use by third parties not having his consent. In this context, 'use' means, in particular, making, offering, putting on the market, importing, exporting or using a product incorporating the design or to which the design has been applied or stocking such a product for those purposes. However, the right to prevent third parties so using the design applies only if this is a result of copying the protected design (Article 19).

However, the use complained of is not deemed to be the result of copying if it results from the independent work of a designer who might reasonably be thought not to be familiar with the protected design.

In such circumstances, the owner of the right will have the burden of proving that the third party did indeed copy his design. In any case, where it is denied by the third party, the owner of the protected design will have to show that his design has been copied by or on behalf of the third party. The only exception is where it is clear, on the face of it, that there has been copying, such as where the designer of the design alleged to infringe the right has previously been an employee of the owner of the protected design. In such a case, the third party may be put to proving that his design was not the result of copying.

Again, these provisions show the desirability of keeping full and accurate records. After all, the third party whose use of the design is complained of may claim that his design was made available to the public first. Alternatively, he may claim that the design right is invalid.

The rights in a Community design are not absolute and are limited by the meaning of 'use', though it must be noted that the description of use in Article 19 is not exhaustive. Furthermore, Article 10 sets out the scope of protection that extends to any design that does not, on the informed user, create a different overall impression, taking account of the amount of design freedom. (See above for the meaning of *informed user* in relation to individual character.)

There are further specific limitations of the rights in a Community design as given below.

Limitations

Article 20 sets out a number of limitations on the rights in a Community design, being:

- acts done privately and for non-commercial purposes;
- acts done for experimental purposes;
- reproduction for citation in teaching, provided this is in accordance with fair trade practice and does not unduly prejudice the normal exploitation of the design and mention is made of the source;
- further limitations apply in relation to ships and aircraft, registered in third countries, that have entered temporarily the territory of the EU – this allows the importation of parts to effect repairs and the carrying out of such repairs.

Exhaustion of rights

A further limitation on the protection of a Community design is the doctrine of exhaustion of rights (Article 21). This means that the owner of a Community design cannot object to further acts in relation to a product to the design that he has put on the market within the EU or has consented to the product being put on the market.

This means that the owner of the right cannot object, for example, to a third party buying products that the owner has sold in Portugal, exporting them to another Member State and reselling them there. The doctrine only applies to products put on the market for the first time in the EU and not where the owner of the right has placed the products on the market outside the EU. He can still use his right to object to the importation of the products into the EU by a third party, even if the third party had bought the products directly from the right owner.

The purpose of this rule, which applies generally to goods subject to IPR, is to discourage right holders from selling those goods at different prices in different Member States, thereby leading to a fragmentation of the single market.

Government use

Where a Member State provides for government use of a national registered design, this may extend to the Community design where the use is for essential defence or security needs. Similar provisions apply in the UK for the UK registered design and the UK unregistered design and similar provision has been made for Crown use of the Community design. These provisions are rarely used. If they are, the owner will be reimbursed for such use.

The registered Community design

Most of the provisions relating to the unregistered Community design also apply to the registered Community design. There are, however, some important differences. Obviously the fact that the design has to go through a formal registration process is one major difference. But there are other differences also, such as the meaning of making available to the public, how long the right lasts for and the scope of protection afforded by the right.

The fact that the right is registered brings other implications such as challenges to the validity of the right and applications to revoke the right. That is not to say, of course, that a defendant might challenge the existence of an unregistered Community design, for example, on the basis that it failed to comply with the meaning of 'design', that it lacked novelty and/or individual character.

Bearing this in mind, the following description of the registered Community design will focus on the provisions that apply only to that right. Where the features of the registered design are the same as for the unregistered design, this will be noted without unnecessary repetition.

What are the requirements for registration as a Community design?

The meaning of 'design' is as for the unregistered Community design, as are the meanings of novelty and individual character, apart from differences in the timing of when these are tested, and there is some modification to the meaning of making a design available to the public.

For the registered design, novelty and individual character are determined at the time of filing the application for registration rather than when the design is first made available to the public.

A priority system applies to registered designs, similar to that for patents and trade marks. This means that advantage can be taken of an earlier application to file elsewhere. For example, the owner of a design might file an application to register the design in one country and will then have a period during which he can file applications in other countries and the design will be considered on the basis of that earlier application. For designs, the priority period is six months. The right to priority applies in relation to States that are parties to the Paris Convention for the Protection of Industrial Property 1883. At the time of writing, there are 174 contracting parties.

Where the priority of an application to file for registration of the design in question is claimed, references to the date of filing the application are to the date of priority.

The date a design is made available to the public is the same as for the unregistered Community design except that disclosures by the designer during the 12-month period preceding the application to file the registration or the priority date, if applicable, are discounted. Therefore, a product to the design may, for example, be put on the market and sold by the designer for up to

12 months and the novelty and individual character will be judged at the date of filing (or priority date if there is one).

References to the designer really mean to the person entitled to the design or someone acting on his behalf or with his permission. For example, products to the design may be placed on the market by a third party who is the designer's (that is, owner's) licensee.

How long does a registered Community design last?

Initial registration is for five years, running from the date of filing the application for protection. Thereafter, registration may be renewed for a further five years and so on until the maximum term of 25 years is reached. The reason why the protection runs in consecutive five-year blocks is that the design may no longer be commercially valuable after a few years, in which case, the expense of further renewals may be avoided.

Note that there is no reduction in the initial five-year term if the priority of an earlier application elsewhere is claimed.

Who owns or is entitled to the rights in a registered Community design?

The rules here are the same as for the unregistered design. The designer is the person entitled to the rights in the design (or designers jointly if two or more designers created the design). Employee-created designs will belong to the employer, unless otherwise agreed.

What are the rights in a registered Community design?

The scope of protection is as for the unregistered variety, that is, it covers identical designs and extends to designs that do not, from the perspective of the informed user, create a different overall impression, taking account of the freedom of the designer in creating his design.

The prohibited uses are as for the unregistered Community design but there is a major difference here. In effect, the unregistered Community design merely gives a right to prevent copying the design. On the other hand, the registered Community design gives the exclusive right to prevent third parties using the design without the rightholder's consent. There is no need to show copying and this means that the right is a monopoly right.

The right to prevent third parties using the design extends also to the holders of conflicting registered designs having later registration dates.[5] As neither the Office of Harmonization for the Internal Market (Trade Marks and Designs) (OHIM) nor the UK Intellectual Property Office (UK IPO) examine applications to register designs for novelty and individual character, conflicts between registered designs are possible. Of course, the holder of the earlier design may bring invalidity proceedings after the later design has been registered.

As regards an innocent defendant who uses the design or one not differing in material details and who has no knowledge of the registered design, this is not as severe as it might seem at first sight. This is because registered designs are published and may be searched for (including online). Anyone considering applying a design to a product has the opportunity to check to make sure there are no registered designs that are the same or very similar. Indeed, this is a recommended practical step that anyone contemplating launching a new product should take, ideally before the design process commences or has got beyond a rough draft.

---

5 See, for example, Case C-488/10 Celaya Empranza y Galdos Internacional SA v Proyectos Integrales de Balizamiento SL, 16 February 2012.

The limitations on the right are as for the unregistered Community design but there are additional 'limitations'. There is a right for a third party to continue prior use. This applies where the third party has commenced use of the design or made serious and effective preparations to do so before the date of filing the application to register (or priority date if there is one). In such a case the third party may continue (or commence) such use but may not grant licences under it. This covers the situation where someone, without knowledge of the registered design, coincidentally uses or make serious and effective preparations to use a design that is identical to or only differs from it in immaterial details. Of course, the third party must not have copied his design from the one that is subsequently registered.

How do I go about registering a Community design?

The process is relatively simple. An application can be filed at the OHIM in Alicante. Online filing is also available, which means that a design may be registered almost immediately. As well as filing direct, the application may be filed through national intellectual property offices, which will charge a handling fee (£15 at the UK IPO).

The information that must be provided is:

- name and address of applicant;
- name and address of agent, if there is one;
- indication of first and second language (second language must be one of the five official languages of OHIM but not the same as the first language);
- description of the type of product to which the design is to be applied (preferably using the OHIM classification system – based on the Locarno system, see below);
- name of the designer (unless he has waived the right to be mentioned);
- one or more views of the design (or two-dimensional specimen if design is applied to a textile, wallpaper, lace or leather);
- description of the design;
- if applicable, a claim to priority and supporting documentation;
- if required, a request for deferment of publication.

The form must be signed by the applicant and the necessary fee paid.

Where a single application is made to register more than one design, they must all belong to the same Locarno class. The Locarno classification system is an international classification system for the registration of industrial designs. This contains 32 classes for goods: for example, Class 8 is tools and hardware and Class 32 is graphic symbols and logos, surface patterns, ornamentation.

It is possible to defer publication of a design for up to 27 months from the date of filing (or priority date if there is one). The advantage of deferment is that the design is not made public until later. This can be useful if products to the design are not to be made available to the public immediately, for example, where the designer has yet to arrange for manufacture or distribution. The reduced initial total fee if deferment is applied for is offset by the fact that the full publication fee has to be paid eventually.

The disadvantages of deferred publication are: first, the right to prevent use by an unauthorised third party requires proof of copying and, second, if publication is not requested within the 27-month period, the right to a registered design will be lost. This may leave a residual period of protection by the unregistered Community design.

The basic procedure is as shown in Figure 7.1 (simplified).

The fee structure (as at the time of writing) is as indicated in Table D.

Renewal fees are €90 for the first renewal, €120 for the second renewal, €150 for the third renewal and €180 for the fourth and final renewal.

The OHIM website contains a useful fee calculator.

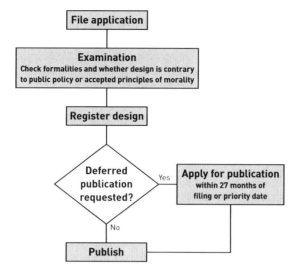

Figure 7.1 Application to register a Community design.

Table D

No. of designs applied for	Registration (per design)	Publication	Deferment (if requested)
1	€230	€120	€40
Additional designs up to 10 additional designs	€115 for each additional design	€60 for each additional design	€20 for each additional design
>11 designs	€50 for each additional design over 11 designs	€30 for each additional design over 11 designs	€10 for each additional design over 11 designs

Invalidity of registered community design

There are a number of grounds for invalidity of a registered Community design under Article 25. Examples are where the design fails to comply with the meaning of 'design', where it is in conflict with an earlier registered design or a protected distinctive sign, where it is not new or lacks individual character or where it is an unauthorised use of a work of copyright. In cases of conflicts with earlier or other rights, only the holder of that right may challenge the validity of the registered design. It may be possible to partially overcome a challenge to validity by amendment of the design.

The UK registered design

The UK registered design is almost identical to the registered Community design. Of course, it only applies in the territory of the UK, whereas the Community design (registered and unregistered) applies throughout the territory of the EU. There are, however, a number of differences and some of the important ones are discussed below.

The UK registered design system was overhauled to comply with an EU Directive aimed at harmonising national registered design law throughout the EU. The legislators had their minds on the later introduction of an EU-wide design so the basic requirements, such as the meaning of design and the requirements of novelty and individual character, are the same as for the registered Community design.

The UK Registered Designs Act 1949 was amended to incorporate the mandatory provisions of the Directive. One option in the Directive related to spare parts, such as body parts for motor vehicles. Member States could continue to protect the design of such parts if they already did so (for example, France). They could liberalise the market to deny protection if they used to protect such parts. The UK already denied protection to spare parts and continued to do so after complying with the Directive. This is in line with the Community design.

Who has the right to the UK registered design?

Unlike the rights to a Community design, the UK registered design has two differences, being:

- where the design is created under a commission for money or money's worth, the person commissioning the design is the first proprietor of the design (that is, the commissioner is the person entitled to register the design as its owner);
- where a design is generated by computer in circumstances such that there is no human designer, the person making the arrangements for the creation of the design is treated as its designer.

The first exception is very important and needs appropriate action. Consider a new design created under a commission that qualifies for protection as a Community design and is to be registered as such and as a UK registered design. Unless there is specific provision for ownership the Community designs will belong to the person creating the design under the commission whereas the person commissioning the creation of the design will be entitled to be the proprietor of the UK registered design. There is real potential for a conflict of ownership.

The second difference is of no practical consequence. It is difficult to envisage a case where a programmed computer is entirely responsible for the creation of a design. If the design in question is generated automatically with no human intervention apart from setting the program into operation, there is still the indirect contribution of the person who wrote the computer program and other items of software used, such as a database of parameters used in determining the design attributes.

Registration of a UK registered design

The process is similar to that which applies to registration of a Community design, with some differences. The fees are significantly less, standing at £60 to register a single design (or £40 to register with deferred publication – applications for publication then cost £20 plus a deferred fee of a further £20). An important difference is that publication may only be deferred for 12 months, after which, if no application has been made for publication, the application will be treated as abandoned. Application is made to the UK IPO and full details of the procedural aspects and forms are available on their website.

Applications to register additional designs cost £40 each or £20 each if publication is deferred. Deferring publication always costs an additional £20 each, whether for a single application or for additional designs.

If a designer intends only to exploit the market in the UK, registration in the UK only is remarkable value. Of course, bear in mind that your UK registration gives you no control over what happens outside the UK. Individuals travelling abroad may purchase and bring back goods to your design and there is nothing you can do about it, unless the design is still protected by the unregistered Community design.

The UK unregistered design right

Part III of the Copyright, Designs and Patents Act 1988 deals with the UK unregistered design right. Note that this right is unlike the Community design and the UK registered design, although there may be some overlap in the protection afforded by these rights.

The definition of 'design' for the UK unregistered design is, under s 213(2) of the Act, 'the design of any aspect of the shape or configuration (whether internal or external) of the whole or part of an article'. Note how this definition looks deceptively simple. It matters not whether the article to which the design is applied is visible during normal use or whether the design has been applied to only part of the article. Of s 213 (which also sets out exceptions and other requirements for protection), Lord Justice Jacob in the Court of Appeal said 'It has the merit of being short. It has no other.'

Clearly, this definition is not concerned with eye-appeal as a protected design might be for the internal part of an article, such as a shape of an ink cartridge for a printer.

What are the requirements for protection?

For protection as a UK unregistered design, it must:

- be a 'design' as defined above, but not an excluded design;
- be original;
- not be commonplace;
- qualify for protection;
- be recorded in a design document or an article has been made to the design.

Apart from the wide definition of 'design', there are a number of exclusions to what can be protected by the right. Methods or principles of construction are excluded, as are shapes that must be that shape so that they can fit or blend in with other articles or parts of articles. Surface decoration is also excluded. Thus, s 213(3) excludes from protection:

a   a method or principle of construction,
b   features of shape or configuration of an article which –

    i   enable the article to be connected to, or placed in, around or against, another article so that either article may perform its function, or
    ii   are dependent upon the appearance of another article of which the article is intended by the designer to form an integral part, or

c   surface decoration.

The first exclusion prevents design right protection from being too strong. The functional definition could be interpreted narrowly but often a number of shapes may perform the same function and, as such, it is unlikely that a narrow meaning will be taken. The 'appearance' exclusion is similar to that applicable to the Community design and the UK registered design and prevents replacement body parts for cars, such as car wings, being protected. That does not mean that the overall shape of the entire vehicle is not protected.

It was intended that copyright was the most appropriate form of protection for surface decoration but this was before the Community design, which can protect surface decoration. In any case, it is difficult to predict the scope of the exclusion. Raised decorative moulding on timber furniture is an example. The exclusion cannot be said to cover two-dimensional designs as a shape cut from a sheet of metal or plastic is, nonetheless, a shape.

Designs must be original and not commonplace

To be protected a design must be original (s 213(1)). This has been held to mean the same as for copyright; that is, the design was the author's own work and not copied from another existing design. The Act gives further guidance and a design is declared not to be original if it is commonplace in the design field in question at the time of its creation. This is not as high a standard as novelty, as in the case of patents or registered designs. For example, in *Ocular Sciences v Aspect Vision Care*,[6] Laddie J accepted that design would be commonplace if it was 'trite, common-or-garden, hackneyed or of a type which would excite no peculiar attention in those in the relevant art'.

The reader should consider whether 'commonplace' means the same as 'individual character'. There is no case law on this but it is at least arguable that the two tests are the same in practice. However, it should be remembered that the UK unregistered design system is completely separate to the other systems of protection.

Whether a design is commonplace is a matter of the existing corpus of designs in the relevant design field at the time of the creation of the design. Note that this is based on the time of creation of the design, not the date that articles to the design are first made available to the public.

The scope of the design field in question is obviously important in determining whether a design is commonplace. It is a matter of taking a reasonably wide view and considering the type of designs of which designers of the articles in question would be aware. For example, designers of conservatory roofs would be expected to be aware of designs of windows, doors, conservatories in general and the material used in their construction. The design field is not limited to contemporary designs and can include designs that have not been used for some time but of which current designers would be likely to be aware, such as decorative features applied to timber window frames in the early part of the last century.

Qualification

A final requirement for protection is that the design must 'qualify' for protection. This is a complicated requirement and can be satisfied in a number of ways. In practice and in most cases, it will not be a problem if, for example, the designer is a citizen of, or usually resident in, an EU country. Where the design is created by an employer or is created under a commission for money or money's worth (that is, something of monetary value), the employer or person commissioning the design, as the case may be, must qualify: for example, a person who is a citizen of an EU country or a company established in an EU country.

If a design does not otherwise qualify for protection, it may still qualify if the person first marketing articles to the design in the EU qualifies, for example, by being a citizen of an EU country or is an EU-based company. The person marketing the articles must be exclusively authorised to put the articles on the market in the UK, even though the actual first marketing may occur anywhere in the EU.

Specific provision can be made to extend the qualification requirements to persons or bodies from countries outside the EU. For example, the Isle of Man, the Channel Islands, Bermuda, the Cayman Islands, Gibraltar and New Zealand.

---

6 [1997] RPC 289 at 429.

How long does the UK unregistered design right last?

Under s 216 of the Act, the maximum duration of the unregistered design right is 15 years from the end of the year during which the design was recorded in a design document or an article to the design was made, whichever was first. However, this period will be reduced if articles to the design have been made available for sale or hire within the first five years from the end of that first calendar year. If this happens, the right runs for ten years from the end of the calendar year during which that first happens.

For example, Fred creates a new design for a mixer tap for a sink during March 2010. He uses computer-aided software in the design process and records the design in a software file all during that month. In August 2012, Fred grants a licence to Albert to make and sell mixer taps to the design. In February 2013, Albert starts advertising and selling the taps. As this occurred during the first five years from the end of the calendar year during which the design was first recorded, the right will last until the end of 2023.

Who owns or is entitled to the rights in a UK unregistered design?

The rules on ownership of a UK unregistered design right broadly follow the rules on qualification. According to s 215 of the Act:

- where the design is created under a commission, the person commissioning the creation of the design will be its first owner; otherwise,
- if the design is created by an employee in the course of employment, the employer will be the first owner; otherwise,
- the designer is the first owner of the design right.
- However, if the design first qualifies for protection by virtue of the person first marketing articles to the design, that person will be the first owner.

Note that a person commissioning the creation of a design will be its first owner. However, this applies only if the designer is paid for his or her work by way of money or money's worth. This is the same as for the UK registered design but unlike the case with the Community design (registered or unregistered), as there is no express provision in the Community Design Regulation vesting ownership automatically in the person commissioning the design.

Where a design, created under a commission, is subject to the UK unregistered design right and the unregistered Community design, the person commissioning the design will be the first owner of the UK design right but the designer will be the first owner of the unregistered Community design. It is vital, therefore, where a design is created under a commission for there to be provision for ownership in the contract between the commissioner and the designer.

In terms of employee-designs, there is no express provision for the basic presumption that the employee will be the first owner where there is an agreement rebutting the basic position that the employer will be entitled, unlike the case with copyright. Of course, there is nothing to stop the employer transferring ownership to the employee.

Where a design is generated by computer in circumstances such that there is no human designer, the person making the arrangements necessary for its creation is taken to be the designer. This is similar to the equivalent provision for copyright but, again, it is arguable that this is unlikely to have any practical effect.

What are the rights in a UK unregistered design right?

The right of the owner, in effect, is simply a right against copying the design without his permission. Under s 226 of the CDPA, the right of the owner is an exclusive right to reproduce the design for commercial purposes by making articles to the design or making a design document recording the design for the purpose of making such articles. A design document may be a drawing on paper or a software file, for example.

Reproduction covers identical designs or designs substantially to the protected design.

An unusual aspect of the unregistered design right is that licences are available as of right during the last five years of its subsistence. This means that during the last five years anyone can reproduce the design and there is nothing that the owner can do to prevent this. However, payment must be made and a licence must be agreed to cover such use of the design. If the parties fail to agree the terms of the licence, they will be set by the Comptroller of Patents, Designs and Trade Marks (the head of the UK IPO). The level of royalties typically might be in the order of 5 to 10 per cent.

In our example of Fred's design for a mixer tap, any person may request a licence of right to make the mixer taps to take effect on or after 1 January 2019. When Albert first negotiated his licence with Fred, he should have taken account of the fact that others could also make and sell the mixer taps during the last five years of the right.

The licence of right provisions do not apply to the right in the context of the design of semiconductor topographies.

Apart from the unregistered design right, licences of right are extremely rare and would usually only be available following an investigation by the Competition Commission, for example, where the owner is guilty of some abuse, such as refusing to grant licences and charging extortionate prices for the articles subject to the right. One important exception is in relation to patents where the patent proprietor may voluntarily signify that licences as of right are available for his invention. The advantage for the proprietor is that this course of action reduces the renewal fees for his patent to half what they should be.

How do I maximise protection of designs?

With any new design, the first thing to consider is what forms of protection are available. It may be that an ingenious design is patentable. If that is a possibility, it is essential to keep it secret until an application for a patent is made.

In any case, it is worth keeping details of the design secret and only disclosing it to persons under a confidentiality agreement, for example, in negotiations with potential investors, manufacturers and so forth.

As usual, with all forms of intellectual property, keep accurate records of all the steps in the design process and any disclosures made. It may be advisable to lodge dated copies of any design document and other documentation with a trusted third party who can give evidence of the development of the design and the design process. For example, a competitor may allege that his design pre-dated yours.

Once you have determined which forms of design rights apply to your design or may be acquired by registration, think carefully about where the design is to be exploited, whether by yourself or by third parties with your consent.

If the design is registrable as a Community design, a UK registered design and/or as registered designs in other countries, decide which routes you want to take to protect your design. It is no good registering the design in the UK only if there is any likelihood of exploiting it in other markets, whether directly or through licensees. Don't forget that if your design is not protected in other countries, others will be free to copy it in those other countries (subject of course to the possibility that the design may be protected in the EU as an unregistered design).

Remember that the unregistered Community design only lasts for three years but registration gives up to 25 years' protection. Look forward and consider what the potential commercial life of your design is and protect accordingly.

If it will take a while before you launch products to your design onto the market, consider whether you should defer publication. If you do, however, make sure you apply for publication within the time limit or you will lose your design.

Remember to note renewal periods and renew in good time, otherwise you run the risk of losing your rights.

How do I get protection outside the EU?

The UK registered design applies in some other countries, such as Bermuda, British Virgin Islands, the Falkland Islands, Fiji and Gibraltar. Some countries extend UK registered designs to their territories subject to local re-registration. Examples are the Isle of Man, Guernsey, Jersey, Malta and Tuvalu. In some cases, local registration must take place within a specified time period of the UK registration. The UK IPO provides information about procedures and details of the local offices.

For other countries, separate applications for registration of your design are required. Alternatively, an application may be made through the Hague System for the International Registration of Industrial Designs through the World Intellectual Property Organization. This is a simplified way of obtaining protection in a number of countries by making a single filing. At present there are 60 contracting parties to the Hague Agreement, including the EU, African Intellectual Property Organisation, Switzerland, Iceland, Norway and Tunisia. A number of EU states are also contracting parties but not the UK.

Individual application is needed for other countries. Some countries operate a *petty patent* or *utility model* system for design protection. The USA protects designs under two systems, *trade dress* (similar to trade marks) and *design patents*. Specialist advice should be sought for international registrations.

The Paris Convention for the Protection of Industrial Property provides for a priority period of six months for designs. This means that novelty requirements for applications in other countries during the six months of the first application will be judged at the time of the first application.

Summary

The Community design (and UK registered design) protects designs that:

- fall within the meaning of 'design';
- are applied to a product or, subject to exceptions, parts of a complex product (for example, that are visible during normal use);
- are new;
- have individual character; and
- are not excluded from protection (for example, being dictated solely by technical function or contrary to public policy or morality).

The UK unregistered design right protects:

- original (not commonplace) designs; being,
  - the shape or configuration of an article, whether internal or external;
  - that are not excluded (functional and dependent appearance aspects or surface decoration); and
  - that qualify for protection.

Unlike the case with the UK registered design and the UK unregistered design right, there is no provision for the commissioner of a Community design to be the first owner of it.

Registration of designs is preferable as this gives monopoly protection, whereas unregistered design right only gives protection against copying.

Registered designs may be renewed in five-year steps up to a maximum of 25 years. The unregistered Community design only lasts for three years while the UK unregistered design right lasts for 15 years, subject to a maximum of ten years of commercial exploitation. Licences of right are available for the last five years on the UK unregistered design right.

At this stage it may be worth thinking about the definitions in practical terms. Look around you, whether you are at home, in the garden, on your street, in a city centre, in the office – wherever. Think of all the things that fall within the definition of 'design' for the Community design (registered and unregistered) and the UK registered design. Do the same with respect to the UK unregistered design. Can you identify any articles that could be subject to both definitions of design? Can you distinguish these from articles that fall within one or other definition only?

Look at the photograph in Figure 7.2. It shows a number of products or articles. Which of these could be protected by the Community design and/or the UK unregistered design right? Assume that the designs in question are new.

Management tips

When appointing a consultant or person who is not your employee to create a design, get a written assignment of all the rights in the design that may exist or be acquired by registration. Strictly speaking, this is not necessary for UK registered design and the UK unregistered design but it is advisable to do so for two reasons. First, for the avoidance of doubt and, second, to cover any other rights that may also apply to the design, such as copyright where different rules apply.

If you have a new design that is dissimilar in one or more ways from the existing corpus of designs, a number of options exist (assuming the other requirements for protection are satisfied):

- do nothing – you may have protection for three years as an unregistered Community design and/or protection for up to 15 years as a UK unregistered design (if someone uses your design without permission, you will need to show that they have copied your design);
- register the design as a UK registered design and/or a registered Community design for five years, renewable up to a maximum of 25 years;
- apply to register the design as a UK registered design and as a Community design or other national design within the six-month priority period.

Although not essential, it may be advisable to use an agent who is familiar with the registered design systems and can advise on whether the design is likely to be accepted for registration and

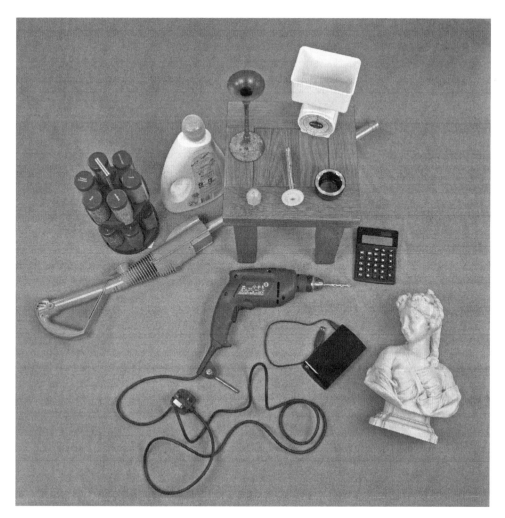

Figure 7.2 The items in the photograph are: a spice rack, wand for vacuum cleaner, plastic washing liquid bottle, table from nest of tables (on which is placed a candlestick, kitchen scales, camera lens adapter, spindle and roller for up-and-over garage door, plastic cap for radiator valve), calculator, bust of young lady, external hard drive and electric drill.

in relation to registration in countries outside the EU. An agent should also be able to handle renewals of registration.

Keep records, even if the design is not registered! Where a design is registered note when renewal is due.

Exercise

Can you identify the design rights that will exist or may be acquired for the following articles? Assume that the basic requirements for protection exist, such as novelty, individual character, not being commonplace, etc.

1. An upright vacuum cleaner.
2. A textured grip for a toothbrush.
3. A new design of armchair.
4. A moulded plastic outer wrapper for foodstuffs.
5. A new car that includes a new shape of engine cover.
6. A software application involving a computer program, visual images displayed on a computer screen and a new typeface.

Suggested answers

1. The external appearance of the vacuum cleaner as a whole may be protected by the Community design and the UK registered design. Component parts may also be protected by these rights if they are new and have individual character, providing they are visible during normal use of the cleaner. The UK unregistered design right may apply to aspects of shape or configuration of the cleaner and parts thereof, even if not visible during normal use. Any surface decoration, such as printed ornamentation or an unusual colour scheme, may have protection under the Community design and UK registered design but not the UK unregistered design right as surface decoration is excluded.
2. Texture may be protected by the Community design and UK registered design and it is one of the examples of appearance given in the legislation for these rights. Texture is not protected by the UK unregistered design right if it is considered to be surface decoration, but it might be protected if deeply profiled so as to be considered otherwise, in which case it could be shape or configuration.
3. Furniture can be protected by all design rights with the following provisos. Any aspect of design classed as surface decoration cannot be protected by the UK unregistered design right. Any aspect of design not normally seen during normal use is excluded from the Community design and the UK registered design.
4. Plastic food trays can be protected by all forms of design right providing the basic requirements for protection are met. Elements out of sight during normal use are excluded from the Community design and the UK registered design, though not the UK unregistered design. Colours, symbols and ornamentation applied to the tray may also be protected except by the UK unregistered design right.
5. The car as a whole may be protected by all forms of design rights. The engine cover may be protected by the UK unregistered right to the extent that it is not excluded under the 'must-fit' and 'must-match' provisions, but not the Community design or UK registered design. Body parts may not be registered to the extent that they are dictated by technical function. Furthermore, component parts of complex articles are not protected by the Community design or the UK registered design where their purpose is to restore the appearance of the complex article. In other words, a replacement wing for a car can be fitted to the car without infringing those rights. Some national systems of design (not the UK, but, notably, France) still protect such component parts.
6. Computer programs are excluded from all forms of design protection, explicitly in the case of the Community design and the UK registered design. They do not fall within the meaning of design for the purposes of the UK unregistered design. Graphic symbols and typographic typefaces are expressly mentioned within the definition of 'product' for the Community design and the UK registered design and can be protected by these forms of protection. Of course, they do not comply with the definition of 'design' for the UK unregistered design.

Chapter 8

Exploitation of Intellectual Property

If a company does not own the building it works in, why should it own the IP it uses?

There are two main types of intellectual property (IP) transactions: assignment, where all rights in the assets are transferred; and licensing, where full ownership is not transferred but permission is given by the owner to a third party to do specified things in respect of their IP assets.

What is an assignment?

Many organisations want the security that full ownership of their core IP brings. Indeed, investors may be more willing to invest in a company that owns its core IP. However, in practice the difference between an assignment, where full ownership of IP is transferred, and an exclusive, worldwide licence can be small. An IP assignment must be in writing and can be for existing or future IP. Assignment is common if an entity does not want to exploit their IP, or does not have the resources to do so. On assignment the assignor will usually get a lump sum. It may be difficult to find a buyer or value early-stage technology as a great deal of money may be needed to develop the invention into a viable product.

What is a licence?

A licence does not transfer ownership of the IP asset but gives a third party the right to do things that would otherwise infringe. The person who grants the licence is called the licensor while the party being given permission to use the IP is called the licensee.

The first thing that you must establish is what sort of licence you are dealing with. There are three types of licence. An exclusive licence where only the licensee, not even the licensor, may use the IP; a sole licence where only the licensee and licensor may use the IP; and a non-exclusive licence, which allows the licensor not only to use it themselves but in addition to license the IP to as many other people as they like. A licence should set out how, when, where, with whom and for how long the IP will be used, and how much it will cost. You can license-out your IP to a third party or license-in another's IP for you to use in developing your own business.

Why do I want to take or grant a licence?

A licence, unlike an assignment, allows the licensor to keep some control over its assets, giving permission to use the IP for some purposes but not for others. Many small firms have not got enough money or sufficient experience in a particular field to sufficiently exploit their IP, making licensing-out a sensible option. Big firms may choose to license-out if the market for their IP is too small to fit in with their business strategy. In addition, rather than take on the difficulty and expense of expanding a business into new countries it may be easier to license to a distributor who is already established in those markets.

The licensor, in return for the use of their IP, can receive either periodic payments called royalties or a lump sum or both. Royalties are usually based upon the net sales of products. They could be a fixed sum, for example, £1 per item sold, or they could be 'stepped', becoming greater as sales increase. If the licensee has an 'exclusive licence' where royalties are to be paid, the licensor is very vulnerable if the licensee doesn't bother to market the asset. Here it would be wise to have either a minimum royalty rate or target sales with a clause in the licence terminating the agreement if these minimum targets are not met. A lump sum is a set amount paid, however successful the product may be. Most inventors are inclined to overvalue their invention. This can cause negotiation problems if the agreement is concerned with early-stage IP where the value is uncertain and where development costs can be high. If the product fails the licensor will gain and the licensee lose out, but if the product is an outstanding success the licensor will be the one to lose. 'Milestone payments' can overcome this problem. As an asset reaches certain 'milestones' along its development, whether it is a book nearing completion or an invention being developed into a prototype, pre-agreed 'milestone payments' are made.

Cross-licensing is where licensor and licensee have access to each other's IP and this form of licensing can create useful collaborations within or between industries. Licensing can also be used to avoid litigation. If an infringer has been running their business using your IP and there is no alternative available for them to use they are in a very poor negotiating situation. They may have to accept your licensing terms in order to avoid expensive litigation.

Licensing trade marks can be of great significance if entering into franchise agreements, joint marketing, co-branding, sponsorships or endorsements. A franchise will, for a lump sum and royalties, include a licence to use a trade mark such as McDonald's for a certain time and in a certain place. The franchisee will get training and help in how to market and run the business, providing the look and feel in line with the franchisor's business. The owner of a famous brand may want to license-out a trade mark or brand in order to increase market penetration and strengthen the brand image, while a licensee may feel that their product would struggle in the market if not sold under a recognised trade mark or brand. There should always be terms ensuring that the licensee use the trade mark as registered, to prevent blurring, and to restrain use as a noun or a verb, such as Google, so that it does not become a generic term and become susceptible to revocation.

What do you want to license?

The first thing you must do is work out what you want to license. After conducting due diligence (see Chapter 9) you should know what is ripe for licensing, and you should have an idea of its value.

If you have IP that you don't use, rather than prune it from your portfolio you should consider licensing it for a third party to use. But beware: you must know why your organisation does not use the IP in question. If it is because it is not part of the business plan then licensing-out may well be sensible, but there may have been another good reason it is not used. If a traditional light-bulb manufacturer invented an everlasting light bulb, exploitation of this new bulb would destroy the market for their traditional product (see Chapter 9). Licensing-out, to what would in all probability be an eager competitor, would be a fatal mistake for the owner of that particular IP.

Finding a licensee

Before you license-out you must find an appropriate licensee and negotiate the terms of the licence. Neither are easy tasks. Licensees can be found by going to trade shows, reading relevant journals and searching the internet. It is important to check that the licensee is solvent, is capable of developing your IP sufficiently and that they fit the image you want for your product. Their reputation may help you sell your product – or it may do the opposite!

Negotiating terms

Negotiation is the art of compromise and the negotiating team should be made up of people who want to increase the size of the cake, not just try to get the biggest slice. At the end of negotiations both sides should feel that they have achieved a fair deal. The team may include scientists and marketing people but negotiation is a skill and a difficult one at that. You must know if it is time to abandon the whole thing and walk out. A licensing lawyer is necessary not to negotiate but to actually draft the terms of the agreement.

The first thing you must do is create a non-disclosure agreement (NDA) so that if you have any sensitive information you can discuss it freely. As with any contract you are free to negotiate any terms that you and the other party agree. However, you need to know not only what your goal is but also the other party's goals and objectives.[1] It might be that rather than money you would both prefer to enter into a mutually beneficial cross-licensing agreement.

It is very important not to be legally bound until everything has been agreed. You do not want there to be any misunderstandings or ambiguity so ensure that all negotiations are 'subject to contract', that is, not legally binding. Once the core terms have been agreed they can be put into writing as a 'letter of intent', but will still not be binding if stated to be 'subject to contract'.

How may the IP be used?

Copyright

Most businesses will (or should) have software licences, whether 'bespoke', where it is specifically produced for them, or 'off-the-shelf'. Off-the-shelf software licensees often include a 'shrink-wrap' or 'click-wrap' notice. These state that by breaking the shrink-wrapped seal or clicking in the box with software downloads the consumer is accepting the terms of the agreement. Terms will often limit its use to a particular machine. Other licence agreements should be under a proper written licence and will usually give the licensee the right to make copies of the work; distribute the work; publish the work; translate, modify or adapt the work, with an agreement about who will own the translation. The licensor can allow the licensee to do any one of these things or a combination of them and in any territory agreed for a specific period. So you can give X the distribution right in France for one year and Y the right to translate the work into German for the rest of the copyright period.

Patents and know-how

The licence to use a patent will usually cover use of any process to manufacture and sell the products. But do not give away too much. If you are licensing a patent make sure you know all the potential uses or 'fields of use'. You may not realise that your drug, intended to be a cure for cancer, can also be used to alleviate the pain of arthritis. Do you really want to allow the licensee

---

1 A.I. Poltorak and P.J. Lerner (2002), Essentials of Intellectual Property: Law Economics and Strategy, 2nd edn, John Wiley.

to be able to use it for this purpose too? Maybe you should limit their use to the cure for cancer, the application that they have paid for? In addition it may be pointless licensing Jim Ltd to use your patent to develop a cure for both cancer and arthritis when the company only has the capacity to develop a cure for cancer. It is better to license Jim Ltd to produce a cure for cancer and let Fred Ltd use your patent to produce the arthritis drug.

Not only should you consider restricting use of your patent to a particular field, market or purpose but you should also consider the territory in which the licensee is being allowed to use your IP. Are you granting Jim Ltd the right to produce or market the drug just in the UK, the EU or across the whole world? Have you actually registered your rights in these territories? If you haven't, anyone can use your IP (apart from secret know-how, which is a contractual obligation) in these countries without your permission. You must also consider the ownership of improvements or modifications to the IP made by either party. Finally, what about other people? Are you happy that the licensee incorporates the IP into the work of others? Are you willing to allow the licensee to sub-license, for others to manufacture or sell the products made from your IP? You may fear that it may be acquired by a competitor or that its reputation will be tarnished if there is an association with a different manufacturer or distributor.[2]

Don't forget that patents often have associated know-how or trade secrets necessary to work the patent. These will need to be licensed with the patent.

Other terms

You need to agree for how long the licence is to last. Is it to be for five years or for the life of the IP? Is there anything that will cause the licence to finish before this date? What will happen if a trade secret becomes publicly available? The licensee, after all, would not want to be bound to keeping something secret that other people could discuss freely. If the licence is for a patent, what will happen if the patent is invalidated or revoked, and what if sales targets have not been met? The licence may also include warranties, an assurance that something is true and maybe also a clause giving the licensor the right to audit the accounts of the licensee. There should be clauses dealing with confidentiality and also any issues relating to competition law.

Summary

A licensing lawyer should be used when creating a licence. A licence should clearly describe the scope or subject matter of the licence, whether it is sole, exclusive or non-exclusive and how long it is to last. The payment terms must be set out clearly and you should consider the position of any improvements and upgrades in the IP. There will in all likelihood be warranties given about the asset and some thought must be given to any maintenance of it. You must also consider what will terminate the licence. It is also important to include a clause stating which country's law will govern the contract and note must be taken of any competition laws that might affect the agreement.

---

2 M. Anderson and V. Warner (2006) A–Z Guide to Boilerplate and Commercial Clauses, 2nd edn, Bloomsbury.

Management tips

- Remember, the licensee is not allowed to do anything with the IP unless you give them permission to do so.
- Retain a copy of all licence agreements.
- If you have a lot of IP assets it might be sensible to have a map of the world with an up-to-date note of your assets marked upon it. In this way you can easily track what IP you control and in which territory.
- You should monitor all licences, making sure that you receive the correct royalties at the correct time.
- It would be sensible to audit the books of licensees to ensure they are telling the truth about sales.
- If you have a registered right all licences must be registered at the national IP office.

Exercise

Sarah has a small company, Innovation Ltd. Linda, one of the company's employees, has just invented a Wisbang, which she is convinced is going to be a revolutionary product producing worldwide sales. The Wisbang is at an early stage of development and Sarah is worried that the company does not have either the resources to make the Wisbang into a viable patented product or the market reach to develop it to its full worldwide potential.

Advise Sarah.

To patent and develop a market for Wisbang will cost a great deal of money. This looks like a prime target for either assignment or licensing.

You should first consider assignment. This is early-stage technology and any assignor will be loath to pay a large lump sum for the Wisbang as there is a great risk involved in its development.

Sarah may be overvaluing the invention but if assigned with a lump sum they will lose out if it does indeed turn out to be an outstanding success. It may be better to license rather than assign and royalty rates must be appropriate.

The first task is to find a licensee. Linda should know people in the field and she should study patent databases journal articles and conference attendees to try to find an appropriate licensee with the resources and capabilities to take on the Wisbang.

Once a potential licensee has been found, a negotiating team, including Linda if she has the right negotiating skills, should be formed.

It will be necessary to explain the advantages of the Wisbang, its commercial application and the advantages of the Wisbang over any alternatives.

During negotiations you must keep in mind what the essential outcomes are. You must know what you need, what you would like and what you don't really want that much.

Remember, if you intend to have a long-term relationship, you need to trust each other.

If the patent is yet to be granted the terms of the licence should have a termination clause taking into account what would happen if the application does not succeed.

Any confidential material must be clearly identified and its future use and disclosure to third parties agreed.

If the patenting or development of the Wisbang needs to be supported it must be agreed by whom, for how long and how much support will be given and at what cost.

Chapter 9

Strategy, Audit, Due Diligence and Valuation

Why does an organisation need an intellectual property strategy?

Will the best product always win?

It is not necessarily the company with the best product that becomes the market leader; it may very well be the company with the best strategy that wins the day. For example, in the mid-1970s Sony developed Betamax, the videocassette tape-recording format. Sony wanted to keep tight control over its patented product and did not freely license its technology for others to use. JVC, a competitor, then created its own tape-recording format, VHS, but JVC used a completely different patenting strategy. Due to their strategic plan, VHS, although in many ways technically inferior to Betamax, became the market leader. The difference was that JVC allowed its VHS to be licensed to numerous competitors. The large number of products using the VHS system and the economy of scale that resulted from this extensive use meant that VHS products became much cheaper and developed a huge market share. VHS became the standard videotape format, making Betamax almost obsolete.[1]

The digital age

In the nineteenth and twentieth centuries value was created by using natural resources, capital and labour in order to create goods that consumers needed or wanted. Industry was staffed by manual workers and output was measured by the number of products manufactured. How things have changed. Manufacturing has declined and intellectual assets have replaced industry as a means for extracting value. Producing intellectual assets has in the past few years been the fastest-growing field of economic activity, showing significant development in creating value for businesses. Today much innovation is due to the successful exploitation of new knowledge and ideas but these intangible assets cannot be treated in the same way as real property. Knowledge and ideas cannot be used up in the way that a product can and such intellectual creativity can, with the advent of the digital era, be replicated accurately and with ease. US companies now invest more than US$1.1 trillion per year in intangibles and it is estimated that in this digital economy between 70 and 90 per cent of the value of most businesses are now in the form of intangibles. This figure can rise to 100 per cent for small technology companies. It has been said that innovation without protection is philanthropy and in order to protect and create value from these intangible assets intellectual property rights (IPR), copyright, design, patent, trade secrets and trade

---

1 There was also an issue of content involved.

marks are an essential tool. Although IPR can protect creative endeavour there is no point in just having these rights without doing something with them. Invention for invention's sake does not pay the bills. You must decide what to do with these assets in order to create value. How well you capture and use the knowledge that is created is crucial to your business. Remember, intellectual or intangible assets are today recognised by many companies as their most important resource. Without IPR to protect their innovation many innovative ventures have nothing to sell or license. In contemporary knowledge-intensive economies, from the world's largest and most powerful companies to the smallest small to medium-sized enterprises (SME) the exploitation of intellectual assets is essential to business.

The board must want an intellectual property strategy

There is good evidence that companies with large, well-managed intellectual property (IP) portfolios are more profitable than those that are IP passive. Most innovative organisations have a business strategy and also an innovation strategy but few have an IP strategy. IPR are intended to reward innovators and if they are not being used to promote commercial success they are not being used to effectively provide this reward. The aim of all innovative organisations should be to turn knowledge into value. So the first issue to be faced is that the company at board level must actually want an IP strategy. They must recognise that an IP strategy provides the framework for acquiring, protecting, leveraging and managing IP and this IP strategy should be aligned with the organisation's business and innovation strategy. However, an IP strategy is not merely having a procedure in place that allows you to file a patent every time an employee comes up with a new idea. Nor is it merely making sure that your trade marks are kept in use, do not become generic names for the products in question or that infringers are warned off. To successfully utilise its IP a business should not just leave employees to cope on a case-by-case basis when problems arise but should have appropriate plans and procedures for dealing with all likely scenarios, with employees knowing what to do and when. An IP strategy will ensure that you file the right patent applications and the appropriate trade marks and renew the most valuable. It will enable you to achieve the goals of the organisation and ultimately help the business to make money. Following the IP strategy will make sure that filing a patent application, which will be published within 18 months, rather than keeping your inventions secret is what you really should be doing to achieve the overall objectives of the firm.

Valuation

We know that IP or intangible assets can be some of an organisation's most valuable assets. Because of this, it is important to have an accurate, or as accurate as possible, valuation of your IP in order to attract investment at the correct level or ensure that you obtain a fair price for your business in a merger (see later). The organisations that are successful are those that create value through innovation and extract that value by strategically leveraging their IP in order to enhance their competitive position. The trick is to use IP systematically over time to help your organisation meet its long-term goals. Whether an SME, start-up or international organisation, all firms need an IP strategy that is in line with their business strategy. Managing the IP strategy efficiently allows the organisation to increase asset value, assess risk, reduce liabilities, improve its competitive position and substantially increase return to shareholders. A well-thought-out, well-managed strategy is the route to financial success.

Chief Intellectual Property Officer with a budget

However, not only must there be a decision taken at board level to develop an IP strategy but an appropriate person must be identified as the Chief Intellectual Property Officer (CIPO) or IP manager. This IP manager should be responsible for facilitating the creation of an appropriate strategy, setting the overall goals firmly in line with and supporting the business plan, and with a budget that will allow them to accomplish these goals. They can only do this after having identified any external competition, obstacles or threats posed by third parties. They can then assemble an IP team with an appropriate budget for the organisation concerned. After the strategy is established the CIPO will then be able to put in place appropriate tactics or plans to implement the overall strategy. As with any strategy, the IP strategy will need to be adjusted and improved as circumstances change so it needs processes in place to ensure that it is periodically reviewed.

What type of strategy is right for your business?

It is not a 'one fits all' type of situation

Developing an IP strategy demands the support of the management of the organisation. It also requires a person or persons to manage the strategy and a budget to enforce it. There is no one IP strategy that fits all businesses and no one strategy will last forever. Your business will change as circumstances change so your IP strategy must change also. It is important to realise that your strategy must fit your organisation as it is now but also be tailored to future aspirations and growth. But remember, your strategy must be realistic, achievable and within the budget set.

What type of organisation are you?

Good ideas can come from anywhere but to make a good idea into a sought-after and saleable product or service requires market insight, sufficient investment, a creative environment, a skilled multidisciplinary team of good managers and the right networks. Your organisation may be good at generating ideas but may not be capable of developing an idea into an innovative product. This may be because it lacks the necessary human or financial capital. In this case your best strategy may be to license or sell your IP or possibly enter into negotiations to create a joint venture with an organisation that possesses the skills that your organisation lacks. But one thing that you must never ever forget is that, no matter how clever an idea is, if the end product is something that no one will want to buy or license there is no point in developing it in the first place.

What do you want to gain from your IP?

What is the business strategy?

Before you can decide what IP strategy is appropriate for your business you must first understand the vision and plan of the organisation as a whole and what its business strategy is. The IP strategy must fit in and fully support the business strategy otherwise there is no point in having it.

It may be that all you want to do in your organisation is to avoid getting into trouble. You may just want to prevent any litigation that would result from infringing the IP rights of others. You may have no intention of gaining a monopoly advantage by protecting your own creative efforts. If this is the case it will be sufficient to educate your employees not to download the software of others or to ensure that they have obtained a licence to use a piece of music on your website. You may, however, want to prevent others using creations, innovations or secrets generated within your business. You could consider publishing your inventions in order to place them in the public domain. This would prevent others from patenting them as they would no longer be new.

Reputation

You may decide to register a trade mark to protect the goodwill you have generated in a sign, image or logo that you use in relation to your products or services. This registration would prevent others from encroaching on the use of the sign in their business and allow you create brand awareness in your product or service. However, you must ensure that these trade marks are used and maintained and there should be a process in place to ensure that you do not inadvertently lose them. You can use other forms of IP strategically to enhance the reputation of an organisation and create a brand image. Some television advertising proudly proclaims the number of patents incorporated within a product such as a vacuum cleaner or car. This is done to show how innovative and therefore superior the product is. You may want to establish a reputation for the safety of your car. Having patents that provide innovative forms of passenger protection, such as air bags or crumple bars, will encourage people to believe that your product is indeed safe.

Protecting secrets

You may need to prevent the leakage of your confidential information, information that gives you an edge over your competitors. To ensure that your trade secrets are protected there should not only be formal clauses in employment contracts specifying that such information is confidential but also some formal means of recording that these secrets exist. What would happen if a key employee with secret information moves jobs or retires? Is there a clause in their contract preventing them giving your secrets to their new employer? Do you even know what secrets they have? You should have a process in place to ensure that your confidential information does not go with them and be lost to your business forever. You should also take care that you are adequately protecting any confidential information that has been imparted to you by third parties. Already you can see the need for some sort of strategy that captures all your intangible property, hard and soft.

Bargaining tool

If your organisation is involved in research you will probably want to patent your inventions to exclude others from using them. However, once you have patented your inventions you can also use this intellectual asset not only to produce a product or process but as a strategic tool. If you want to use another's patents but in return they would like to use yours, having a patent is an asset that can be used in negotiations to encourage a favourable cross-licensing agreement. If you have infringed another's IP rights you may be able to use your IP as a bargaining tool in negotiations in an attempt to avoid expensive litigation. Patents can be used not only to block your competitors and control the behaviour of consumers or suppliers but they can also reduce the cost of borrowing as they are an asset that can be valued (see later) and used as security. Trade marks can not only be used to create customer loyalty and form strategic alliances with customers or suppliers but as an asset that can be traded or exchanged.

Where do you fit in?

Once you have established ownership of IP you must decide what you want your IP to do. Do you just want your IP to help you to avoid liability or to improve the branding and marketing of your products and your organisation? Do you want it to protect your investment in R&D or do you want to go further and use it to generate revenue?

You must first establish your market. Are you positioned in an expanding market? Did you listen to your existing customers and improve the performance of an established product or make it more simple or convenient to use? Alternatively, have you invented something completely new? Is yours a new product creating a new market? Do you want quality or quantity? Does your plan require you to generate a large number of IP assets of varying quality or a small number of high-value assets? How do you intend to create value? Do you want to sell products you have made based on your IP, extracting a premium price for them due to your monopoly or semi-monopoly position? Alternatively, do you want to sell or license your IP to others for them to make products that incorporate your IP? What about the IP of others? Do you want to use your IP to negotiate access to technology of third parties or do you want it to increase assets or attract capital? Maybe you want to create a spin-out company but a decision about what to do with your IP must be made, otherwise there will have been no point in having gone to the bother of protecting it in the first place.

What strategies are available?

Julie Davis and Suzanne Harrison define five levels of strategy in their book *Edison in the Board Room* (2001). They classify these strategies as: defensive, cost control, profit-centred, integrated and visionary, while Michael Gollin, in *Driving Innovation* (2008), added a further 'no strategy at all' to the list. Your business may or may not fit into any of these categories, but it does provide a useful way of thinking about where you are in the strategy league table.

No strategy

Surprisingly, this no-strategy strategy could well be adopted intentionally by an organisation. After careful study of the market and any competitors in the relevant sector, it may be decided that doing nothing about IP is the appropriate strategy to adopt for your type of organisation at this stage of its development. A no-strategy strategy may certainly be the cheapest approach in the short term and indeed if your business is low risk it may be the best policy in the long term too.

You may feel that a trade mark is unnecessary as you can rely on an established reputation or goodwill, an unregistered right, to draw in customers. You may be in a sector where invention is unusual and feel that any copyright that you generate in your business is unlikely to be misappropriated by others. You may also have concluded that the only people likely to infringe your IP are your customers and as it is generally thought to be an unwise business decision to sue your customers there is no point in protecting your IP. It is, after all, ineffectual to protect your IP if you have no intention of enforcing it if it is infringed. However, if you are trying to create a strong brand, even though you may have the unregistered right to your name, get-up or image, registering your sign and logo is cheap, easy and sensible. If you want to be involved in creating innovation, protecting any new invention by patents or new products by registered design right rather than relying on an unregistered design may be desirable. So some strategy is needed.

Although a no-strategy strategy could be a deliberate and indeed a sensible decision, that is rarely the case. Such a strategy is usually found either because management is unaware of IP or is unable or unwilling to invest the necessary time and money, with the associated training of their staff that is needed, to protect their intangible assets. This IP gap can unfortunately lead to crucial intangible assets being lost to the business with competitors being able to use the organisation's creations freely and without constraint. The organisation may also find that its employees leave with valuable trade knowledge that has been neither categorised as confidential nor recorded. Consequently, such valuable information will be lost to the organisation forever. It may also be found that the organisation has unintentionally failed to secure ownership of the copyright in works it has commissioned from contractors or that its domain names have been taken by others. Finally, such a no-strategy strategy exposes the organisation to an increased risk of incurring large costs due to employees infringing the IPR of third parties. As Robert Pitkethly points out, 'An IP strategy is not something that a small company cannot afford to have, but rather something it cannot afford to be without'.[2]

---

2 Robert Pitkethly (2006), UK Intellectual Property Awareness Survey 2006, a preliminary report prepared for the UK Intellectual Property Office. Available at: www.ipo.gov.uk/ipsurvey.pdf.

Defensive

Companies using this defensive IP strategy see IP as a legal asset, not as a business asset. They will therefore use IP for defensive purposes only. The aim of such a strategy is to protect and build a portfolio that will act as a shield to protect the organisation's own core products and services. Such a strategy will also attempt to maintain freedom to operate, ensuring that the organisation is not prevented by the IPR of others from operating in their core field.

To act as an effective defence the company must ensure that they know what IP they actually own. They must then have a procedure in place to maintain it, making sure renewal fees are being paid when they become due. Such organisations will want to encourage the creation of new IP in order to protect the core business of the organisation and may well put into effect an incentive system to encourage researchers in the organisation to disclose patentable inventions. Defensive organisations want to minimise risk so they will be careful to ensure that they don't infringe the IP of others. They will need to train their employees not to use the software or patented inventions of others in developing their own products unless the appropriate licences are in place. If such infringing use of others' IP is discovered it can lead to litigation that, if successful, can cost a great deal of money in damages and legal fees as well as harm to a firm's reputation. Not only that but all the effort and expense the company invested in researching and developing their product may well have been wasted. It may be possible to negotiate a licensing deal with the rightful owner but an infringer will not be in a strong position to make a good bargain. In 2006 it cost RIM, the manufacturer of the BlackBerry, US$612.5 million after NTP accused them of patent infringement. An infringer will face the prospect of an injunction that could in effect close their business down. If they cannot incorporate an alternative to the IP they infringed in the development of their product, an infringer will be over the proverbial barrel. They will have to accept a licence on whatever draconian terms the claimant offers as part of a negotiated settlement entered into to avoid being sued.

An organisation with a defensive strategy will probably spend quite a lot of money in filing patent applications and enforcing their IP but they may not know what of their IP is important and what is not. Although they will employ outside legal professionals to protect their core IP there will usually be no licensing-out of non-core intangible assts. This is a missed opportunity. If they licensed-out assets that they do not use they could extract value from the IP generated within their organisation in an efficient manner rather than just having to bear the cost of creating and protecting it. Using such a defensive strategy, an organisation may end up with a large IP portfolio that is difficult to manage and that contains a great deal of unused IP that many parts of the organisation are unaware exists. It is expensive to protect IP and it is highly inefficient to protect IP that is not creating value.

Cost control

This strategy is still fundamentally defensive but the organisation will in addition try to minimise the cost of creating and maintaining their IP. It can cost a great deal of money to obtain and maintain a patent for its 20-year life cycle. In his book, *A Better Mousetrap* (2007), Graham Barker states that a Patent Cooperation Treaty application of 26 pages valid in eight European states for ten years would cost about €47,000, including patent attorney costs, renewal fees and translation costs. Even if worth patenting at the time the patent application was filed, it should be questioned whether maintaining it for the full 20-year life of the patent is worthwhile. It has been estimated that only about one in four inventions that could actually be patented, fulfilling the criteria of being new, non-obvious and of industrial application, should under this strategy actually be filed. The rest will not add value to the business.

An organisation employing a cost-control strategy will screen their portfolio, having established clear criteria of what core IP they need to protect, and they will concentrate only on the most valuable to their core business. They will prune their portfolio, getting rid of all unnecessary or unused patents, trade marks and designs. They will still encourage their employees to disclose inventions but they will have a strategy that weeds out non-core elements at an early stage. Consequently, they will only protect some of the inventions and designs generated within the organisation. Remember you need a market. There is no point in renewing the patent for an anti-wrinkle cream if nobody is likely to buy it as other creams have been developed that do an obviously better job at fighting wrinkles. There is no point in keeping a trade mark that has lost its reputation in its market or a design that has become unfashionable and lost its attraction.

In order to do this pruning of an IP portfolio, someone needs to find out if the IP is still being successfully used in association with a defined product. It will need an IP committee both to attend to pruning and also to make decisions in line with the business strategy about which inventions will be patented, which trade mark or design will be applied for and which will be renewed.

Using this cost-control strategy, organisations will have established in which countries they intend to market their products and so will know where they will need to file patents, designs and trade marks. They will have to ensure that the strategies applied to each territory are in accord with each other and that they are all in line with the overall business strategy. In order to control costs the IP committee should also consolidate the use of patent attorneys overseas, using only the minimum number necessary in each country to handle the IP in use in each territory in which they already market or intend to market their products.

Profit-centred

This strategy is appropriate for organisations that are beginning to see their IP not just as a legal but as a business asset. They recognise that value can be derived from the IP itself not just the products made from it. This strategy provides the benefit of the defensive strategy with the added benefit of a return on investment. Take a car manufacturer, such as Volvo. Due to their strategy of concentrating on the safely of their cars, their research scientists spend a great deal of time researching into making their products safer.[3] What should they do if, during the course of their research, they accidentally discovered something that improved road performance? Many highly valuable inventions have, after all, been discovered by accident; take, for example, the invention by Fleming of penicillin. Should the Volvo employees object that 'Our core business is making safe cars – we are going to ignore our discovery of a way to improve road performance as it does not relate to our core business'? An organisation implementing a profit-centred IP strategy would say, 'Certainly not'. They would want to embrace the road-performance discovery and create value from it – but how?

Licensing is a fantastically efficient use of an organisation's non-core IP. If money and time has already been invested in developing an intangible asset, even if your organisation does not wish to exploit the result, it is rational to do something with it to add value to your business. It is not expensive to negotiate a licensing deal and such profit-centred organisations recognise that at very little extra cost unused assets that have value to others can be licensed out. Their non-core or under-utilised IP will then be actively supporting the business rather than being pruned or abandoned. It is desirable to have a licensing department that is separate from the legal department. Such a licensing department will be tasked to actively look for licensing opportunities such as our improved road-performance invention. It has been estimated that for companies using the profit-centred strategy at least 1 per cent of their revenue could be generated by this method of creating value. This profit-centred strategy needs decisions as to what and what not to patent or protect.

---

3 Robert Cantrell, IP Think Tank.

This results in strategic IP management. The CIPO together with the IP committee may, with a view to creating revenue, decide to patent inventions such as our road-performance idea. This invention would be protected not as a core product but purely with the intention to license the patent to others. The patented invention can then be successfully integrated into other people's products, creating revenue for the organisation. However, for this level of strategy to be established top management must be involved.

If such a strategy is adopted, the CIPO must make sure that there is a regular royalty audit. It is common that a minimum royalty be paid under a licence deal and so there should be a process in place to make sure that it is actually being paid. Under such a profit-centred strategy there will be a process for detecting infringers. If infringement is found to have occurred, rather than rush into expensive litigation, negotiated settlements should be sought that may include 'encouraging' the infringer to take out a licence in order to avoid legal action being taken against them. Remember if you have IP you should enforce it. If you are not going to enforce it, why have it? But enforcing it does not always require expensive litigation.

Integrated

An integrated strategy requires that an awareness about and an understanding of the importance of IP is found through the entire organisation. Such an approach encompasses not only the employees but can even affect the structure of the organisation itself.

Employees

There will be an IP or innovation culture in organisations adopting an integrated IP strategy. Employees will have been trained to consider IP as crucial to the business, not just a legal issue or one that is only considered when making decisions about the funding of new R&D projects. IPR in this sort of organisation are not even seen merely as a value-creation asset that can be licensed or sold. In the sort of organisation that uses an integrated IP strategy the whole organisation understands that IPR can be used strategically not only to obtain finance or collateral for loans but also to make the whole business function effectively.

Good information on and communication about IPR is needed in organisations adopting this type of strategy. This is especially important in large companies. In 2012 IBM had 6,478 patents issued to it in the USA alone.[4] With this many patents in an organisation it is important that employees can obtain information about them. Easily available, clear and up-to-date information about an organisation's intangible assets will ensure that researchers do not waste their time working in an area in which their own organisation already has a patent or other such rights. Negotiators should know what their organisation already owns. It would be a complete waste of time and resources to enter a licence deal with a third party when there is already something owned by the company that could be used just as effectively. So that employees can find out what IP an organisation owns, there should be a user-friendly database of all IPR in an organisation's portfolio.

But knowing what your own organisation is doing is not enough. It must be someone's job to study all the relevant external IP databases so that you are always aware of what other firms are doing. You must know who is beginning to patent or register designs in new areas that could lead to them developing new and competing products. With such information, you can take appropriate and speedy offensive or defensive action. After deducing a competitor's strategy you may, if you do not want to patent in those particular areas, decide to defensively publish technical disclosures that you have previously been keeping confidential. This publication would

---

4 IFI CLAIMS Patent Services.

provide prior art, thus destroying novelty in a competitor's invention. They would then be prevented from obtaining a patent that would have created a monopoly for them and a barrier to entry for you.

Structure

In an organisation adopting an integrated strategy, IPR may even at times affect the corporate structure of the organisation itself. Such an organisation may decide to create a subsidiary, Research Ltd, the function of which would be to conduct R&D. Any resulting IP generated from that research would be transferred to an IP holding company, Holding Ltd, which would then transfer chosen IP to another subsidiary, Exploitation Ltd, which would be devoted to exploiting it.

It is not always wise to only rely on IPR that is developed in-house. If the organisation lacks expertise in particular areas and the IPR of a third party, Sweet Ltd, would be a useful asset, Sweet Ltd should be approached to see if their IPR could be licensed or assigned. However, maybe a merger with Sweet Ltd would be more beneficial to all parties. Alternatively you could consider entering into a collaborative innovation agreement with other companies or universities working in the area where your organisation lacks expertise. Collaboration gives you access to people and skills that you would otherwise be unable to access. Remember: no matter how innovative your organisation, most of the bright people don't work for you, so buying in their expertise is a very sensible move.

Monitoring

Part of an integrated strategy will be concerned with detecting infringement. Not only should the CIPO, after discussion with the appropriate departments, have policies in place to ensure that all trade marks and domain names are registered for all the relevant goods or services of the organisation, but they should make sure that patent, design right, trade mark and domain name monitoring systems are implemented. This can be done in-house if there is capacity within the organisation, otherwise specialised watching and maintenance services are available for a fee.

An integrated strategy adopts an integrated approach to IP throughout the organisation. This strategy requires not only the exploitation of IPR generated by the organisation but the identification and acquisition by assignment or licensing of IP developed by others.

Visionary

There are very few organisations that would claim that they had implemented a visionary IP strategy but those that have are in effect 'staking an IP claim to the future'. They have fully integrated their IP strategy with their business strategy but their ambition is greater than that: they want to shape the future of IP itself. Such firms do not just want to anticipate trends, they want to change the laws relating to IP and influence the strategy of their competitors to ensure that they are in the forefront of innovation in their field. They will ensure that they have IP where innovation in their sector is going, not where it has been.

Companies such as these will encourage disruptive technologies, getting their inventors together to brainstorm in order to create new ideas. They will invent a car to replace the horse and cart and then the electric car to replace the petrol car. They will invent the mobile phone, creating a market where none existed before. These companies will know the value of their own IP assets, the value of open source or access to the IP of others that can be gained by cross-licensing, etc., and they will understand that their portfolios have a defensive value. Finally, they will have processes to detect infringement and they will know if these process are working.

To create an IP strategy

You must know what to protect, in what order and when. You need to know how to protect it and where geographically you need protection, taking into account the need to keep within a budget.

There is no point protecting something that is only going to be used internally or in geographical areas where you do not intend to market your product. There is also no point in registering rights that you cannot enforce or where it is unlikely that you will ever discover that infringement has occurred. You need to know if your IPR, your software or your patented inventions are likely to be incorporated into a third party's product or whether you are going to develop your IPR into a product to manufacture and sell yourself. You need to know the strength of your IPR, whether your IPR can be easily reverse-engineered or designed around. You must understand your competitors and how your products are differentiated from theirs. You must also understand your own organisation. Do you have a well-established reputation with a large portfolio of brands, patents, know-how and databases with your own distribution channels, or are you a small start-up with no track record which is still at the point of searching for a distributor?

You must establish an internal IP strategy

You must try to value your IP (see later). This can often be a very difficult task as at the beginning of the life of an invention or a mark it is often impossible to know if will be a huge international success or a total flop. But your accountant should nevertheless try to assess the value of the goodwill in your business or the value of a patent. They can do this in line with current accounting standards, taking into consideration the legal scope of any patents, that is the rights a patents covers, what products or processes it protects, how easily it can be enforced and what weaknesses it has. Also to be considered are when rights such as design and patents will expire and in what countries the rights are valid. You must coordinate all relevant information or else it will not be possible to know how to allocate resources and you must educate all staff with regular meetings. There must be effective coordination between the heads of the business units, sales, marketing, distribution and manufacturing. In this way there will be input from each department with regard to the organisation's wider strategy so that everything can be synchronised. However, the first thing you must do is create the team.

Create the IP team

In many organisations IP is seen as a legal issue and is left to the lawyers. However, this is unwise if you want to maximise value creation. If you leave your IP strategy to the lawyers they are likely to be focused on assessing and minimising risk; this is, after all, what they are trained to do. Their focus will be not to align the IP strategy with the business strategies of the organisation but risk reduction.

If the firm is research active the input of technical people is crucial. There is a tendency, however, for inventors to overvalue the importance of their inventions. There is also a risk that they will focus their attention on their pet R&D projects.

To ensure that there is an effective IP team the team should be headed by one person, the CIPO or IP manager. The CIPO should be in ultimate control of implementing and managing the IP strategy. How many other people are involved of course depends on the strategy adopted but let us assume we are in an ideal world and that your organisation can assemble a multidisciplinary team to help your CIPO. Ideally the team should include people from all fields with a variety of skills and knowledge but all with knowledge of IP. The best teams will include, but not be limited to, researchers, lawyers who know about business and business people who know about the law.

Gather the relevant information needed to develop the strategy
Before you can gather the correct information there are some things you need to know.

What is the business strategy of the firm?
If the strategy of the organisation is innovation its main aim must be the generation of IP. It must also be forward-thinking, with innovation projects planned that will replace those that expire. Remember a patent lasts at the most 20 years and a registered design has a maximum life of 25 years. It is also essential that you have sufficient resources in people, technology, time and budget for what is being worked on and that an IP strategy is created for any new product.

If the strategy of your organisation is to create product differentiation based on quality it is essential that the manufacturing side knows of this and does not aim at cost-cutting with a focus on producing the cheapest product. If you want to produce a luxury car it may well be worthwhile spending money on R&D to produce and protect expensive refinements, but if that makes the car too expensive for the target market such research is counterproductive and may result in a loss of market share. You may want to innovate to make your car cheaper to make. You may, like Volvo, claim that safety is your main concern, but whatever it is you must know what the vision of your business is and all the departments must work collaboratively with that vision in mind.

What are the business strategies of your firm's competitors?
You must also know what your competitors are up to. But first you must identify who your competitors are. Your competitor may have a completely different business strategy from yours but still be a competitor. Starbucks, the coffee company, owns all the retailers that trade under the Starbucks trade mark. There are advantages and disadvantages to this business model but one of the advantages is that Starbucks has immediate control over its outlets. If, for instance, it wanted to change its logo or trade dress it could implement this change when and where it chose to do so. In comparison, a competitor in the coffee shop industry, McDonald's, franchises all their outlets. Any alteration to the franchise agreement would have to be agreed upon, hence McDonald's do not have the flexibility of Starbucks and are not able to force franchisees to swiftly change aspects of their shops.

To help you identify competitors you can search available IP databases, many of which are free, in order to see who is registering rights in certain sectors. A search of the trade mark register by class of goods or the Espacenet database of patents filed by product category will help you to find out who is working in your field. This search may also help you to identify gaps in the market that, if filled by you, could enhance your organisation's competitive position. Not only may you in this way identify new products or opportunities or invent around the inventions of others, but you may also be able to detect areas that your organisation could use to create barriers to entry for competitors.

You want to find out what IP your competitors have, how strong it is, how long it will last and where they have protection. If you ignore the developments of your competitors, you do so at your peril. At one time Polaroid was the market leader in instant photography. Their business model was based not on the cost of the cameras sold, but profit made from the price charged for the replacement film. Polaroid did not keep their eye on technological developments and innovate to incorporate them. With the advent of the digital camera, providing instant access to large numbers of photographs at a very small cost to the consumer, there was no longer any call for their expensive and cumbersome technology. Polaroid went insolvent in 2008.

Now you must establish what IP your firm controls or will control in the future
You must create a comprehensive inventory of all patents and patent applications, trade marks, trade secrets, designs, copyright, databases and strategic agreements with customers and suppliers. You must know for how long each IP right is going to last in each territory it is registered.

You should make sure you have a procedure for updating this list as IP is created or pruned. There should be a named individual having responsibility for ensuring that all IP is captured. There should be a procedure for employees to disclose inventions. Even if the decision is made not to file patent, records of each invention disclosure should be kept. Ideally you should be able to match each IP right that you own or license with a specific product.

Analyse it all

The assumption may be that you will retain your core intangible assets and license-out or sell non-core IP. But it is not as simple as that. There may be some assets, although non-core, that it would be wise to retain under your control. Consequently there are some other things that you need to know.

What IP will offset the threat of substitutes?

Imagine that you manufacture and sell good-quality electric light bulbs. The consumer needs to replace this product periodically, consequently you have a ready and stable market for your core product. If one of your employees invents an everlasting light bulb, is this a cause to break out the champagne and rejoice? Maybe it isn't. Even if you patent this product worldwide, once everyone has replaced their existing light bulbs with one of your everlasting light bulbs or once the 20 years of your patent protection runs out and others can manufacture the bulb freely, you will have lost your core market in replaceable light bulbs totally and forever. You may be well advised to keep the invention a secret and preserve your monopoly in light bulbs that need to be replaced.

Alternatively, if your employee invents a light bulb of inferior quality but that could be sold at a substantially lower price, should you just ignore the new invention? In deciding not to patent this inferior light bulb you will be giving others the opportunity to exploit it as a substitute and cheaper alternative to your product. This could cause your business irreparable harm. It may be sensible to try to acquire rights to the third-party inferior light bulb or even the whole company that owns it, not to exploit it yourself but purely to prevent the bulb being used by others as a substitute for your core product.

What IP may be used in negotiations with competitors?

Do not discard IP that might be useful to others.

Is there existing IP of others that covers what you want to do? Rather than spend time trying to invent round it you could negotiate a licence so that you can use it. There may also be assets that you own that can be used in cross-licensing or used to create patent pools. Opportunities may also be available to enter into joint ventures. Do not ignore any of your IP assets by concentrating only on those that have been registered. You could find that your database of customers has enormous value to an advertiser, far more than any patent you may possess.

If negotiations to license another's design or patent break down because the owner is demanding too high a price or unreasonable conditions, do not despair. You should check how much longer the right has to run. Remember, designs last at most 25 years and the maximum term of a patent is 20 years. It might just be worth waiting until the invention enters into the public domain and you can use it freely. If you cannot wait for the term to end, can you design round it? Alternatively, can you object to its registration or have it revoked? Also, make sure that you have established that it is registered in the territory you want to use it in. You may find that it is registered in the UK but you want to use it in the USA. In that case you can use it freely as long as you do not import products in which it is incorporated into the UK. One very important thing to keep in mind, however, is that while you are waiting for your competitors' rights to expire, your competitors are playing the same waiting game with yours.

What IP will give you freedom of action?

You may want to register IP, a design or patent purely in order to prevent others registering a similar asset. This will give you freedom to work in a certain area without encroaching on the rights of others. A cheaper alternative, as far as patents are concerned, may be to publish disclosures. Once disclosed the information becomes part of the prior art and novelty will be destroyed, preventing another patenting the invention. Alternatively, you may want to enter into a licence agreement or buy another's IP outright. Whatever tactics you use, it must be established that there is a procedure to retain freedom to operate and that it is being followed and that the person responsible for implementing the procedure is identifiable.

You need a vision of your strategic objectives

You have determined when, why, how and what IP you are going to protect. You have a budget, having decided on the level of financial and human investment the organisation is willing to make. You must now educate your workforce on your IP strategy and develop a company IP culture to promote your vision.

This need for education applies not only to the innovators of the IP and the management who will manage it, but to the employees in general. Employees need to know what they may and may not do. They must not only know that they are not to use another's software without an appropriate licence but that confidential information must be kept secret, as well as why this is important. You must ensure that you have a user-friendly database for all of your IP rights, including those that have been licensed-in and licensed-out, and that all signed agreements are recorded so that the workface can access the information if and when necessary. It may be a good idea to have an email generated, say every two weeks, to inform all relevant employees of all IP activity.

It is wise to have an up-to-date internet policy that can be adjusted to take into account new technologies. Employment contracts need to be aligned with IP policies and you must keep abreast of any changes in legislation such as the patent and copyright Acts. There needs to be a procedure in place to manage any disputes.

Creating value

The profits of a business are traditionally generated by a careful balance between sales volume, selling price and the cost of production. Consumers chose to buy your product because they have decided that due to the price, quality, appearance, ease of use or reputation of your product it is the best choice for them. You may decide to license your brand not only to obtain royalties, but to increase brand awareness or increase capacity. Licensing-out not only means that you get money under the terms of the licence agreement but, by being used by other organisations, it can increase market share of your product or create value by enhancing your reputation. The Virgin brand is extremely well known but it covers many areas of endeavour. Virgin is run almost like a group of franchise businesses that range from air and rail travel, hotel and leisure, music, clothes and financial services to soft drinks, to name only a few. The businesses being run under the Virgin trade mark are, in effect, all independent companies but all benefit from the Virgin reputation.

Value can be obtained via licensing by obtaining royalties. In addition, if organisations have competing products or overlapping inventions or if there are several patent holders with rights in different aspects of a product, such as a mobile phone, a cross-licence can create value not by obtaining royalties but by granting the right to use each other's IP. Intellectual assets can also be used to create patent pools where, for instance, two or more organisations cross-license each other and then agree to license a bundle of patents to third parties. Patent pools are an excellent way to avoid the problems associated with patent thickets or standards. Organisations can acquire the right to use all the IP rights in the patent pool that are essential to make a product in one licensing agreement, therefore reducing the transaction costs associated with negotiating numerous licences. Licensing is a specialist art and licensing lawyers should be involved from the beginning. After all, it will cost much less to get it right at the start rather than to try to sort it all out later after something has gone wrong. But, although licensing needs the input of specialist licensing lawyers, a licence is in effect a business deal. The people who know about the business are the ones who should be involved in negotiating a licence deal and, although involved from the early stages, the lawyers only come into their own at the point when a contract needs to be drafted. Hence, when entering into licensing deals you need not only lawyers to write the agreement, but technical people, and business people to negotiate a workable deal.

Approach to infringement

Your approach to infringement must take into consideration two aspects. Enforcement – what you will do if someone infringes your IP, and defence – what processes you have in place if it is discovered that you or your employees have infringed a third party's IP (see infringement).

Someone has infringed your IP

We will begin by thinking about enforcement. Your infringement strategy must include some way of finding out whether your rights are being infringed. There is no point in spending money and effort creating a brand or filing for a patent if you are unlikely to find out if anyone is infringing your right. You must have some process in place for detecting infringers. Trade mark or brand erosion is quite easy to police. By looking on the internet you can quickly find out if your mark or a confusingly similar one is being used on the same or similar goods. Alternatively you can hire a trade mark, copyright or patent monitoring service. Such services can be quite an efficient way of detecting whether other people are using your trade marks or designs but detecting patent infringement is far more difficult. To determine if your product patent has been infringed, you may not only have to search the internet for potential infringers but when found you may have to go to retail outlets, buy the 'infringing' product and reverse-engineer it in order to detect whether your inventive concept has been used. Infringement of process patents is almost impossible to detect as you need to have access to the 'infringers' factory to see if the process they are using does indeed fall within the claims of your patent. Remember that if infringement is found you may not only apply for an injunction to prevent the infringement continuing but you can claim damages from the infringer.

You may, during your IP audit, discover some IP that you were unaware that you had. Before you prune it, just check to make sure that it is not being used in someone else's product. If it is, there may be a little (or big) windfall in store. Watching services should be used in each country you trade in, but remember it is no use detecting infringers if you don't have the money to do something about them if you find them.

Once you have a method of detecting infringement you must decide what your approach to enforcement is going to be and not make decisions on an ad hoc basis. Is your strategy to take an aggressive approach to infringement, suing every infringer that you catch, or are you going to sue only the low-hanging fruit, the ones who will not fight back? You must have a process so that you know what to do if infringement is found. If you are a large organisation you may adopt the former approach of suing everyone, but a small company may be ill-advised to enter into litigation lightly. You must only start the legal process if it is really worth it to you to do so. The infringer must have enough money to pay any damages you claim and you must have enough money to cover any legal costs in case of a counter-attack. It is at this point that you must contact your trusty legal adviser.

Issues that can cause difficulties are that different countries have different legal systems. In the UK the loser pays litigation costs but these can be limited to £50,000 if a case is brought in the Intellectual Property Enterprise Court. In the USA even the winning party may have to pay its own costs. This can amount to an enormous sum. What will be your strategy if you find that there are not just one but many infringers of your IP? Do you go for the big organisation to frighten off the others or do you go for a small organisation who will give in without much of a fight (probably the safer option)? Do you have access to insurance? It is unlikely that you will be able to get insurance unless you have a proper IP strategy and procedures in place. You must keep in mind that you should only sue if it is worth it. Do you need to protect your products or reputation or gain damages? This might be the time to enter into negotiations to agree a licensing deal or a negotiated settlement with the infringer. A good lawyer will be essential to help you through this difficult time.

You have infringed another's IP

What do you do if you find that you have to defend yourself against an accusation that you have infringed third parties' rights? Do you have a process in place to deal with an accusation of infringement? What would you do if you suddenly found out that there is to be an injunction taken out against you? Do you have a defence to copyright infringement? Are you using your own name in an accusation of using another's trade mark? Are you going to try to claim that the patent should not have been granted in the first place? You need to contact your lawyer, and quickly.

Keep revising the strategy

Is your strategy working?

Although the bottom line is that money is being made, there are many ways to assess whether the strategy is working effectively. More than one way of assessing effectiveness should be used in order to get the complete picture. Key performance indicators should include things that are easy to measure, such as the number of patents filed or trade marks registered and how quickly disclosures are dealt with. However, you also need to know about things that are more difficult to assess: for example, the scope and quality of patents granted, whether they are protecting pioneering technology, whether the IP could affect a competitor's ability to operate in the future or whether it could be used in licensing deals.

Keep updating your strategy. If business decisions require a change in the product you make, ensure that this is reflected in the treatment of your IP. You need to have frequent meetings between the R&D, business, marketing units and lawyers. You must be aware of what is likely to happen in the future, for instance when your patent runs out. When Eli Lilly's anti-depressant drug Prozac went off patent in 2001, the company's share of new prescriptions dropped by 73 per cent in two weeks as generic alternatives flooded the market. That drop, or something similar, should have been anticipated and reflected in both the IP and business strategy of the organisation. It is important to keep asking what IP assets we have, how long they will last, what we need and what does our competitor have. Does our IP provide a competitive advantage and are we maximising value?

Audits

Why have an audit in the first place?

Most people think of financial records and balance sheets when they hear the word 'audit'. An audit, however, is not confined to the world of accountants. The word originates from the Latin *auditus*, meaning a hearing. The reasons for conducting an audit vary, but basically an audit allows you to know what assets you have and what controls you have in place over those assets. The information obtained from an audit is a powerful management tool allowing you to identify IP and establish policies in order to create value from that IP. An audit may be conducted in preparation for a takeover or merger, when a licence agreement is being entered into (see due diligence) or, horror of horrors, it may be needed if legal action is looming and you need to enforce or defend your IP rights.

The audit as a management tool provides a systematic review of all the IP assets and agreements, practices and procedures that have been put in place to promote the business plan. During the audit all registered or unregistered intellectual assets that are owned or used by the business will be recorded. A log should be kept of when such assets were created and how they are maintained, used, protected and enforced. In addition, a record should be kept of any agreements, practices, policies and methods of ensuring that the policies are being adhered to. The management audit will examine the entire IP portfolio in order to ensure that the law is being followed and to assess any risks, minimise costs and consider whether certain assets should be licensed, sold or pruned.

Internal audit

Timing

Once you have developed an IP portfolio you should establish procedures to make sure that each time new IP is created it will be logged. If you don't keep track of such things, they will be forgotten and lost to you. You must also have policies in place to help you to decide what assets should be protected and procedures to ensure that they are maintained, with any fees paid at the appropriate times. Regular IP audits will give you the information necessary to allow you to make the most of your intellectual assets. Not only should an audit be conducted to give you a picture of your IP assets when you are creating your IP strategy to fit into the business plan, but you should also conduct one each time the plan is significantly altered. In fact, internal audits should be undertaken at regular intervals as part of your normal business management.

Basic steps

The reason you are conducting the audit will determine how detailed it needs to be. A pending legal action will need a more diligent, focused and thorough audit (see due diligence) than when it is part of a regular management process. The type of business you run and your business plan will also be important factors in determining your approach to the audit. But, for whatever reason it is conducted, the audit will include a list of all IP assets and a review of the practices and processes applied to your projects, third-party agreements and products. Remember, you really do not want to find yourself in a situation where you thought that your patent, design or trade mark was safely registered only to find that it had not in fact been registered or that the registration had been accidentally allowed to lapse. You also do not want to find out too late that an employee inadvertently used their own name rather than the company name when registering your rights. To prevent surprises like these you need appropriate procedures in place and these procedures need to be audited on a regular basis.

Asset listing

Registered IP

PATENTS, DESIGNS AND TRADE MARKS

Make sure you have a list of all registered and pending patents, designs and trade marks in all the countries in which they are or will be registered. Keep a record of all maintenance fees and dates of renewal. For patents, make sure you have a log of the inventors, filing dates, numbers and status of the patents. Also, for all IP, keep an accurate and up-to-date record, with copies, of all licence agreements, whether they are agreements that allow you to use a third party's IP or a third party to use yours. Look at all relevant patent design and trade mark databases and keep a list of any competing patents, similar designs or confusingly similar marks being used by third parties.

Unregistered IP

It is also important to log all your unregistered marks such as unregistered signs, packaging, get-up, etc., that may be copied by others.

COPYRIGHT

It will be impossible to list all the works of copyright that your business has created as copyright will protect everything from the most insignificant memo to the webpage of the business. There should be a copyright policy in place. A good approach is to separate the copyright works into different categories such as advertisements, training materials (which could include anything from books and manuals to training videos demonstrating how to use machines), webpages and software. It is worth trying to prioritise which are most important or core works for your business by looking at the business plan. You must keep records of the date the work was created. The date is needed to ascertain the length protection will last and may be used as evidence if there is a dispute over copying. You should also have the name of the author with information as to their status. It is important to know if they were an employee or commissioned when they created the work. If they were commissioned, was an assignment or licence of the copyright agreed, and if so what were the terms? A copy of the agreement should have been retained.

TRADE SECRETS/CONFIDENTIAL INFORMATION/KNOW-HOW

It is very difficult but still important to keep track of all the secrets or confidential information that is used in a business. Such sensitive information can range from customer lists and client relationships to new inventions. If you don't keep good records of your trade secrets and know-how you may very well lose them. Employees must, for instance, know what is regarded as a trade secret and that information must be stored appropriately in order to retain its status (see Chapter 3). But know-how must be protected too. If a key employee leaves and know-how is stored only in their head, it will be lost to your business forever. Confidential information should be classified according to its importance to the business and each grade should have policies dealing with access to and sharing of the information. Highly confidential information should be restricted on a 'need to know' basis with a record of who has had access to it. It works well if one named person is in control of all such information; but remember, you must keep track of who that one person is. They should be tasked with identifying, grading and tagging sensitive information and giving it an appropriate level of protection. There should be secure records kept that are stored safely and password-protected, with a clear description of trade secrets, know-how or confidential information and when and by whom it was created or developed. All records must be kept up-to-date and old confidential information should be destroyed.

You must be concerned with how you keep your own confidential information but you must also consider third parties. If you have disclosed sensitive information to third parties or they have disclosed their sensitive information to you this information must be used and stored according to the terms of the agreements, copies of which should be retained.

POLICY AND PRACTICE REVIEW

You should periodically review your confidentiality policies to make sure that they are still appropriate. If there is an invention disclosure system you should make sure that there is easy access to invention disclosure forms in order to make it easy for inventors to comply. Make sure that confidentiality agreements are included in contracts of employment and that all employees not only are aware of the importance of adhering to the policies but that they are indeed following them. There is no point in having brilliant policies if no one knows about or complies with them. Employees must have a clear understanding of what is confidential, what can and what can't be done with such information and the consequences of a breach. If you have a 'clear desk' policy they must know that you will really blow up their briefcase if they leave it on their desk overnight and what disciplinary action will follow.

PROJECT/PRODUCT REVIEW

When projects are initiated it is often hoped that products will be developed. Before expensive IP protection is sought the audit will need to judge not only whether any future product resulting from these projects is likely to result in a viable product, but whether that product is likely to become a commercial success and be worth protecting. It must also be remembered that if, for instance, an inventive concept can easily be kept secret it may not be worth spending the time and money patenting it. It is also essential to know about other people's IP. The audit should identify any IP that belongs to third parties that may affect your freedom to operate. Any licences to be taken or collaboration to be considered to get round this problem must be identified at this point.

Your audit should make sure that the high-value products in the business are well protected and gauge the cost of this protection over the expected marketable life of the product. There should be a list of all IP, copyright, trade marks, design, etc., that relates to each individual product. The audit should make clear whether these rights are going to last for the full expected lifetime of the product or if, as with a patent or design right, they will last only for a limited number of years. An assessment should be made of the likelihood of the product being infringed and indeed how likely it is that such infringement will be detected. For example, it is almost impossible to uncover infringement of a process patent but far easier to expose infringement of a product.

BUSINESS PLAN/IP STRATEGY

The audit will ensure that there is a procedure to identify IP assets and policies and make sure that they are being used according to the business plan. To this end the IP strategy must be regularly reviewed. The audit should ensure that there are up-to-date processes for implementing strategic decisions about IP assets, their valuation and exploitation in accordance with the aims of the business. If there are no plans to use non-core IP, consideration should be given as to whether these assets could be exploited in some other way such as sale or licensing, or merely abandoned.

LICENSING

Most clever ideas have been created outside your business, no matter how innovative you are. That does not, however, mean that you cannot use the creations of others in your business. Licensing, whether it is you licensing the creations of others or others licensing yours, is an important aspect of commerce. It is estimated that total global licensing revenues will reach US$500 billion by 2015. The audit should check that there has been no breach of the licences' terms and ensure that all royalties have been paid in line with the agreements.

ENFORCING OR DEFENDING IP RIGHTS

If you are undertaking an audit in connection with an infringement action, you do not need a full audit. Looking at the IP or agreements involved in the action will be sufficient. But you will need the advice of lawyers. IPR prevent other people using your IP without your permission and prevent you from using other people's IP without theirs. Some people feel that IPR are like scarecrows defending the territory upon which their rights are based from encroachers. There is not much point in having these rights unless you do more than just treat them as a threat. Not only must you back the threat up with legal action but you must be able to find out about the infringement in the first place before you can defend your rights. This is where a watching service to identify infringement may come in useful. Whether you use a watching service or not, you must have systems in place such as the regular searching of patent, design and trade mark databases, both to reduce the chances of you accidentally infringing third parties' rights and to identify any infringement of your own rights.

You must check that both you and the third party are abiding by the terms of any licensed-in or licensed-out agreements. You must have a strategy for dealing with infringement if or when it occurs. Will your strategy be to fight all infringement or only some, and if so, which? You must also have systems and processes in place to keep track of the stages of any legal actions that you may become involved in. The most important issue for an audit to address if there is a claim of infringement of a registered right is that you actually own the right and that it is still valid. You cannot sue if you have failed to maintain the right by paying the appropriate fees. The situation is more complicated if you are claiming infringement of an unregistered right such as a design right, copyright or passing off. It would be wise to immediately get the advice of your lawyers before contacting the other 'infringing' party.

Due diligence

Why do due diligence?

Most companies need to use IP developed by others. It may be software to run their accounting system or a patent that is essential to produce their core products. Not only may the bought-in technology be essential to them when running their business, but they may have spent a great deal of money acquiring it. Such companies do not want to find that what they have acquired is either useless or that using it has caused them to infringe another's IPR. One of the aims of due diligence is to reduce the risk of becoming embroiled in costly legal battles with a resulting hefty bill for damages. Even worse, you may end up facing an injunction that will prevent you from using the acquired IP that you have already incorporated into your core product. Apart from the legal costs and disruption involved with legal actions, they can cause reputational damage to a company and a consequent reduction in share price.

Almost every time you commercialise your IP there will be some sort of a due diligence procedure undertaken. You may be agreeing a licence or taking part in a merger, but whatever it is the status of the relevant assets must be established. How detailed the process will be depends on why the information is needed, but keep in mind that this can be an expensive operation. You must assess how much you are willing to pay for what you are going to get. Despite having regularly conducted an IP audit with good records being kept, you may still find that you can't answer all of the questions asked by the due diligence team. It will, nevertheless, be a much quicker and more efficient process than if you know nothing about your IP and this will reduce your costs enormously.

The due diligence process will usually involve lawyers but there may also be accountants involved in valuing the rights being inspected. Be careful to ensure that the status of any confidential documents are well understood so that there is no accidental leak. Such documents must be clearly marked as confidential according to their category of sensitivity (see Chapter 3). The team will not only examine patents, copyright, designs and trade marks but also any IP licence or option agreements, R&D contracts or consultancies relating to the relevant IP rights. Sometimes a definitive answer to questions posed cannot be given. If, for instance, a patent is being considered it is impossible for anyone to guarantee that there is no prior art. All that can be done is to diligently search and swear that nothing was found; you can never guarantee that there actually is nothing.

What is IP due diligence?

Due diligence is a snapshot where the IP assets and liabilities of an entity in relation to an IP transaction are identified and verified.

To conduct a due diligence process it is necessary for the team to identify the type of business involved and all the material or core IPR for the proposed transaction. Rights that are core or material for a business are rights that if no longer available would have a serious effect on the running of the business. Most companies will have most if not all types of IP but if it is a pharmaceutical company the core or material IPR are likely to be patents; if it is a fashion house it is likely to be design; while a software company will be producing copyright material as their core product. Everyone should know what IP is material to their own business, but how have you come to that conclusion and do you really know just how important it is? How are you defining materiality? Is it how much it would cost to replace your IP, the turnover it creates or the cost to your business if you could no longer use it? However, just because certain IP is core to the business as a whole does not mean that it is relevant to this due diligence report.

The due diligence procedure exposes strengths and weaknesses in the relevant IP, showing what warranties the sellers can give and what warranties or indemnities the purchaser should be seeking. The team will need to fully understand what transaction or agreement is at issue. They need to make sure that the right bits of IP get transferred but the wrong bits don't and that any *relevant* problems or defects are detected during the procedure. Much of the process of due diligence is composed of an informed judgement. There can never be a 100 per cent guarantee that all defects have been uncovered. If, however, during the process you can't answer all the relevant questions, the potential purchaser or licensee will see this lack of information as increasing their risk, causing them to require warranties or indemnities.

The due diligence team will look at the validity of the rights, the authority to use them and how long they can last. They will also make a judgement about the strength or weakness of the rights and how vulnerable they are to challenge, how easily a competitor can copy or design around a right or even whether a competitor can use their own IP to block your freedom to operate. Such a block could prevent the product being exploited, making it valueless.

You need to make sure that the relevant people in your organisation are available to talk to the due diligence team to help them assess the true value of the IP. Choose these people carefully, however, as different people will have different views. The IT people will think differently from those in marketing and the researchers will have different priorities from those in sales. If representatives from all the key areas are consulted, the team, with the assistance of the CIPO, will, it is hoped, be able to make an informed judgement.

If the object of the due diligence report is an international transaction or your IP is registered in foreign territories, lawyers or patent agents from these jurisdictions may need to be involved in order to advise on any local laws. This will of course increase the costs, but luckily most contracts are drafted in English and so at least the costs of translation can be avoided.

The process

Identification of IPR that are material or core to the transaction

Just because certain IP is core to the business as a whole does not mean that it is relevant to this due diligence report. The team need only deal with IP relevant to this particular transaction. We are not just talking about registered rights, but contracts and licences that allow the business to use third-party IP must also be considered. Keep in mind, however, that a right such as a trade mark or patent may be material in one country such as the UK but if there is no intention to market or license any product using the IP in other territories it will not be material elsewhere.

It will be necessary to go through each right in detail in order to establish whether or not it is material to this transaction. If you have kept good records it should be easier for you to identify what rights are material and by giving the due diligence team this information you can reduce your costs and make the process more efficient.

Confidential information, know-how and trade secrets

Just because a right is not registered does not mean that it is of no value. Many of the most valuable intangible assets are protected via secrecy rather than registration. The due diligence team will want to be able to access all relevant confidential information, know-how or trade secrets that are used in connection with the core products or services. The team will want to examine the policy adopted for categorising the sensitivity of the information, where and how this information is stored and who knows about it. They will want to ensure that there are NDAs and restrictive covenant in employees' contracts of employment, in agreements with consultants and any other party that has access to the sensitive information of the business (see Chapter 3). They will want copies of all relevant agreements and licences where the business is entitled to use the confidential information, know-how or trade secrets belonging to a third party and where a third party can use such information belonging to the business. They are also likely to ask about any future confidential information that will need to be licensed in or out.

Registered and unregistered marks

REGISTERED TRADE MARKS

The due diligence team will want to examine the trade mark registers in all the countries where the trade mark is used, noting the classes in which the goods or services are registered. They will also check to see if different versions of the mark are being used. If the marks are not being used as registered this could affect their validity, so the team will have to assess whether the mark is likely to be invalidated for non-use. They will check to see when the mark was registered and establish that fees have been duly paid and when they are next due to be paid. They will make a list of all the products upon which the marks are being used to establish that the goods are being used in the class in which they are registered and will look to see if the mark is vulnerable to claims of invalidity or revocation on any other ground. Trade marks can be assigned or licensed and so any licence agreements must be recorded and copies retained. Not only will the team look at existing marks but they will also examine any searches relating to relevant applications that have not yet been granted and how likely they are to be granted.

UNREGISTERED MARKS

Just because you have not registered a mark as a trade mark does not mean that a name, logo or get-up is not still of value (see Chapter 2). Such unregistered marks, if relevant, still need to be considered in the due diligence process. It is important to keep details of all the unregistered names, marks, logos, slogans or get-up, the products upon which they are used and the countries in which they are marketed.

Third parties

One of the main purposes of the due diligence procedure is to ensure that you do have the right to use IP that you claim you have. Any third parties who may also have rights to these marks must be examined in detail. A list must be kept of any marks that you have licensed-in and copies, dates and terms of these agreements should be made available to the due diligence team. They can then check that the agreements are still in force and the terms of the agreements have been complied with.

Internet domain names

In the internet age most organisations use domain names in their marketing. A list of the exact domain names, dates of registration and the countries in which they have been registered should be available for the team to inspect. If possible, keep note of any third parties who have registered a name that is substantially similar to the trading name or unregistered marks of your business.

Copyright

There is a great deal of copyright material used within a business. This material may have been created in-house by employees, commissioned from independent contractors or bought or licensed-in from third parties. In all likelihood your organisation has licensed-in both computer software and hardware. Bought-in accounts and payroll software may be essential to your business but many businesses do not regard such software as an IP asset that should be considered in the due diligence procedure. You must still keep records of any fees and licence terms involved, even in off-the-shelf software. You need to know what this software is, where and by whom it is being used and have details of the licence agreement.

Much material generated within a business, such as day-to-day memos, is of little relevance to the business but some, such as leaflets, brochures or webpages, will be of great importance even to a firm that does not feel it deals in copyright work as its core business. It is important that your copyright policy demonstrates how employees are educated about copyright so they know how to treat copyright both created within your business and licensed-in. The policy should stipulate that, if created in-house, the author, their status and the date of creation of works are recorded. Remember, if work is commissioned, the copyright belongs to the author and so you should arrange for copyright in commissioned work to be assigned to the business and dated copies of the assignment should be retained. The due diligence team will insist on having access to these assignments. Almost more importantly than knowing what to do with copyright generated in-house, employees should know how not to infringe the copyright of others and how to obtain rights clearance where necessary. The team will want to know that you are using any copyright that belongs to others legitimately so all licences must be available for them to inspect, as should all licences where third parties have licensed your copyright material. Finally, the due diligence team will need to know if there is any copyright infringement litigation either proceeding or pending. They will want to assess the likelihood of these claims succeeding.

Databases

A database could be the most valuable asset that your organisation owns. You should keep up-to-date details of all databases used by your business, whether in electronic or paper form. Details that need to be kept are the creator or owner of the database, the date and place of creation, plus a detailed description of each database created in-house. If a database has been licensed either in or out a copy of the licence should be kept. If there has been any infringement or challenges to the database, these should be kept on record.

Patents

In the big scheme of things very few businesses will create patentable inventions, but they are likely to use on a daily basis products, anything from mobile phones to bicycles, that incorporate patents. Where an invention is made a patent is one of the strongest IPR available, giving a complete monopoly to the proprietor for up to 20 years. Whether your business owns the patent or merely licenses it, if the patented product or process is core to the transaction at issue certain details must be available for the due diligence team. The right to sell or license must first be established. Next it must be verified that the patent is in force, having been maintained with all fees being paid, and how long the patent still has to run. If the innovation is to be used in other countries, evidence of successful filing (or failure to file and, if so, why) and when the patent will expire in those countries is required. The team will want to establish the strength of the patent and so will want to know whether there are any issues such as prior disclosure that could bring into question the validity of the patent. If there have ever been any opposition or invalidity proceedings these are of great importance. If the patent has survived such attack it indicates a strong patent. The team must be told if any legal proceedings are pending. They will need to assess the chance of success as this is an important risk factor that will require warranties or indemnities being made. If the patent is still at the application stage, not having yet been granted, they will need to know at what stage of the process that application has reached and when it is likely to be granted. You should also be able to tell the team about any objections made to the application so that they can assess how likely it is to succeed. Finally, copies of any licensing agreement must be readily available.

Registered designs and applications to register

Registered designs should be treated in the same way as patents. If a registered design is core to the relevant transaction you should establish that it is in force and is registered in the countries in which you wish to use it, and know when it will expire and when it needs to be renewed. Any challenges, past or pending, to its validity must also be disclosed so the team can assess the risk.

Valuation of IP

Valuing an IP right is a difficult exercise.[5] Certainly, it is not an exact science and there is no right answer. Rather, it is more an art than a science. Applying different methods and even the same method applied by different persons may give wildly different results.

It may seem an impossible task to calculate the value of IP. For example, how much is a patent worth? The answer could be nothing, if nobody is interested in buying the patented product or taking a licence to make or commercialise it. On the other hand, it could be worth tens or hundreds of millions. Kodak had to pay Polaroid nearly US$1 billion in damages and interest when it infringed the latter's instant photograph technology. Even the IPR of a failed company can be worth buying. A recent example is the sale of the IPR (primarily trade marks and goodwill) belonging the well-known camera retailer Jessops to Peter Jones (of *Dragons' Den* fame) for over £500,000.[6]

---

5 The UK IPO produces a helpful booklet titled 'Agreeing a Price for Intellectual Property Rights', April 2011. Available at: www.ipo.gov.uk/iprpricebooklet.pdf.
6 Arguably, this was a fantastic bargain; time will tell.

Why value intellectual property?

Before looking at possible approaches to valuing an IPR, it is not unreasonable to ask why it should even be done at all. Some of the reasons are as follows.

- It may be important to calculate whether a royalty rate under a licence is appropriate and proportionate.
- A company involved in the acquisition of another company will need to value that other company's IP, which might be a significant or substantial part of the overall value of the company's assets. The same applies where IPR are to be acquired in other situations.
- It may be important or prudent to include IPR on a company's balance sheet.
- The value may be required for reasons of taxation.
- It may be important to estimate the value of a right in legal proceedings so as to assess damages or in order to settle a case of alleged infringement.

Methods of valuing intellectual property

How much is an IP right worth? This is not unlike the proverbial 'how long is a piece of string?'. Before getting into quantum theory, we have to come up with workable ways of finding an acceptable answer, bearing in mind that the methods we can choose from may result in very disparate values.

There are three main methods, two of which are forward-looking and, consequently, subject to numerous different interpretations or estimates. The other, however, looks at historical data wholly or mainly. The main methods are:

1. Cost method – how much it has cost to create the IP right.
2. Willing buyer and willing seller approach, including looking at comparable licences where these exist.
3. Economic benefit method (or cost–benefit approach).

Sometimes the choice of method will be influenced by what the purpose of the exercise is. For example, for the purposes of taxation it may be beneficial to show the value as small or large depending on the circumstances. If you are trying to sell it, you will want it to appear expensive. If you are a potential licensee negotiating a royalty figure, you will want to minimise its value.

Cost method

This method takes the value as the cost to acquire the right. This is not as simple as it may first sound. It is not just a question of adding up the fees to apply for and register the right concerned. There are a number of other costs involved, some of which may be hard to separate from other costs of the business organisation concerned.

For example, there are the costs of research and development, paying consultants and professional advisers and even allowing for bonuses for employees and, in rare cases, setting aside money for employee compensation under patent law.

There may be other costs such as the cost of acquiring rights in subsidiary IP, such as where rights in designs and trade marks are commissioned or acquired for designs and trade marks that are incorporated in a patented product. Know-how may also have to be acquired. Market research may be involved. This may contribute to the decisions to pursue a path leading to the IP right.

Other costs may include the organisation's fixed and fluctuating on-costs, such as costs of offices, administration, plant and production facilities, insurances, auditing, depreciation, etc. The costs of setting up or expanding a department to handle the exploitation and further development of the right may be relevant.

At its simplest, the cost method consists of working out the expenses associated with registering a patent, design or trade mark, being the fees payable to the relevant office and the fees payable to a lawyer, patent or trade mark agent responsible for handling the application and registration, and where the right has been registered for some time, the fees associated with renewing the rights.

If all the other direct and indirect costs mentioned above are to be included, the exercise becomes much more complex. Where the subject matter is particularly complex or requires significant research and development, such as in relation to pharmaceuticals or computer software or other cutting-edge technology, these other costs can far outweigh the costs associated with registering the right.

EXAMPLE OF COST METHOD

To give an example of the cost method in action, say that a company, Gardenwares, makes and sells garden equipment. It engages a design consultancy to come up with a new wheelbarrow design. The design has an inventive wheel mechanism and overall the wheelbarrow has an unusual appearance. The company has obtained a UK patent for the wheel mechanism and registers the overall design as a UK registered design. The company also decides to market the new wheelbarrow as the Shifteasy and registers that name as a UK trade mark. The value of the design is, based on the cost method, set out in Table E.

Thus, the total value of the IPR associated with the Shifteasy is £18,569.17. Of course, this may bear little or no relation to its actual value but is nevertheless a valid method of calculating value for some purposes, such as taxation. Note: 'UK IPO' is the UK Intellectual Property Office and fees payable do not allow for subsequent renewal fees that will become due. It is assumed that all applications proceed without problems such as amendment, opposition or rejection. No allowance has been made for VAT where applicable. If the fees and costs have been incurred some time ago, an uplift will be required to calculate the present value.

Table E

Cost detail	Amount (£)
Design consultancy fee	5,475.00
Solicitor's fee in drawing up the assignment of IPR to Gardenwares	525.00
Patent costs	
Patent agent fees	3,763.80
Fees paid to UK IPO	250.00
Registered design costs	
Patent agent fees included above	–
Fees paid to UK IPO	60.00
Trade mark costs	
Trade mark agent fees	1,207.87
Fees paid to UK IPO	200.00
Gardenwares' employee and management costs	
Employee and managers costs	6,750.00
Overheads at 5% (office costs etc.)	337.50
Total costs	18,569.17

Where the right is a soft IP right, it is the costs of producing the right that are important as there are no costs of registration (apart perhaps from depositing copies with third parties for evidential purposes). For example, the cost of producing a work of copyright such as a literary or artistic work includes the costs of materials, facilities and equipment needed to create the work and, of course, the costs of the time spent by the author of the work. There may be other subsidiary costs such as management costs and the legal costs associated with assigning or licensing the copyright where the author is not an employee.

Whether the total costs relate to the creation of hard or soft IP, the totality of the costs, however based, usually bear no relation to the value of the right. They are not even an approximation of valuation in the commercial sense. This approach may, however, in some cases, give a formula for working out a value that may be useful in some situations.

An artist may spend 200 hours creating a large landscape painting. She may cost her time at £10 per hour and cost of materials used is £260. The contribution for the use of her studio is £65. Her painting is worth, on the basis of the cost method, £2,325.

In practice, the painting may sell for much more or much less, if it sells at all. There may be other sources of income derived from the copyright in the painting, such as where limited-edition copies are sold or rights to copy the painting are granted to publications such as magazines. So the actual value of the painting may vary from nothing to many thousands of pounds.

Some inspired guesswork may be needed to determine the actual value. This may not be as hit or miss as it sounds and the artist may have a track record of selling her paintings and rights under them. This takes us to our next method of valuation.

Willing buyer and willing seller

If I own an IP right and you want to buy it or use it under a licence, how much would you pay me? I write books about IP law. From past experience I know I can earn a few thousand pounds from each edition of such a book. If my subject was contract law, I know the total annual sales for contract law textbooks is much greater but there are more titles available. If I wrote the leading text on contract law, I would probably earn several times more than in the case of the leading text on IP law, because more students study contract law than IP law.[7]

Armed with this information and knowledge of past experience, I know the sort of royalty I can expect from publishers and this helps to negotiate between publishers. However, sometimes the highest rate on offer may not give the greatest income. Other factors are at play, such as the standing and market reach of the publisher and the sale price of the book. Whether the book is available online or in print form only is another factor. Thus, I have some idea of the value of my work of copyright. This does not take into account the costs of writing the text and the costs of publication, distribution and marketing.

Valuation of rights that endure for a long time, such as copyright, is one thing. A further problem for rights that are quite limited in time, such as patents and designs, is another matter.

Patents have a maximum life of 20 years. This is compromised in the case of pharmaceutical patents as it takes several years for the necessary licences to be obtained before the patent can be exploited (although a five-year extension is available in such cases to compensate for this). But when the right expires, anyone may make the product or use the process, as the case may be.

Anyone buying the rights under a patent or design has to go through a complex process of valuing the patent or design. This will inevitably require detailed examination of the market over a period of time. A judgement may be made, often on the basis of past experience, that the type of product or article has a shelf life of only a few years, perhaps because of changes in fashion. After a while, the public tend to tire of something that was new not so long ago.

---

7 At the present time, contract law is a compulsory subject for law students and many students in other disciplines also take contract law. IP law is not a compulsory subject but, in the authors' view, it should be, for all students, whatever their discipline.

A judgement will have to be made as to the size of the relevant market and potential market share. The degree of novelty and inventiveness may be issues, as well as whether the product or article fulfils a long-felt want or is capable of generating a new market altogether. Alternatively, it may well sit alongside current products and compete with them for market share.

Whatever the position, a lot of estimation is involved. Suppose I have invented a new software-implemented method of making computer screen images appear three-dimensional, allowing the view to move around the image and change the viewing angle. The potential market is enormous. But how many will buy the software? Will persons want it as an add-on to the their existing imaging tools? What if camera manufacturers want to build it into their image sensors or camera software?

COMPARABLE LICENCES

Where comparable licences exist these might be useful as a rule of thumb, though some caution is required as no two IP rights are the same. A patent or registered design is a monopoly right but the potential market might be quite small: for example, in the case of a patent for heavy machinery for the manufacture of carpets. On the other hand, a patent might appear to be a simple improvement upon existing technology yet there is a substantial market for it, such as the case of communications software to be used in mobile phones. Another factor is the strength of the right. Could it be vulnerable to a legal challenge? If it is a patent, are the claims so narrow that others can easily engineer around it? The strength of bargaining position of the parties is another issue.

In many cases, one or other party will already have similar licences and so will know what a 'ball-park' royalty rate will be. They will know of their own licences and, perhaps, those of competitors. They may have negotiated licences for similar technology in the past. Patent and trade mark agents may be quite knowledgeable when it comes to typical rates as they will have been involved in assignments and licensing of IPR and, of course, litigation where damages or accounts are assessed.

One source of information about typical royalties is litigation where compulsory licences and the terms of licences of right are established. A good many of these are determined by hearing officers in the Patent Office.

Typically, royalty rates for hi-tech inventions are much higher than for mechanical technology or improvements thereto. Patent licences tend to be higher than trade mark licences and these again are usually higher than licences for designs. Pharmaceutical licences tend to be high, taking account of the massive investment in creating and developing new products. Exclusive licences for copyright works tend to be around 10 to 20 per cent.

Factors to consider when negotiating licence royalties or the transfer or rights of ownership include:

- the duration of the licence and its scope;
- the rights involved and their remaining duration;
- the territorial scope of the rights: for example, in the case of a patent, does it apply to the UK or to a number of other countries? If the right is a registered design or trade mark, is it registered in the UK only or within the European Union and/or other countries?
- whether licences have already been granted under the rights;
- the right to any improvements made by the licensee or person acquiring the rights;
- whether know-how will be transferred and assistance with working the rights;
- how and when royalties or other fees will be paid and whether access to accounts will be given to confirm sales figures;
- how infringements will be dealt with: for example, will a licensee be able to bring proceedings for any infringement affecting him?

VALUATION OF IP

Comparable licences can give a rough guide but no more. They may be unhelpful in most cases and a bare royalty rate can be quite misleading. Little other than the royalty rate may be known in most cases.

Cost–benefit approach

This approach looks at the anticipated costs and benefits from a project over the expected lifespan of the project. A discount rate is applied to allow for the fact that the difference between the cost and the benefit could have earned income by investing in other ways, for example, by investing on the stock market or in a high interest account.

Costs include the initial costs of acquiring the IPR and subsequent renewals of registered rights. Other costs, which may be very substantial, include the costs of plant and machinery to manufacture the product in question, materials and supplies, associated staff costs and professional fees, factory and storage space, maintenance, distribution costs, marketing costs and so on. Overheads must also be allowed for.

The benefits include, of course, the income received on units sold, either by retailers or direct sales. There may also be fees and royalties received from licences granted. For example, licences may be granted to manufacturers in other territories where the IPR are in force.

A cost–benefit analysis uses a formula to calculate the overall value (known as the net present value, or NPV) of a project. That formula may be expressed as:

$$NPV = \sum_{t=0}^{N} \frac{R_t}{(1+i)^t}$$

where t is the relevant year, R_t is the difference between costs and benefits for year t and i is the discount rate. N is the number of years of the project.

Let us return to our earlier example of Gardenwares and its Shifteasy wheelbarrow. Say that the costs and benefits are as shown in Table F, which also shows the calculation of the NPV for the project based on a product lifespan of ten years. The first year costs include the costs of acquiring the initial IPR of £18,569.17, the costs of setting up the manufacturing capability, marketing costs and other associated costs. Subsequent years' costs also include the costs of renewing the IPR where required and acquiring rights elsewhere. Production and distribution costs are

Table F

Year	Costs (£k)	Benefits (£k)	Net cash flow (benefit − cost)	Present value (net cash flow/(1 + 0.05)^t
0	78	67	11	−11
1	37	98	61	58
2	35	156	121	110
3	37	198	161	139
4	42	276	234	193
5	38	245	207	162
6	30	220	190	142
7	29	195	166	118
8	19	120	101	68
9	11	75	65	42
			Total NPV	£1,021(k)

included each year. The benefits include royalties from licensing the technology in other countries. It has been assumed that the capital would have earned 5 per cent interest and this is used as the discount rate. There may be costs (and benefits) associated with winding up the project at the end of its useful life, such as disposing of plant and machinery, cleaning and modifying premises and selling off surplus stock and materials. Any remaining wheelbarrows may be sold off at a heavily discounted rate.

Thus the total NPV is just over £1 million. This can be taken as the value directly and indirectly associated with the IPR. It might be the sort of value used in negotiations for the acquisition of the rights in question, not that a buyer would want to pay anything like that amount – he would hope to generate some profit himself from the venture!

Although this seems a much more accurate approach than the cost method of the willing buyer and seller approach, it must be remembered that most of the sums are speculative. They may be based on past experience of similar products. In practice, income figures may be very different in practice. At least this method gives some idea of the value of the project, much of which may be the result of having the IPR in the underlying technology. Of course, other factors may have an impact. These include the success or otherwise of marketing, consumer resistance and the possibility of rival products that may or may not infringe those IPR.

Another feature of this method is that the value changes from year to year, taking account of the first year heavy expenditure and the reduction in the number of years before the IPR lapse or expire or when alternative technology overtakes the product.

Summary of key points: strategy

There should be one person in charge with ultimate responsibility but with the backing of an appropriately skilled team. You should be clear about what the business strategy is and must be able to implement the IP strategy to synchronise with that. You should complete a full IP audit of all IP both registered and non-registered and establish a process for keeping this data up-to-date. You should be clear about how to create value from exploiting your IP and have a process for pruning unused IP. A database of all licences both in and out should be kept with a process for keeping this data up-to-date. You should be sure that you have freedom to operate and this must be checked regularly. There must be a policy and procedures for educating your employees into the IP culture and vision of the business. Employment contracts should fully reflect the IP policy. Finally you should have a process for monitoring infringement with an enforcement and defensive infringement strategy and remember you should review your strategy regularly.

Summary of key points: audit

The audit will look at who is responsible for IP in the business and who are the company's external IP advisers. The audit will establish whether the appropriate IP policies and procedures are in place. It will look at what IP rights there are (registered or unregistered), their validity and status. There will be an assessment to establish what the most valuable rights are. The audit will also consider whether licences have been given or received, the terms of these licences and whether the terms are being adhered to. Finally the audit will review any legal proceedings and assess the outcome of any pending applications or legal actions.

Summary of key points: due diligence

Make sure that you understand why due diligence will be conducted. You may be negotiating to sell your entire company or planning to create a joint venture. Whatever the reason you need to keep copies of all the documents mentioned above so that the due diligence team can make a proper judgement about whether the transaction should be entered into or not. They will not take things on trust but need proof. If you cannot supply proof, this may lead to you having to give undertakings and warranties. Remember if the IP contracts that you have entered into cannot be transferred after a transaction such as an acquisition; they have no value to the acquirer so they will pull out of the deal. You need to be able to show that you own the IPR used in the business either because you created them in-house or licensed them in. If you licensed-in you must be able to prove that such a licence is not affected by a change of control or consent clause but will carry on after the transaction has been completed. You will have to show that you are not infringing any third-party rights and that you are aware of the importance and strength of any threatened litigation or issues associated with employees' rights. You must also demonstrate that your business is not involved with any regulatory, competition or data protection problems.

Summary of key points: valuation

Each method may have its own uses for particular purposes. Where the owner of IPR wishes to raise capital or income from the sale of those rights, or where they are involved in a company merger or acquisition, some sort of value must be placed on the rights. Where rights are being assigned or licensed, both parties will want to carry out a valuation exercise. It would be prudent to carry out a valuation using the cost method and a cost–benefit analysis. Where they exist, comparable licences may provide a touchstone.

For example, a buyer would want to estimate how much the seller has paid to acquire the rights and would also want to know how much profit exercising those rights would be likely to generate.

If Gardenwares was to sell its rights to the Shifteasy wheelbarrow in year one, a potential selling price range would be something between the costs of acquiring those rights (£18,569.17) and the NPV (£1,021,000). A buyer wishing the exploit the rights would pay nothing like the NPV. A more likely price could be around £100,000 to £250,000. Of course, a buyer might have carried out his own valuation and have come up with a very different NPV figure.

A final check of comparable licences might come up with a typical royalty figure of 12 per cent of net sales income. A unit sales wholesale price of £35 with an estimate of an average of 15,000 unit sales per year for ten years would give a total income of £630,000 (undiscounted figure). This suggests somewhat less than the cost–benefit approach and might suggest an acquisition value nearer £100,000.

Whatever method is used to value IP there are some other factors that need to be considered. They include an assessment of the strength of the rights, whether legal action is likely to defend those rights or attack infringers and the likely outcomes. Taking a patent to court can be extremely costly for the losing party. An audit may be carried out (see earlier in the chapter). This may highlight strengths and weaknesses, such as where the rights have been litigated. For example, in a previous legal action, the claims of a patent may have been amended or some claims invalidated. A limitation may have been imposed on a registered trade mark. Other factors are whether registered rights have been properly renewed and the remaining duration of those rights.

Management tips

- Make sure your IP strategy is in line with your business strategy and is updated regularly.
- A good IP team is essential, with a CIPO with vision.
- Make sure you have defined your most important goals.
- Get advice on the best way of protecting your assets.
- Identify the best collaborative partners.
- You should keep the audit report confidential within the company.
- You should ensure that the different departments involved, research, marketing, sales, are willing to act on and follow up any issues raised.
- Make sure you use the audit to feed into any future business plan of the organisation in order to create new business opportunities.
- Make sure that people who give the information to the due diligence team know about IP.
- Make sure everyone involved understands the importance of the transaction.
- Ensure that you know what is material for this particular transaction.
- Have proof or copies of everything that you are going to be asked about.
- Be prepared to involve foreign lawyers if necessary.
- All companies should have a risk committee and directors will be in breach if they do not identify risks related to IP.

Exercise

A strategy is coherent action backed up with a good argument. What is the main challenge that you face when creating an IP strategy, what approaches could you take to overcome the problems and what steps will support that approach?

Chapter 10

Infringement of Intellectual Property Rights

In previous chapters, we have seen what acts constitute an infringement of intellectual property rights (IPR). The aim of this chapter is to pull together and summarise those acts and to look at further issues that apply to infringement of IPR, such as the distinction between 'soft IPR', such as copyright, and 'hard IPR', such as patents.

It is also important to reflect upon the potential defences to infringement and to acts that may be performed without the owner's permission that do not, nevertheless, infringe the right concerned.

We will also examine the practical steps that may be taken to stop acts alleged to infringe IPR and to obtain evidence of infringement to support legal proceedings. It is important to note that it may be some time before a full trial of the issues can take place. Under some circumstances it may be vital to put a stop to infringing activity immediately, otherwise irreparable harm may be done by the time the case comes to court.

Other issues to be considered are the choice of court or forum to bring proceedings for infringement and the territorial nature of IPR.

By the end of the chapter you should be able to answer the following questions:

In summary, what rights are given to the owner of the various IPR?
How do those rights compare and contrast?
In what ways are those rights infringed?
What is meant by the terms 'soft IPR' and 'hard IPR'?
What are the main differences between 'soft IPR' and 'hard IPR' when it comes to infringement?
What can I do to strengthen my position in relation to my IPR?
What court or forum is most appropriate in which to bring an action for infringement?
How do I obtain evidence of infringing materials and activities?
Can I bring an action for infringement in a foreign country?

Summary of intellectual property rights and infringement

It should be apparent by now that some of the IPR are subject to formal registration. These include registered trade marks, patents and registered designs. These are often referred to as 'hard IPR'. Other rights come into being informally: for example, copyright comes into existence the moment the work in question is created. There is no need to do anything. The right is not subject to any formalities. That is not to say that nothing should be done to keep records and take other measures such as placing a copyright notice on copies of the work, as we will see later.

IPR that are not required to be formally registered are often known as 'soft IPR'. They include copyright, rights in performances, unregistered design rights, goodwill protected by the law of passing off and information protected by the law of confidence.

Another distinction between the various IPR is whether they are provided for by legislation or exist at 'common law' or equity. Statutory IPR include copyright and similar rights (often referred to as neighbouring rights, which include database rights and rights in performances), registered trade marks, patents and registered and unregistered designs. Those not provided for by legislation are fewer and include goodwill protected by the law of passing off and information protected by the law of confidence.

It should also be noted at this stage, as should be apparent from the previous chapters, that subject matter can often be protected by more than one IP right. For example, written information may be protected by copyright and the law of confidence. A new and inventive widget may be protected by patent law and design law. The same subject matter may be protected by one right but later that protection gives way to a different form of protection. For example, a new invention should be protected by the law of confidence until such time as a patent is applied for and details of the invention are published by the intellectual property office. Patent protection should take over, assuming a patent is granted in due course.

The differing nature of IPR can explain the differing nature of the forms of infringing acts. As 'hard IPR' are registered, these rights give monopoly rights that are infringed by a person carrying out a prohibited act irrespective of any knowledge of the subject matter or the fact of registration. The reason is that these rights are published in registers that can be consulted by the public. If a person infringing the right did not know about the register entry and did not know of the existence of the protected subject matter that does not prevent infringement, though it may be relevant to remedies available to the owner of the right.

On the other hand, copyright infringement requires an act of copying or one of the other acts circumscribed by the copyright. The infringer must have had access to the protected subject matter whether by seeing it or taking a duplicate copy. Lack of knowledge of the existence of the subject matter cannot infringe, however close the second work is to the first. The same applies to unregistered design rights.

Goodwill protected by passing off is somewhat different in that lack of knowledge of the goodwill provides no defence; though again it could have a bearing on any financial compensation payable. However, having said that, most cases of passing off involve deliberate and calculated similarities in name or get-up. Often, it will concern an attempt to get as close to a well-known name or get-up as one can get without falling foul of the law. These attempts are not often successful.

Summary of infringement of intellectual property rights

In general terms, the rights of the owner of an IP right are associated with the forms of infringement of those rights. For example, the owner of a copyright has certain exclusive rights that are infringed by a person carrying out an act that falls within those rights without the licence of the copyright owner in relation to the whole or a substantial part of the work, whether directly or indirectly. There are usually some defences to infringement, such as public interest or express defences or acts that may be performed without infringing the right in question.

It might be useful at this stage to set out the forms of infringement of the various IPR, defences and non-infringing acts in a table in summary form before proceeding further.

Table G contains broad definitions only as a guide and lacks some detail. For full descriptions, please refer to the appropriate chapter.

Table G

IPR	Infringement	Defences and non-infringing acts
Registered trade marks	Using in the course of trade a sign identical or similar to a registered trade mark in relation to identical or similar goods or services. The use must be such as to cause confusion in the eyes of consumers unless the sign and trade mark and the goods or service are identical. A further form of infringement is where, without due cause, there is unfair advantage taken of the trade mark or detriment to it	Use of one's own name, use to describe accessories etc. There is also a doctrine of exhaustion of rights whereby the proprietor's rights are exhausted in respect of goods placed on the market within the EU by him or with his consent
Goodwill protected by the law of passing off	A misrepresentation causing damage to the goodwill associated with a name, sign or other get-up	Limited own name defence
Confidential information	Use or disclosure of confidential information without the authority of its owner to the detriment of the owner	Public interest defence
Patents	Making, selling, using, importing, keeping etc. a patented product. Using or offering for use a patented process (a form of knowledge required). Making, selling, using, importing, keeping etc. a product obtained directly from a patented process. Supplying or offering to supply the means relating to an essential element of the invention to put the invention into effect (a form of knowledge is required)	Acts carried out for private and non-commercial purposes, experimentation, extemporaneous preparation in a pharmacy of a medicine, or in respect of ships or aircraft temporarily in the relevant territory. Certain acts in respect of farming. Limited right to repair (really a matter of whether the patented product is being 'made'). Prior use. The doctrine of exhaustion of rights applies

continued

Table G Continued

IPR	Infringement	Defences and non-infringing acts
Copyright	Performing an act within the owner's exclusive rights in relation to the whole or a substantial part of the work, directly or indirectly, without the licence of the owner. These acts include copying, issuing copies to or communicating the work to the public, making an adaptation, etc. Some of these acts only apply in relation to certain types of work. Authorising another to infringe is itself an infringement. There are also numerous secondary infringements. For example, possessing or dealing with infringing articles, most of which apply only in the course of business. Copyright authors (which may not be the present owners) also have moral rights which may be infringed, for example, by failing to identify the author or by making a derogatory treatment of the work in question	There are numerous non-infringing acts set out in the CDPA, known as the permitted acts. These include fair dealing, certain uses in education or by libraries or archives, certain special acts which apply to computer programs and databases, etc. There is also a limited common law defence of public interest.
Databases protected by the database right	Extraction and/or reutilisation of the contents of the database	
Rights in performances	Performers have 'non-property rights' which are infringed in a number of ways, such as: recording etc. a live performance without the consent of the performer; making a copy of, making available or issuing to the public, etc. recordings of qualifying performances without the consent of the performer. Performers also have 'property rights' including reproduction, distribution, rental and lending and making available to the public. Performers also have moral rights which may be infringed, for example, by failing to identify the performer or by making a derogatory treatment of a performance. Persons having recording rights have broadly similar rights to performers with whom they have an exclusive recording contract	There are a number of permitted acts such as criticism, review and news reporting, incidental inclusion and certain acts in relation to education

Registered design rights	Using a design or one which does not produce a different overall impression on the part of the informed user. Use includes making, putting on the market, importing or exporting or keeping for those purposes a product incorporating the design	Acts carried out for private and non-commercial purposes, experimentation, or in respect of ships or aircraft temporarily in the relevant territory. In the context of repair of a complex product. Prior use. The doctrine of exhaustion of rights applies
Unregistered Community design	As above but only if the use in question arises from copying	As above
Unregistered UK design right	Reproducing the design by making articles exactly or substantially to the design or a design document to enable such articles to be made, without the licence of the owner. Authorising another to do the above is also an infringement. There are also secondary infringements, such as importing, selling etc. for commercial purposes.	If the act in question also infringes copyright, design right is not infringed. Taking a licence of right during the last 5 years of the right

Note
Some forms of infringement of copyright and rights in performances carry criminal penalties. There are other criminal offences related to other rights for acts which do not generally infringe the right as such. For example, falsely marking a product as being patented. Other forms of defence may be to challenge the validity of the IPR.

What can I do to strengthen my position in relation to my intellectual property rights?

People tend to infringe IPR for a number of reasons. Some infringe in the belief that they will not be found out or will be able to escape the long arm of the law. Others may infringe through ignorance, wilful or otherwise. Yet others may infringe because they believe that whatever they are doing is outside the scope of protection.

There are a number of ways in which you can strengthen your rights and ensure you are in a good position to deter would-be infringers or, if your rights are infringed, be in a strong position in any consequent legal proceedings.

The five key principles are:

1. Make sure you have all the rights you can acquire.
2. Keep accurate and thorough records.
3. If you rely on the law of confidence make sure others are made aware of that and are made subject to an obligation of confidence.
4. Place notices on articles, products and copies of your works that you put on the market.
5. If you license your rights, make provision for assistance from licensees in litigation, in appropriate cases, such as infringements carried out in the licensed territory.

We can now look at each of these in more detail.

Acquisition of rights

Some IPR are automatic and free from formalities. Copyright is a good example. That does not mean that nothing needs to be done to strengthen the right, as we will see later.

For rights subject to registration, such as patents, registered trade marks and registered designs, apply for registration. In some cases, failure to do so can be devastating. For example, if you fail to patent a product invention, as soon as you put the product on the market, others will be free to copy it (assuming there are no other rights, such as a design right – but even if there is, that will only protect that design and not the invention as such).

If you use a trade name or logo, register it as a trade mark. If you fail to do so, you will have to rely on the law of passing off and will have to prove goodwill, misrepresentation and damage. There are numerous examples of passing off claims failing because the claimant has failed to prove the existence of goodwill or that he or she will suffer damage. On the other hand, if you have registered the name or logo as a trade mark and someone uses an identical sign in relation to identical goods or services you have nothing to prove. Such use infringes per se, even if the defendant did not know your name or logo was registered as a trade mark. Other uses, such as using a sign similar to the trade mark for similar goods or services, simply require proof of a likelihood of confusion on the part of consumers. A third alternative is use that takes unfair advantage of or damages the reputation of a registered trade mark.

Consider which overseas markets you want to operate in and/or license third parties to do so and make sure you have adequate protection in all the relevant territories. If the expense of registration in numerous territories is daunting, remember that there is a right to priority in some cases. For example, you may apply for a patent in one country and delay applications elsewhere for up to 12 months; your invention will be judged on novelty as at the time of your first application.

The priority period can be used productively in finding organisations willing to invest in the subject matter or take licences to exploit it. You may decide to exploit the rights within the EU but grant licences to others to exploit in other parts of the world. For example, you may grant a licence to a company based in Australia to manufacture and sell articles to your protected design, limited to the territory of Australia and New Zealand. Clearly you need to register your design as a registered Community design and seek protection in both Australia and New Zealand.

If you engage others to create or help create the subject matter, make sure you provide for ownership of, or entitlement to, the relevant rights. Remember the rules where employees, self-employed consultants or third-party design companies are involved. In many cases you will need to obtain an assignment of the rights in question and impose an appropriate obligation of confidence or a non-disclosure agreement. In the context of employees, even if there is no doubt as to ownership of or entitlement to the rights, it may be important to deal with the position should an employee leave. Consider using reasonable covenants in restraint of trade.

Keep accurate and thorough records

What would you do if you complained about someone who copied your work of copyright who then claimed that he was the first to create the work, or one substantially similar, and you had copied his work? The authors know of such a case. The person who was the original author did not keep a copy of the work when it was created. It only existed at that stage in electronic form on magnetic disk. Later he wrote over it to reuse the disk!

To continue the copyright theme, make notes of who made it and their status or position, when it was made and to whom and when it was disclosed. Keep a copy of the work as it was made and further copies of subsequent modifications and developments. If it comes to a legal fight, make sure you can submit convincing and admissible evidence of your rights.

One approach is to lodge copies with someone who can provide evidence of the work and its date of creation. A number of organisations exist to do this that can provide affidavit evidence in the case of a legal dispute. Alternatively, use a trusted third party to retain copies or use the simple expedient of posting copies to yourself using recorded delivery. Keep them sealed until they can be used in evidence.

Confidentiality

The law of breach of confidence gives protection to trade secrets, which can include business information as well as secret processes. Trade secrets can be protected by ensuring that persons to whom the secret or information is disclosed are aware of its confidential nature and that they must not use the subject matter or disclose it further without the express written permission of the owner. Sadly, all too often it can end up in the public domain and others will become aware of it and want to use it or disclose it further. There may be a remedy against the person responsible for the breach of confidence but the situation is not at all satisfactory as regards 'innocent third parties'.

In some cases, there is no need to expressly impose an obligation of confidence where the relationship between the parties is one in which an obligation of good faith will be imputed automatically, such as between a client and legal adviser. But in other cases, emphasise confidentiality before allowing others access. Do not rely on the courts to imply an obligation of confidence. The case of *Carflow Products (UK) Ltd v Linwood Securities (Birmingham) Ltd* demonstrates this admirably, where a prototype steering-wheel lock was shown to a potential buyer before an application had been made to register the design of the lock.[1] The court declined to imply an obligation of confidence on the buyer. Looking at the circumstances objectively, such a person would probably think that steps had already been taken to apply for formal protection.

Of course, if the information concerns a patentable invention or a registrable design, it make sense to apply to register it. But, before doing so, it is vital to protect it by imposing an

---

1 [1996] FSR 424.

obligation of confidence on those to whom it is disclosed. If someone owing such a duty does indeed disseminate the information in breach of the duty, that will be ignored when considering the novelty of the invention or design for a period of time. For example, if an application is made to patent an invention, any disclosures made in breach of confidence will not prejudice novelty if the breach occurred within the six months prior to filing an application for a patent.[2]

Apply notices to copies, articles and products

A basic rule is to make others aware of your rights, their scope and nature. It should be clear to persons seeing copies of your work or products made to your patent or design rights just what rights apply to them. Awareness needs to be reinforced by making it clear that infringement will not be tolerated. Simply putting an appropriate sign indicating that an article is subject to a registered design with the registration number and the identity of the owner shows that the right is taken seriously.

Apart from indicating that you take your rights seriously, there is a secondary reason why a notice should be placed on copies, articles or products as the case may be. Although ignorance of the existence of an IP right will not prevent a finding of infringement, it might affect the remedies available to the right owner. This applies to most IPR, whether or not based in statute.

For example, in relation to a patent, damages or an account of profits are not available against a defendant who was not aware of and had no reasonable grounds for supposing that the patent existed.[3] There are two further points. Simply marking a product with the words 'patent' or 'patented' is not sufficient to fix a defendant with knowledge of the existence of the patent. There must also be a reference to the patent number. Finally, it is an offence to claim that an invention is patented when this is untrue.

A further example is that damages are not available under copyright law if the defendant, at the time of the infringement, did not know and had no reason to believe that copyright subsisted in the work in question.[4]

Finally, where proof of copying is important, consider incorporating information into a work that will not usually be spotted by an infringer. There are a number of variations on this. For example, in an Australian case on computer programs, the makers of the Apple II microcomputer had embedded the names of the programmers in the memory devices in the machines. When faced with this evidence, the defendant could no longer maintain that his lookalike computers did not contain copies of the Apple programs.

In another case, the existence of fictitious entries in a database of lawyers could only be explained by the fact that the defendant had made a copy of the claimant's database.

The Ordnance Survey relied on stylistic features on its maps, referred to as 'fingerprints', to show that they had been copied by the Automobile Association. The case was settled out of court for some £20 million.[5] Some map-makers include deliberate mistakes to trap copyists.

Licensees

Owners of IPR often grant licences to others allowing them to manufacture and commercialise copies, articles or products subject to the rights. A licence will sometimes also grant the right to use the owner's trade marks or get-up.

We have seen that there are two main types of licence, the exclusive licence and the non-exclusive licence. The former grants rights that can be exercised by the licensee to the exclusion

---

2 Section 2(4) of the Patents Act 1977.
3 Section 62(1) of the Patents Act 1977.
4 Section 97(1) of the Copyright, Designs and Patents Act 1988.
5 *Guardian*, 6 March 2001. Available at: www.guardian.co.uk/uk/2001/mar/06/andrewclark.

of everyone else, including the right owner. Non-exclusive licences are appropriate where the owner wants to grant the same rights to a number of licensees, such as usually happens in the case of computer software.

It is important to note that licences can be limited in duration, in the scope of rights licensed and limited territorially. For example, the owner of a literary work might grant an exclusive licence to X to make and sell copies of the work in the UK, the USA, Canada and Australasia for a period of ten years only and then grant an exclusive licence to Y to translate the work into Spanish and to make and sell copies in Spanish-speaking countries in Central and South America for 25 years.

IP licences contain all manner of terms and are usually quite complex documents, dealing with all sorts of eventuality. The licence is, however, an opportunity to provide for actions to be taken in the case of suspected infringement.

The licence should contain provisions as to policing the right in question, informing each other of potential infringements and, in appropriate cases, making test purchases. Again keeping proper records is an important aspect, as is making them available to the other party to the licence. In many cases, a licensee will have a right to commence legal proceedings, particularly in the case of an exclusive licence. In some cases, non-exclusive licensees can also bring an action if the licence so provides. Where proceedings are brought by a licensee, it is normal for the owner to be made a party to the action. The licence should cover apportioning the costs and any monetary award between the licensee and licensor.

What court or forum is most appropriate in which to bring an action for infringement?

If the owner of an IP right thinks it is being infringed, the first step would be to contact the person he believes is infringing the right and inform him in writing, giving some information about the right in question and the form of infringement alleged. The communication may be in the form of a letter before action. It may be that the infringement in question is inadvertent and it might be possible to agree payment for past infringement and grant a licence covering future exploitation. Any such communication must be expressed to be without prejudice.

Of course, under some circumstances, the owner of the right may not be prepared to grant a licence: for example, in the case of a trade mark or a patented invention where the proprietor of the patent intends to work the invention himself and not grant licences.

In terms of some forms of right, being patents, registered trade marks or designs, some care must be taken to avoid triggering a groundless threats action brought by the alleged infringer or other involved person. Legal advice is almost always essential even at an early stage.

Alternative dispute resolution

Failing resolution, the owner of the right will have to decide where to bring proceedings. However, it may be that the dispute is one suitable for alternative dispute resolution (ADR). Litigation normally results in a win/lose outcome, whereas ADR may bring about an outcome where both parties have a satisfactory resolution. An example is where the alleged infringer agrees to take a licence or where the parties agree to cross-license technologies. There are a number of forms of ADR, including mediation and conciliation.

ADR has a number of advantages over litigation. It tends to be less expensive and can deal with matters such as where infringement is alleged in a number of different jurisdictions.

The Centre for Dispute Resolution offers dispute resolution services. The UK Intellectual Property Office (UK IPO) also offers a mediation service.[6]

---

6 Centre for Dispute Resolution: www.cedr.com; UK IPO: www.ipo.gov.uk.

The UK Intellectual Property Office

Under s 74A of the Patents Act 1977, on request from the proprietor of a patent or any other person, a patent examiner of the UKIPO may provide a non-binding opinion as to whether a certain act infringes a patent or whether the patent is invalid for lack of novelty or inventive step. This might be a useful first step that could encourage the proprietor or an alleged infringer to settle the case rather than pursue full and expensive legal proceedings. Of course, any opinion is not binding and is without prejudice to any subsequent proceedings. This service may be particularly useful where the technology underlying the invention is not too complex, such as a patent for a mechanical invention. It is not appropriate in the case of biotechnological inventions or computer-implemented inventions. At the time of writing the fee chargeable for an opinion is only £200.

The Comptroller of Patents also may rule on numerous statutory provisions in relation to patents, such as opposition, amendment, determination of the right to a patent, employee compensation, reinstatement, etc. In some cases, the Comptroller may decline to rule on the issue where he thinks it more properly dealt with by the court.

Hearing officers at the UK IPO have jurisdiction to decide cases under trade mark law and, in very limited cases, design law. Trade mark law in particular generates much work for the hearing officers and there is also an appeal system under trade mark law in which appeals may go before the 'Appointed Person', rather than to the court. As one might expect, hearings at the UK IPO are less expensive and costs awards are relatively small. Many cases are 'paper hearings' where the parties submit their arguments and evidence on paper. Trade mark cases usually concern opposition, invalidity and revocation hearings.

The Patents County Court

The Patents County Court was established in 1990 to provide a less expensive alternative to the Patents Court in the High Court for less complex cases. It has a limit of £500,000 on awards it can make. Where a case is likely to be complex and require taking evidence from numerous witnesses, including expert witnesses, the Patents Court is more appropriate. Where the damages sought are likely to exceed £500,000, again the Patents Court is the most appropriate forum.

The Patents County Court operates two tracks: a small claims track and a confusingly named twin-track. The small claims track is most suited to lower value cases not exceeding £5,000. Costs are strictly controlled and are not available in most cases. That is, each party usually bears their own costs as opposed to the normal rule whereby the losing party pays the costs of the successful party as well as their own.

The small claims track was introduced in 2010 and came into effect on 1 October 2012. It is intended to be useful for SMEs and entrepreneurs with low-value claims. It might be suitable, for example, where a photographer claims that the copyright in one of his photographs has been infringed.

The small claims track can be used for disputes involving copyright, trade marks, passing off and unregistered designs. It cannot be used for claims involving patents and registered designs.

The remedies available under the small claims track are limited, typically to an award of damages and an injunction to prevent further infringement. Applications for search orders and interim injunctions may not be brought under the small claims track. (Remedies are covered in the following chapter.)

The Patents Court in the High Court (now the Intellectual Property Enterprise Court)

The Patents Court is part of the Chancery Division of the High Court. It is the main court of first instance in IP cases and there are no limits on the remedies available. It also hears appeals from the Comptroller of Patents. Some IP cases, such as copyright, normally go to the Chancery Division itself but this is a technicality. The courts are for all intents and purposes the same.

The Patents Court is appropriate for complex cases involving difficult issues such as the validity of a patent or where the damages sought are in excess of £500,000. The Patents Court encourages parties to consider using ADR as a means of settling a dispute.

Other courts and forums

In England and Wales, appeals from the Chancery Division go to the Court of Appeal. In Scotland, cases go to the Court of Session (which has an Outer House and an Inner House). In Northern Ireland, there is the High Court of Northern Ireland. For all of the UK, the final appeal is to the Supreme Court.

However, where the issues at hand involve the interpretation of a provision under EU law and its meaning is not clear, a court may refer questions to the Court of Justice of the European Union for a preliminary ruling. For example, where the meaning of a provision in a EU Directive is not beyond doubt, a court in the UK may seek a ruling from the Court of Justice, which the UK court will then apply to the facts of the case before it. There have been many such references under the trade marks Directive.[7]

The European Patent Office and the Office for the Harmonisation of the Internal Market have various divisions and Boards of Appeal. These are important in cases where an application to register a Community trade mark or design or an application for patents under the European Patent Convention have been refused by the examiner or a third party brings opposition proceedings.

How do I obtain evidence of infringing materials and activities?

If an owner of an IP right thinks it has been or is being infringed, he will need to think about gathering evidence to bring to the court to support his case. It may be appropriate to apply to the court for a search order permitting the owner's solicitors to enter the defendant's premises to make copies of evidence, which may be copies of alleged infringing works and associated information such as records of the number of infringing copies made or imported. Search orders are discussed in more detail in the following chapter.

Often there is no need for a search order and it may be a matter of simply buying or downloading alleged infringing copies. It is important to document fully such activities.

Where the right in question is a trade mark or goodwill protected by passing off, 'trap orders' may be considered. For example, by placing an order for the owner's goods or services and seeing whether the defendant's are offered instead. In an old example, *White Hudson & Co Ltd v Asian Organisation Ltd*, there was evidence that persons in Singapore asking for 'red paper cough sweets' were offered the defendant's sweets that had similar wrappers.[8]

If the alleged infringing goods, products or articles are being marketed by a secondary infringer, such as a retailer, a court order may be granted requiring the secondary infringer to identify the person from whom he acquired the items.

Can I bring an action for infringement in a foreign country?

Questions of jurisdiction are complex. In relation to the EU, there are some basic rules under the Brussels Regulation on jurisdiction and the recognition and enforcement of judgments in civil and commercial matters, 2000.[9] The basic rules can be briefly stated thus:

> A defendant should be sued 'at home', that is, in the court in the Member State in which he is domiciled.

---

7 The UK Trade Marks Act 1994 was implemented to conform with this Directive.
8 [1964] 1 WLR 1466.
9 There is an equivalent Convention covering the EEA countries, called the Lugano Convention.

As an alternative to this, a defendant may be sued in another EU Member State where the action concerns the infringement or anticipated infringement of an IP right, if that takes place or may take place in that other Member State;

A further alternative is where there are two or more defendants domiciled in different Member States and the claims against each are so closely connected that it is expedient to hear them together to avoid the risk of irreconcilable judgments resulting from separate proceedings – they can all be sued in the Member State in which any one of them is domiciled.

A major qualification to all the above is where the case involves the registration or validity of a registered trade mark, patent or design – the case must be brought in the Member State in which it is or will be registered.

The Community trade mark and the Community design both have rules of jurisdiction that supplement the above rules.

To give some examples:

Alex lives in London and is the owner of the copyright subsisting in a photograph of the Eiffel Tower in Paris. He uploaded his photograph on Google Earth. He discovered that Fritz, who lives in Germany, has downloaded the photograph and is selling in Germany t-shirts bearing a copy of Alex's photograph. Alex may only bring legal proceedings in Germany.

As above, but Fritz has a stall near the Eiffel Tower and is selling his t-shirts from the stall. Alex may sue Fritz in Germany or France.

As above, but Fritz has a partner in his t-shirt venture who is called Sarah and is domiciled in England. Sarah applies the copies of the photograph to blank t-shirts provided by Fritz and then sends them to Fritz in Germany who exports them to Italy to be sold by Luigi. All three are 'partners in crime' and are aware of what they are doing. Alex is spoilt for choice. He may sue in England, Germany or Italy.

Donna is an inventor and she has UK, French and Spanish patents for her latest new widget invention, which she obtained under the European Patent Convention. Each of the resulting national patents are, therefore, identical. Acme Inc is a large US corporation with subsidiary companies in the UK, France and Spain. Each of them is infringing the respective patents in those countries. Donna can choose any of those three countries.

As above, but each of the subsidiary companies has entered a defence alleging the relevant patent is invalid. Donna must bring separate legal actions in the UK, France and Spain.

The last example shows how urgent it is for the adoption of a single European patent that would allow the whole matter to be determined in a single Member State. One eminent judge, Lord Justice Jacob, described the present system as 'Kafkaesque'. There have been plans for a single European patent since the 1960s. There seems to be more impetus now, so hopefully it will come into being in the not-too-distant future.

Management tips

Bear in mind that registered rights are monopolistic in character while unregistered rights require proof of copying or other acts involving access to the original work or article. Therefore, if you can obtain registration, seriously consider doing so. Bear in mind, of course, that patent protection can be very expensive depending on the territories for which protection is sought. In a few cases, it might not be commercially viable to patent an invention.

If you have a patent or registered design, mark products or articles with the fact that it is patented or registered as a design and also put the registration number alongside. This makes it almost impossible for an infringer to claim that he was not aware of the fact of the patent or registration. This will prevent an infringer escaping an award of damages through lack of knowledge.

If you have a registered trade mark, use the ® symbol next to your trade mark. If you have not registered your trade mark, use the ™ symbol instead.

If you have a work of copyright, place a prominent copyright notice, such as © 2013 Fred Smith.

Be aware that you may commit a criminal offence if you falsely represent that you have a patent, registered design or registered trade mark.

If you apply to patent an invention, be aware that you may apply in other countries for patents for the same invention within 12 months. This can be important in terms of financing the costs of patenting and giving some time to seek funding.

If you suspect your rights are being infringed, consider ADR (if the other party agrees to this). If ADR is not possible, consider using the services of the UK IPO, for example, to obtain an opinion about validity or infringement.

IP litigation can be very expensive. Make sure you use the most appropriate forum. If you are seeking damages of less than £5,000 consider using the small claims track in the Patents County Court.

Exercise

What type of court or other forum would be most appropriate for each of the situations described below?

1. Tecksoft has a UK patent for a software communications system. Sales of this system represent more than half of Tecksoft's turnover. Its arch rival Industar has started marketing a similar system.
2. Simon is an expert on medieval history. He has self-published a book on the subject in paper form. In the first year, he sold around 200 copies at £10 each. He has just discovered that Lee has made an electronic copy of the book and has sold 500 copies online at £5 each.
3. Kerry created a new and unusual design for a garden seat to be made from stone-effect concrete. The design included a motif applied to the edges of the seat. Kerry registered the design as a Community design. She granted an exclusive licence to Steve to make seats to the design that he could sell throughout the UK, France and Germany for a period of five years. At the end of the five years, Kerry renewed her Community design for a further five years but has discovered that Steve has continued to make the seats after the expiry of the licence agreement. Furthermore, Steve has created his own design of motif and applied that to the seats. It is very attractive and has increased the total sales of the seats.
4. Nick is a professional photographer. He took a photograph of four girls in swimwear doing handstands at the water's edge on a beach on a sunny day. He published his photograph in a

book of photographs of people on holiday, which he made available for purchase from his website. Later, he discovered that the Tourist Information Centre at Skegthorpe had copied the photograph in its publicity material, available as a flyer in the tourist office and on its website. Nick thinks he is entitled to substantial damages in excess of £10,000 and also damages for breach of his moral right to be identified as the author, as the copies do not carry any attribution as to the identity of the photographer. Nick is so incensed by the tourist office's behaviour in all this that he rejected all offers to negotiate a settlement.

Suggested answers

1. Patent litigation can be vastly expensive. As Tecksoft and Industar are arch rivals, it is highly unlikely that both would agree to ADR. Indeed, that would be likely to be unsuited to this sort of case as there are likely to be difficult issues to resolve such as whether the patent in question is valid, especially as it probably involves computer programs. Industar is almost certain to attack the validity of the patent. The outcome of the case could have very serious implications for either party. This is a case that would be most suited to the Patents Court in the High Court.
2. The value of Simon's claim is relatively small, certainly less than £5,000. Furthermore, it would appear that the case will not involve difficult questions of law and, therefore, the case would be most suited to the small claims court in the Patents County Court.
3. As Kerry and Steve have been contracting parties, they already have a working relationship, although Steve should not have continued to make the seats after the expiry of his licence from Kerry. This situation looks perfect for ADR. A mediator might be able to come up with a solution that suits both Kerry and Steve. It could be that Kerry agrees to grant a new licence to Steve to allow him to continue to make the seats, possibly at a reduced royalty (as sales have increased). Steve will register his motif as a Community design and assign the design to Kerry, retaining the right to use it under a licence, allowing her to license that design to other manufacturers in countries other than those in which Steve exploits the designs.
4. It does not seem likely that ADR would be agreed to by Nick. As the claim is for at least £10,000, this is more than the small claims track of the Patents County Court, but the multi-track system would be suitable. There are unlikely to be any complex issues of copyright subsistence or of evidence requiring expert witnesses. Therefore, commencing action in the Patents Court in the High Court would not be appropriate.

Chapter 11

Remedies

The remedies available for infringement of intellectual property rights (IPR) have developed over the centuries. There is now a whole range of remedies, some of which may be claimed together while others are mutually exclusive. There are even some remedies that may be available against a person threatening to bring legal proceedings for infringement. Some measures are interim measures, designed to put an immediate stop to an alleged infringing action, but sometimes it may be just to maintain the status quo pending a full trial of the issues. Bear in mind that it may take several months or even a number of years before a case comes to court for final determination.

There is a Directive on the enforcement of IPR,[1] although the UK more or less already complied with the remedies set out in the Directive. In order to fully comply, some UK Regulations were brought in, which included a methodology for assessing damages and providing for disclosure orders in Scotland to match what was previously available in the rest of the UK. The Directive takes the European three-factor approach in that remedies should be effective, proportionate and dissuasive (Article 3(2) of the Directive). This can be seen as an overriding principle.

The key measures in the Directive are:

- rights of owners, licensees, bodies such as collecting societies to bring enforcement actions;
- orders to obtain evidence, such as search orders, and disclosure of information about infringement;
- the availability of injunctions to prevent ongoing or future infringement including interim measure prior to the full trial;
- orders for the destruction of infringing articles and equipment used to make infringing articles;
- awards of damages appropriate to the actual prejudice suffered by the owner and, where the infringer had acted unintentionally and without negligence, payment of pecuniary compensation if the full measure of damages would cause him disproportionate harm and pecuniary compensation appears reasonably satisfactory;
- payment by the unsuccessful party to the successful party of his reasonable and proportionate legal costs as a general rule providing equity does not allow this;
- a requirement for disseminating information about the case and award if requested by the winning party (although judgments are published, recent case law shows that a publicity order may be particularly appropriate to be placed on the losing party's website).[2]

---
1 Directive 2004/48/EC of the European Parliament and of the Council of 29 April 2004 on the enforcement of intellectual property rights, OJ L 157, 30 April 2004, p. 45.
2 For example, in Samsung Electronics (UK) Ltd v Apple Inc. [2012] EWHC 2049 (Pat), the judge ordered that the defendant publicise on its UK website the fact that the design of its iPad was not infringed by the claimant's Galaxy tablet computer.

This chapter looks in more detail at remedies. Some remedies are potentially available for all types of IP right. Examples include injunctions and damages. However, it is important to note that some remedies are not available for all forms of IP right. For example, additional damages might be available for flagrant copyright infringement but are not available at all for patent infringement, no matter how deliberate and brazen.

Before looking at each type of remedy in more detail, see Table H for a list of the remedies that may be available for infringement of the various rights.

By the end of this chapter, you should be able to answer the following questions.

What remedies are available for infringement of IPR?
What forms of remedy are available in relation to each type of IP right?
How can I stop infringing activities pending a full trial?
What are interim injunctions and search orders?
What is a *Norwich Pharmacal* (disclosure) order?
How are damages calculated?
What are additional damages?
What are groundless threats of infringement proceedings?
What criminal penalties are there for infringement of IPR?

Summary of main remedies

Table H

Intellectual property rights	Remedies	Notes
Trade marks	Injunctions Damages Accounts Delivery up of infringing goods, etc. may be available	'…or otherwise, as are available in respect of infringement of any other property right' (s 14(2) Trade Marks Act 1994)
Passing off	Injunctions Damages Accounts Delivery up of articles etc. to which name or mark subject to goodwill has been applied	
Confidence	Injunctions Damages Accounts Destruction order, for example, of articles made using information subject to confidence	
Patents	Injunctions Damages Accounts Delivery up or destruction	*continued*

Table H Continued

Intellectual property rights	Remedies	Notes
Copyright	Injunctions Damages Accounts Additional damages	'…or otherwise, as are available in respect of infringement of any other property right' (s 96(2) Copyright, Designs and Patents Act 1988)
Database right	As per copyright	
Performers' rights	*Performers' property rights* Damages Injunctions Accounts Additional damages may also be available *Performers' non-property rights and recording rights* Injunctions Damages	'…or otherwise is available to the plaintiff as is available in respect of the infringement of any other property right' (s 191L Copyright, Designs and Patents Act 1988) As for breach of statutory duty – s 194 Copyright, Designs and Patents Act 1988 Delivery up generally available
Design rights	*UK unregistered design right* *UK registered design* *Community design*	As for copyright (s 239 Copyright, Designs and Patents Act 1988) Injunctions, damages or accounts '…or otherwise is available to the plaintiff as is available in respect of the infringement of any other property right' (s 24A(2) Registered Designs Act 1949) Injunctions, damages or (in the UK at least) accounts, seizure orders
Moral rights	Injunctions Damages	As for breach of statutory duty – s 103 (copyright) and s 205N (performers' rights) Copyright, Designs and Patents Act 1988

Preliminary actions

Where the owner of an IP right suspects the right is being infringed, there are a number of courses of action that he may consider taking. Bear in mind that it may be some time before legal proceedings are concluded (often two or three years or more) and, in the meantime, the owner or his licensees may be suffering considerable economic damage by the activities of the alleged infringer.

The owner may want to stop the alleged infringer's activities immediately, long before a court will rule on whether infringement has actually taken place. He may also want to obtain vital evidence of infringement, especially where there is a danger that the alleged infringer will destroy evidence or remove it from the jurisdiction of the courts once he is aware that legal proceedings are a possibility. The owner may suspect that counterfeit goods or infringing copies or articles are being imported into the UK or other EU Member State where he has IPR in other parts of the EU.

The law has developed two particular mechanisms to help: the interim injunction and the search order. HM Revenue and Customs also have powers to seize counterfeit goods and other infringing articles being imported into the UK and there are equivalent powers in other EU Member States.

A further form of order is the *Norwich Pharmacal* order (so named after the case that gave rise to the order). This requires the person to whom it is addressed to disclose information to the claimant. It might typically be information as to the identity of the supplier or importer of infringing goods or articles. Special provision is also made in relation to persistent infringers who distribute or give access to pirated material, such as films or music.

These remedies and orders are discussed below, before we look at the main remedies in more detail.

Interim injunctions

An injunction is one of the most important remedies available and is an order of the court requiring the defendant to stop carrying out or not to commence a specific activity or to do some positive act. Normally, in the context of IPR, an injunction is an order to stop infringing a right or not to embark on some activity which, if carried out, would infringe. We will look at injunctions in more detail later but in terms of preliminary actions, the interim injunction is very important.

The interim injunction usually orders an alleged infringer to stop carrying out some activity alleged to infringe an IP right until the case comes to a full trial. At the full trial it is likely to be substituted for a permanent injunction if the alleged infringement is proved.

It must always be remembered that injunctions are discretionary remedies. Where a rightowner seeks an interim injunction, even if it appears at that stage that he has a strong case, an interim injunction will not necessarily be granted. The judge from whom such an order is requested must seek to balance the harm done to either party if he grants or refuses the request.

The leading case on interim injunctions in IP cases is *American Cyanamid Co v Ethicon Ltd*,[3] involving the alleged infringement of a patent for surgical sutures. The House of Lords confirmed that the object of the interim injunction was to protect the claimant from the harm he would suffer if the activity in question was allowed to continue until the full trial of the action. However, the potential harm to the claimant must be balanced against the harm to the defendant if it is subsequently found that he was not infringing the right after all. He would have been prevented from carrying out a lawful activity. In either case, the harm suffered might not be adequately compensated by an award of damages.

If an interim injunction is granted, the claimant has to give an undertaking to pay damages if he loses at full trial. A number of other issues may influence the court's decision, such as whether the defendant would have sufficient funds to pay damages if he lost. The whole exercise is something of a balancing act.

At an application for an interim injunction, the court will not usually have all the evidence and full legal argument, but nowadays, the strength of the parties' position will be taken into account as it appears at that time.

To sum up, the current position as regards interim injunctions is as follows:

- The grant of an interim injunction is a matter of discretion and depends on all the facts of the case.
- There are no fixed rules.
- The judge should rarely attempt to resolve complex issues of disputed fact or law.

---

3 [1975] AC 396.

- Major factors to be taken into account are:
  - the extent to which damages would be likely to be an adequate remedy and the ability of the other party to pay;
  - the balance of convenience;
  - the maintenance of the status quo; and
  - any clear view the court may reach as to the relative strength of the parties' cases.

Search orders

It may be that the claimant can obtain evidence of infringement openly, such as by making test purchases of articles or material alleged to infringe his IPR. During the lead-up to a trial, there is provision for disclosure of material and documents and the like from each party. However, in some cases, the claimant may suspect that there is other evidence that can only be obtained by means of a court order allowing a without-notice search of the defendant's premises. This might be the case where it is suspected that a defendant will destroy or conceal evidence. This could include pirate copies, machines used to make infringing copies such as a mould, a punch with a representation of the claimant's trade mark or a plate for making infringing paper copies. Other material may provide details of the source, sales and distribution of goods or articles and prices and income derived.

Where such material is suspected to exist, a claimant may apply for a search order. If granted, a search order will enable him, accompanied by his solicitor, to enter the premises where the offending materials and articles are kept and remove them, or have copies made, so they can be produced at the trial. Strict rules now apply to search orders. As with interim injunctions, the claimant has to give an undertaking in damages should it turn out that the defendant was not infringing the rights in question.

Following concerns that the search order was being too freely used there is now a standard form of order and strict rules that must be complied with. For example, the order must be exercised by a neutral supervising solicitor experienced in the use of search orders and the order must not be exercised against premises where it is likely that an unaccompanied woman is present unless the search party includes a woman.

Other factors include:

- The order should be executed during normal office hours so that the defendant can take immediate legal advice.
- A list of items taken should be made, giving the defendant an opportunity to check it.
- If the order contains an injunction restraining the defendant from informing others (for example, co-defendants), the period should not be too long.
- In the absence of good reasons otherwise, orders should be executed at business premises in the presence of a responsible officer or representative of the defendant's company.
- Provision should be made to prevent the claimant going through all the defendant's documents (for example, where the parties were competitors and the claimant could thereby gain useful and sensitive information about the defendant's business unrelated to the alleged infringement).

A final point to note is that there is a general right not to disclose information that would expose a person to criminal prosecution. This is called the right against self-incrimination. However, as some civil infringements of IPR are also criminal offences, there is an exception to that right. An example is in the case of a secondary infringement of copyright, such as importing or selling infringing copies of a work that might also be a criminal offence under copyright law. There are similar issues under trade mark law. For example, selling counterfeit copies of film DVDs bearing registered trade marks will infringe civil rights under trade mark law and may also attract criminal liability. In such cases, a defendant cannot hide behind the rule against self-incrimination to refuse to hand over evidence of the civil wrong on the basis that it would also expose him to criminal liability.

Rights of seizure

There is a limited right of seizure exercisable by copyright owners and in relation to performers' rights. The right may be used typically where infringing copies or articles are being sold at a temporary market or a car boot sale. Before exercising the right, the police must be informed.

More importantly, HM Revenue and Customs have powers of seizure of items such as counterfeit goods, copies or articles being imported into the UK. Council Regulation (EC) No 1383/2003 of 22 July 2003 concerns customs action against goods suspected of infringing certain IPR and the measures to be taken against goods found to have infringed such rights.[4] The powers may be exercised in one or more Member States of the EU. Other specific provisions for seizure are contained in the relevant legislation such as s 111 of the Copyright, Designs and Patents Act 1988 and s 89 of the Trade Marks Act 1994. HM Revenue and Customs publish a notice on these provisions.[5]

Where an owner of an IP right suspects counterfeit or infringing goods or articles are being imported, he may make an application for seizure. Customs authorities may also act under their under their own initiative and stop goods in transit and inform the relevant IP right owner so that he can make a formal application to have the goods seized. The applicant must undertake to pay all costs including the costs of destruction if eventually ordered and pay compensation to the owner of the goods if they are found not to infringe the right claimed.

Norwich Pharmacal orders

An order for discovery against a person who is not a wrongdoer but who may have information identifying the wrongdoer or evidence of a wrong. The name comes from the case of *Norwich Pharmacal Co v Commissioners of Customs and Excise*,[6] where the claimant sought information from Customs and Excise as to the identity of companies importing chemicals alleged to infringe the claimant's patent.

Prior to 2006, there was no equivalent order in Scotland but this was changed as a result of the European Directive on the enforcement of intellectual property rights.

Special provisions for persons routinely using the internet to infringe copyright

The Digital Economy Act 2010 brought in provisions aimed at tackling the problem of subscribers to internet services who routinely infringe copyright on a significant scale, for example, by distributing or facilitating access to copyright works online. The fine detail will be set out in an initial obligations code, a draft of which has been published by OFCOM.

The basic mechanism is as follows:

1. A copyright owner who considers a subscriber to an internet service has used the service to infringe his copyright (or has allowed another person to use his access service to infringe copyright) may submit a copyright infringement report (CIR) to the service provider.

---

4 OJ L 196, 2 August 2003, p 7.
5 HMRC Notice 34 Intellectual Property Rights. Available at: www.hmrc.gov.uk (search under intellectual property rights).
6 [1974] AC 133.

The CIR will include details and evidence of the apparent infringement, including the subscriber's IP (Internet Protocol) address (this alone does not give the identity of the subscriber).

2. The service provider will then notify the subscriber within one month. This will include information about the apparent infringement and subscriber appeals system. The notification must also include information about copyright and its purpose, advice or information about how to obtain advice as to lawful access to copyright works and how to protect his service against unauthorised use. Further information may be required to be given, such as a statement that the copyright owner may apply for a court order to discover the subscriber's identity and may bring proceedings against him. Service providers must keep copyright infringement lists of subscribers who receive multiple unchallenged CIRs.
3. If the copyright owner so requests, the service provider will supply a copyright infringement list for the period specified showing which subscribers have a threshold number of CIRs without identifying those subscribers.
4. A copyright owner may then to apply to the court for a *Norwich Pharmacal* order to discover the identity of the infringing subscriber or subscribers. If the order is granted, the copyright owner may bring proceedings against that subscriber or those subscribers. It appears from the draft initial obligations code that a 'three strikes' regime will apply before an application can be made for a court order for disclosure of the subscriber's identity (that is, three notifications sent to the subscriber within a 12-month period).

Main remedies available for infringement of intellectual property rights

In most cases, the owner (or licensee having the right to bring an action) will want to put a stop to the infringing activity. That is why the injunction is usually sought and usually granted if the court finds that infringement has occurred, is taking place or is likely to take place in the future. Other remedies available are damages and, as an alternative, an account of profits. Orders for delivery up and/or destruction of infringing materials may also be available and orders to publicise the fact of the finding of infringement. Other remedies exist depending on the nature of the right, such as additional damages and actions for groundless threats of infringement proceedings.

Injunctions

An injunction is granted to a claimant to prevent future infringements of IPR. Even if a claimant is successful at trial an injunction is not always granted. It is an equitable remedy and, as such, is discretionary. It may not be imposed in a case of breach of confidence where the information has subsequently entered the public domain.

In some cases, a claimant may be a 'patent troll', a person who has obtained a patent with no intention of working it himself. Instead he uses the right to threaten others with litigation unless they pay licence fees, which are often extortionate. Patent trolls are common in the field of computer software. Even the well-known online auction site eBay has been threatened by a patent troll.[7]

An injunction will not be granted if it is not possible to be precise about its terms. It must not be so wide as to prevent the defendant doing something that he may legally do. Nor must it be vague or ambiguous: its scope must be clear to the defendant; bearing in mind failure to comply may result in an action for contempt of court.

---

7 eBay Inc. v MercExchange LLC 547 US 388 (2006) where the US Supreme Court refused to grant an injunction.

A basic test for imposing an injunction is laid down in an old case, *Shelfer v City of London Electric Lighting Co*, being:[8]

1. if the injury to the claimant's legal rights is small; and
2. is one that is capable of being estimated in money; and
3. is one that can adequately be compensated by a small money payment; and
4. the case is one in which it would be oppressive to the defendant to grant an injunction;

then damages in substitution for an injunction may be given. However, this is a 'good working rule' and the court's discretion under it is not limited. The interests of third parties and the public also can be taken into account.

A proprietary injunction is one granted on the basis that the claimant has proprietary rights in relation to property in possession of the defendant. For example, if it is alleged that a person has unlawful possession of property, the owner may apply to the court for a proprietary injunction ordering that person not to dispose of the property.

It has been confirmed, however, in *Twentieth Century Fox Film Corp v Harris*,[9] that such injunctions are not available in IP cases. To grant such an injunction would be to accept that all the property and income derived from the infringement belonged to the owner of the IP right. This would be out of all proportion with the harm suffered by the owner (for which damages are available) or the profit made by the infringer (for which an account of profits may be available). For example, the profit made by the infringer would be the income less the cost of making and commercialising the infringing copies. From this a further reduction might be appropriate to allow for overheads and on-costs and, possibly, taxes paid on the infringing copies.

Injunctions against service providers

Under s 97A of the Copyright, Designs and Patents Act 1988, injunctions are available against online service providers, including internet service providers. Injunctions are available against service providers having actual knowledge that someone is using the service to infringe copyright. In determining whether a service provider has actual knowledge, account is taken of all matters that in the circumstances appear relevant, including whether he has received a notice, for example, sent to his email address.

Typically, an injunction granted under this provision will order the service provider to block access to a subscriber's account that is being used to infringe copyright.

A recent example of a successful application for injunctions against service providers was the case of *EMI Records Ltd v British Sky Broadcasting Ltd*,[10] in which a number of music and film companies applied for injunctions requiring the defendant internet service providers to block or at least impede access by their customers to a number of P2P (peer-to-peer) file-sharing websites.

Damages

Damages are, as a general rule, awarded so as to place the defendant in the position he would have been in but for the wrong, inasmuch as a monetary award can do this.

Assessment of damages

The Directive on the enforcement of intellectual property rights contains a formula for assessing the quantum of damages payable by a person infringing those rights.

---

8 [1895] 1 Ch 287.
9 [2013] EWHC 159 (Ch).
10 [2013] EWHC 379 (Ch).

First, where the infringer knew or had reasonable grounds for knowing that he was engaged in an infringing activity, he shall pay damages appropriate to the actual prejudice suffered by the holder of the right resulting from the infringement.

A court shall taken into account all appropriate aspects, such as the negative economic consequences, including profits lost by the holder of the right and any unfair profits made by the infringer. In appropriate cases, elements other than economic factors shall be taken into account, such as moral prejudice caused to the holder of the right by the infringement.

As an alternative and where appropriate, the damages may be assessed as the royalties or fees payable had the owner authorised the activity in question: that is, if the infringer obtained a licence to carry out the acts in question.

To assist in the exercise of assessing damages in this way, it is usual to look at comparable licences where such exist. What would a willing licensor and a willing licensee have agreed upon as a reasonable royalty or licence fee?

To give an example, say that a published photograph is reproduced in a magazine without permission. Say that 50,000 copies of the magazine have been sold and a typical licence fee would be around 2 pence per copy, then damages might be assessed at $50,000 \times 2p = £1,000$. This is exactly the sort of case that would be suitable for the small claims track in the Patents County Court, as mentioned in the previous chapter. There may also be issues of moral rights and further damages might be awarded for breach of moral rights, such as the right to be identified as author.

However, the owner of the copyright in work used without permission may not have intended that it should be published at all. For example, the work in question might be a private diary. In such a case, damages might be assessed on the basis of the unjust profits made by the infringer together with an amount to compensate for the harm done to the copyright owner. There might also be an award of additional damages, discussed later.

The Directive goes on to say that, where the infringer did not know and had no reason to believe that he was involved in an infringing activity, a court may nonetheless order the recovery of profits or damages, which may be pre-established. As far as law in the UK is concerned, damages will not be awarded against a defendant who did not know and who did not on reasonable grounds suspect that the right in question existed. However, this does not prevent an order for an account of profits.

Accounts

The purpose of the remedy of an account of profits is to prevent unjust enrichment of the defendant. The value of an account is the profit made by the defendant attributable to the infringement. It is not the value of or income derived from the infringing articles or materials.

Legislation relating to infringement of copyright and related rights, patents, designs and trade marks provides for an account of profits as an alternative to a claim for damages. The claimant will have to decide which, although he may set out his claim in the alternative. An account of profits is also available for breach of confidence and the tort of passing off.

An account of profits may be a useful alternative where it appears that the defendant has made more profit than would normally be awarded as damages.

A limiting factor in the usefulness of the remedy is that it may be difficult to isolate the profit made from infringing activities from income derived from other sources, for example, where the defendant is otherwise engaged in lawful activities.

Additional damages

Additional damages may be available where the infringement in question is blatant and deliberate. An example is where the defendant has deliberately carried out acts of infringement on the basis that the benefit he will receive will outweigh any award of damages if successful proceedings are brought against him. Another situation where they may be appropriate is where the owner of the right had no intention of commercialising the subject matter, for example, where it is a private diary.

The legal test for whether additional damages may be available requires the court to consider the flagrancy of the infringement and the benefit accruing to the defendant. The award of additional damages is discretionary.

A claim for additional damages may only be made alongside a claim for ordinary damages. Additional damages are not available if the claimant elects for an account of profits. As the term 'additional damages' suggests, they are additional to ordinary damages only.

Additional damages are not awarded often. One example is the case of *Williams v Settle*,[11] in which the defendant, a professional photographer, was commissioned by the claimant to take photographs at his wedding. The claimant became the owner of the copyright in the photographs. The father of the claimant's wife was later murdered and the defendant sold photographs of the wedding group, showing the murdered man, to the press. The claimant was awarded damages of £1,000, which were far in excess of the measure of ordinary damages that would have been awarded, as the claimant had no intention of publishing the photograph and the defendant received a relatively small sum for the copy of the photograph from the newspaper.

Publicity orders

Almost all court hearings in IP cases are open to the public and the vast majority of cases are published. Many are published in full with various sets of law reports. Nowadays, most judgments are available online. In rare cases, the court may be cleared of the public: for example, in a breach of confidence action where some secret information must be disclosed in oral evidence.

Article 15 of the Directive on the enforcement of intellectual property requires that, where requested, measures must be taken to disseminate the decision in an IP case at the expense of the infringer. This includes displaying the decision and publishing it in full or in part. Furthermore, Member States may provide for additional publicity measures that are appropriate to the particular circumstances including prominent advertising.

In a design case, where Apple Inc unsuccessfully sued Samsung Electronics (UK) Ltd for infringement of its Community design, the court ordered Apple to publicise the decision on the homepage of its website and in newspaper and magazine advertisements for one month. Apple failed to comply strictly with the order and the statement in its publicity materials was misleading. The Court of Appeal ordered that the correct statement be used and extended the time for it to be displayed on the website.[12] Apple was also punished by a higher award of costs than usual against it in the appeal hearing.

Groundless threats

It can be expensive to defend an IP infringement action. It is all too easy for the owner of an IP right to threaten to bring proceedings against someone who may, when faced with potentially large costs, decide to cease the activity complained of, even though it is not at all clear that the claimant will succeed in the legal proceedings. This is especially true where the person threatened is not the alleged primary infringer but is, for example, a retailer stocking the articles in question for sale.

---

11 [1960] 1 WLR 1072.
12 Samsung Electronics (UK) Ltd v Apple Inc. [2012] EWCA Civ 1430.

To prevent or deter owners of IPR adopting bullying tactics against, in particular, retailers, importers or distributors, the remedy of groundless threats actions exists.

Where a person threatens another with litigation for the infringement of an IP right, a(ny) person aggrieved by the threats[13] may in some circumstances bring an action for groundless threats of infringement proceedings. This remedy is particularly important in terms of monopoly rights such as patents, trade marks and designs (including the UK unregistered design and registered design and the Community design). It does not apply to copyright and related rights, breach of confidence or passing off. However, threats made in relation to these rights could in some cases be met with an action based on unlawful interference with contract.

The scope and nature of the remedy varies depending which form of IP right applies. However, the remedy does not apply in all cases. Some types of threat cannot give rise to a groundless threats action, such as a threat of patent infringement proceedings where the allegation concerns the making or importing of a patented product. There are some defences to the action. A patent proprietor faced with a groundless threats action will have a defence if he shows that the patent is valid in the relevant aspects and the acts concerned indeed do infringe the patent.

There are differences in the action depending on the right involved although the remedies available if the threats are found to be groundless are the same in all cases and are:

- a declaration to the effect that the threats are unjustifiable;
- an injunction against the continuance of the threats; and
- damages in respect of any loss that the claimant has sustained by the threats.

Licensees

To refresh our memories, remember that an exclusive licensee has the exclusive right to carry out the licensed acts even to the exclusion of the owner of the right. A non-exclusive licensee has the right to carry out the licensed acts but others may be licensed to carry out the same acts and/or the owner may also carry out those acts unless the licence provides otherwise. Remember also that licences, exclusive or otherwise, may be limited in relation to specific acts, to specific territory or for a specific period of time.

Exclusive licensees have a right of action in relation to an infringement affecting the licensed right. This is concurrent with the right of the owner and they have all the rights and remedies as the owner. The licence may provide for the division of any damages or accounts awarded. Typically, the owner will get an amount equivalent to the royalty or fee he would have been entitled to had the infringing acts been licensed by him.

Normally, non-exclusive licensees do not have a right of action but there are some exceptions. Where a copyright licence expressly so provides, a non-exclusive licensee also has a right of action where the infringing acts are within the scope of the licence.

Non-exclusive licensees under a trade mark can bring an action if, having been called upon to take action, the proprietor refuses or fails to do so within two months, unless the licence provides otherwise.

In a slight variation, for the Community design, a licensee can bring an action if the licence agreement so provides but an exclusive licensee can bring an action if the right-holder, having been given notice, fails to bring an action within an appropriate time.

---

13 Some of the legislation uses the term 'a person aggrieved' while other legislation uses 'any person aggrieved'. The difference is of no practical effect.

Moral rights

Moral rights apply to original works of copyright and films and performances. Breaches of moral rights are actionable by the author, film director or performer as the case may be. Bear in mind that these rights (the right to be identified and the right to object to a derogatory treatment) cannot be assigned during the person's life. The false attribution right may be actioned, of course, by the person falsely attributed.

There is also an artists' resale right applicable to certain forms of copyright work but this right can only be managed through a collecting society.

Breaches of moral rights are treated as breaches of statutory duty, which means that, typically, injunctions and damages are available. There may also be orders for delivery up or destruction. In terms of derogatory treatment, a court may, if it thinks it an adequate remedy, order that a disclaimer be used to disassociate the author or director from the treatment of the work.

Assignment of rights of action

Normally, assigning the right in question or specific acts under the right gives the assignee the right to bring legal proceedings if the right in question has been infringed. In some cases, the owner of a right may assign a particular act to a collecting society that will enforce that part of the right. Thus, rental rights and the right to perform a work in public are usually assigned.

Criminal offences

At one time IP infringement was a matter left to the owner of the right to bring civil proceedings to enforce his rights. Largely, this is still the same today but piracy and counterfeiting have become such major problems that specific criminal offences have developed that are aimed at tackling these activities that have attracted the attention of criminal organisations.

The serious criminal offences that carry heavy penalties apply to copyright and related rights and trade marks. There are no specific criminal offences directly related to breach of confidence or passing off. Offences under patent law are relatively minor and cover situations such as where a person marks as patented products that are not patented or falsely gives the impression of having a business connection with the Patent Office or of being a patent agent or attorney.

Copyright offences are not strict liability but require that the accused must know or have reason to believe that, for example, he was dealing with infringing copies. The maximum penalty is imprisonment for a term not exceeding ten years and/or a fine. There is no limit to the value of the fine if tried in the Crown Court. Some offences under trade mark law carry lesser maximum penalties.

There are some equivalent offences for rights in performances in connection with illicit recordings but these carry lesser penalties, either a maximum of six months' or three months' imprisonment and limited fines. There is also an offence of falsely representing authority to give consent to a performance.

'Having reason to believe' is an objective test. It is a question of whether the ordinary reasonable person having knowledge of the facts known to the accused would have the relevant reason to believe.

The important trade mark offences, such as applying to goods a sign identical to or likely to be mistaken for a registered trade mark, with a view to gain or to cause loss to another, also carry a maximum penalty of imprisonment for a term not exceeding ten years and/or a fine. Although almost of strict liability, it is a defence to show belief on reasonable grounds that the use in question was not an infringement of the trade mark.

There are also some minor offences under trade mark law such as falsely representing a sign to be a registered trade mark. Similar penalties apply to registered designs.

There are no criminal penalties associated with the UK unregistered designs or the database right; although, as with other rights, other forms of criminal law may be applicable such as the law of fraud or trade descriptions law.

There is a general privilege against self-incrimination in civil proceedings. Thus, a person may refuse to give evidence in a civil case that would show or tend to show that he had committed a criminal offence. However, that privilege does not usually apply in civil proceedings involving IP. A typical example of this exception to the general rule is where a search order is being executed against a person suspected of civil infringement and documents subject to the order tend to show that copyright offences have been committed. That person cannot engage the privilege to refuse to hand over the documents.

Management tips

If the alleged infringement is likely to do real harm that cannot be remedied by an award of damages in a full trial, contact your solicitor with a view to applying for an interim injunction.

Consider applying to the court for a search order if you think this is the only way of obtaining evidence of infringement. But be aware that these are not granted lightly and must be executed by a solicitor with appropriate training and experience. In many cases, it will be possible to obtain evidence without a search order: for example, by simply buying copies of the article or work alleged to infringe.

If you bring a legal action for infringement, you will have to prove your damages. Keep full and accurate records of your sales, profit, licence fees, etc.

If you elect to apply for an account of profits, be aware that it might be difficult to isolate the profits made by virtue of the infringement from other non-infringing activities carried out by the infringer.

Seek legal advice before threatening an alleged offender with legal action to avoid precipitating a groundless threats action.

Make sure that licences have provisions dealing with infringement actions, such as the division of damages between the parties and practical consideration such as which party will bring the action, joining the other party as co-claimant, providing assistance, etc.

Check that your activities do not infringe the rights of others, particularly as there is a low threshold for some of the criminal offences associated with IPR.

Exercise

Matthew designs, makes and sells greetings cards to which he applies his own registered trade mark. Recently he noticed some fake copies of his cards on sale at a market stall run by Rodney. They also bear a sign that is identical to Matthew's trade mark. The market was a traditional market held weekly in Smalltown. What action should Matthew take?

As the market is a regular one, Matthew cannot exercise the right of seizure but he could buy some of the cards to retain as evidence and to confirm that they are indeed fakes. If he confirms that they are fakes, he could apply for a search order to search Rodney's premises to secure evidence of the quantity of infringing cards in case Rodney removes them if alerted beforehand. The evidence might show the source of the cards if Rodney has bought them from a third party.

If, for example, the fake cards are imported by a shipping company, if the company refuses to disclose the original source, Matthew could apply for a *Norwich Pharmacal* order to enable him to bring proceedings against that person.

Matthew might also want to inform Trading Standards and/or the police as it is possible that Rodney has committed criminal offences under copyright law and trade mark law.

If a reasonable person would suspect the cards were fake, the offence under copyright law would be made out. For trade mark law it might be a matter of Rodney showing on reasonable grounds that he had reason to believe that the use of the sign on his cards did not infringe Matthew's trade mark.

If criminal convictions follow, this fact can be put in evidence in any civil action brought by Matthew. He is likely to ask for an injunction to prevent further dealings in the fake cards and damages that might be based on how much Matthew would have charged for permission for the cards to be made and sold by Rodney and a court order for delivery up of any remaining cards and their destruction.

Bibliography

Arena, C.M. and Carreras E.M. (2008) *The Business of Intellectual Property*, Oxford University Press.
Bainbridge, D.I. (2012) *Intellectual Property*, Pearson.
Barker, G. and Bissell, P. (2007) *A Better Mousetrap*, abetterMousetrap.co.uk.
Blaxill, M. and Eckardt, R. (2009) *The Invisible Edge*, Portfolio.
Davis, J.L. and Harrison, S.S. (2002) *Edison in the Boardroom: How Leading Companies Realize Value from Their Intellectual Assets*, John Wiley.
Gollin, M.A. (2008) *Driving Innovation: Intellectual Property Strategies for a Dynamic World*, Cambridge University Press.
Greenhalgh, C. and Rodgers, M. (2011) *Innovation, Intellectual Property, and Economic Growth*, Princeton University Press.
Griffiths, A. (2011) *An Economic Perspective on Trade Mark Law*, Edward Elgar.
Hart, T., Fazzani, L. and Clark, S. (2009) *Intellectual Property Law*, 5th edn, Palgrave Macmillan.
Li, X. and Correa, C. (2009) *Intellectual Property Enforcement: International Perspectives*, Edward Elgar.
Parr, R.L. and Smith, G.V. (2005) *Intellectual Property: Valuation, Exploitation, and Infringement Damages*, John Wiley.
Poltorak, A.I. and Lerner, P.J. (2002) *Essentials of Intellectual Property: Law Economics and Strategy*, 2nd edn, John Wiley.
Stone, D. (2012) *European Union Design Law: A Practitioner's Guide*, Oxford University Press.
Thorne, C. and Bennett, S. (2010) *A User's Guide to Design Law*, Routledge.

Index

A
absolute grounds for refusal 21–2, 24, 37
advertising 1, 21, 84–5, 102, 127, 137
    campaigns 23, 27, 34–5, 87
    comparative 28, 37
    extensive 13, 34
    prominent 202
    slogans 82
    television 151
    website 25, 86
African Intellectual Property Organisation 139
African Regional Office 59n22
Agreement on Trade-Related Aspects of Intellectual Property 7
application procedure 62–3
    trade mark **33**
assets 74, 144, 146, 148–9, 151–2, 155, 159, 166, 169, 178
    business 153–4
    fastest-growing 52
    freezing order 31
    intangible 168
    intellectual 160, 163
    IP 143, 147, 156, 162, 165, 167
    listing 164
    valuable 13, 40
    value 171
attorneys 22–3
    Chartered Institute of Patent Attorneys 23
    fees and costs 77, 153
    Institute of Trade Mark Attorneys 23
    overseas 154
    patent 22, 42, 46, 62–3, 67, 70
    trade mark 21–2, 37;
    see also lawyers
audit 74, 146–7, 162, 165, 171, 177
    internal 163
    IP 11, 161, 163, 166, 176
    report 178
    royalty 155

Australasia 187
Australia 33, 184, 186

B
bad faith 17–18
Bainbridge, D. 93
Barker, G. 153
Berne Convention for the Protection of Literary and Artistic Works 1883 6, 92, 106, 118
brand 12–13, 13n1, 29, 82, 157, 161
    awareness 36, 151, 160
    famous 32, 144
    luxury 26–7
    own brand 28, 35
    strong 152
    unique 20, 35
    value 23
    well-known 20
Brazil 32, 75
breach of confidence 40, 42–3, 50, 59, 104, 186, 199, 201, 203–4
    action for 7, 41, 48, 202
    law of 3, 185
British 6, 92
    Brands Group 13
    Commonwealth 7
    goods 12
British Horseracing Board 112, 117–19
British Library 120
British Sky Broadcasting Limited 99, 200
broadcaster 88
broadcasting 4
    British Sky Broadcasting Limited 99, 200
    Rome Convention 1961 107n62
    Southwold Corporation 111
broadcasts 2, 6, 9, 79, 83–4, 98–9, 107, 109
    radio 87, 89, 111
    satellite 88
business information 47, 49, 185
    Reed Business Information 19

INDEX

C

Cadbury 13–14
    Crunchie bars 28
Calvin Klein 13
Canada 98, 187
Chartered Institute of Patent Attorneys 23
Chief Intellectual Property Officer 149–50, 155–7, 167, 178
China 25–6, 32–3, 45, 61, 75, 100, 106, 126
Coca-Cola 2, 13, 16, 75
Community design 8
    unregistered 6, 122
Community Trade Mark (CTM) 18, 21, 24, 32–3, 36
compensation 68, 79, 198
    appropriate 49
    employee 171, 188
    financial 10, 180, 193
confidential information 9, 40, 160, 164, 181
    access to 11, 44, 168
    disclosure 46, 48, 106, 151
    exploitation 49
    law 41
    possession of 43
    sensitive 45
confidentiality 7, 40, 42, 45, 58, 76, 185
    agreements 41, 43, 46, 48, 59, 64, 138, 165
    clauses 49, 146
    destroyed 48
    duty of 11, 51
    policies 165
consumers 1, 10, 12–13, 15, 17–21, 27–8, 38, 148, 160, 181
    behaviour 151
    confused 4, 33, 35, 37, 39, 184
    disadvantaged 53
contrary to public policy 17, 58, 127, **133**, 139
copyright 2, 6, 53, **81**, 124–5, 133, 136–7, 140, 145, 148, 152, 158, 164–6, 173, 179–80, 182–3, 184–5, 191, 195, 203
    70 years after death 11, 92–3, 108
    Acts 79, 160
    artistic 82, 85–6, 96
    assignment 9, 91–3
    Crown 116
    database 113–18, 120–1
    justification 3, 80
    law 70, 107–8, 197, 206
    literary 4, 8, 87
    material 104, 167, 169
    monitoring service 161
    music 9, 86–7
    offences 204–5
    owner 94–5, 98–9, 201–2
    programs 75, 101–2, 110–11
    in photographs 105, 188, 190
    protection 10, 42, 57–8, 78, 83–4, 89, 97, 122
    sound recording 88, 109
    subsistence 112, 114, 186, 192
    works 5–6, 103, 106, 174, 185
Copyright Designs and Patents Act 1988 79, 83–6, 89, 93, 99, 114, 135, 138, 182, 186, 195, 198, 200
copyright infringement 4, 9, 27, 35, 82–4, 86–7, 92, 95–7, 99–101, 103–5, 109–11, 116, 169, 180, 194, 200
    defence 162
    report (CIR) 198–9;
counterfeit 1, 29
    articles 10
    drugs 29
    DVDs and CDs 29, 197
    goods 27, 29, 78, 100, 105–6, 195–6, 198
counterfeiting 29, 110, 204
counterfeiters 1, 29
Court of Justice of the European Union (CJEU) 117–19, 127–8, 189
crime 41, 108
    cyber 105
    partners 190
    prevention 46
    in the workplace 106
criminal convictions 110, 206
    laws 49, 205
    liability 198
    organisations 204
    penalties 106, 183, 194, 205
    prosecution 105, 197
    remedies 104
    sanctions 29, 105
criminal offences 10, 22, 37, 76, 95, 105, 107, 183, 191, 197, 204–6
customers 2, 11, 13, 35, 40, 44, 53, 58, 78, 102, 106, 152, 158, 200
    accounts 112

customers *continued*
    average 38
    Community 25
    lists 159, 164
    loyalty 151
    potential 46
    preferences 50–1
    trade 19
    UK 25, 34

D

damages 36, 47–9, 67, 70, 73, 79, 100, 153, 162, 166, 170–1, 174, 184, 186, 191–3, 194–5, 197, 199–200, 203–4, 206
    additional 201–2
    award 31–2, 188, 196, 202, 205
    cap 74
    claimed 161
    entitlement 110
    for lost sales 69, 104
    not awarded 105
    sought 189
databases 2, 32, 79, 98, 106, 118–21, 157–8, 169, 182
    copyright 6, 114
    customers 159
    lawyers 186
    licenses 176
    parameters 134
    patent 60, 64, 147
    protection 3, 112–14, 117
    right 180, 195, 205
    structure 115, 116
    trade mark 164, 166
    user-friendly 155, 160
Data Protection Act 1998 40
Davis, J. 152
deception 10, 17, 35
    deceptive 24, 135
defences 4, 8, 26, 29, 37, 48, 70, 72, 74, 95, 102–5, 110, 161–2, 180, 181–3, 190, 203–4
    available 30, 96
    effective 153
    essential 130
    permitted 59
    potential 179
    public interest 47
descriptive 14–16, 21–4, 30, 34–5, 37–8, 71
    not descriptive 21, 24, 26

dispute resolution 36
    alternative 74–5, 104, 187, 189, 191–2
    Centre for 187
distinctiveness 15, 30
distribution 114, 118, 132, 182, 197
    agreements 25
    channels 157
    costs 173, 175
    network 12
    right 108, 145

E

eBay 27, 29, 199
E-Commerce Directive 27, 99n41
economic benefit 1, 10, 171
Europe 16, 75
    Human Rights Act 46
    inventor 67
    patent law 7–8, 55, 57–8
    patent ownership 68
    period of protection 61
    trade within 21
European Common Market 25, 59
    authors 106
    countries 24–6, 59n22
    customs authorities 105
    Parliament and Council 99n41, 113, 193n1
    patent law 55
    protection 62
    states 61, 153
    three-factor approach 193
    unitary patent 59, 190
European Court of Justice 27, Directive 198
European Economic Area (EEA) 98, 112, 115, 117, 189n9
    non-EEA countries 98
European Patent 59, 190
    Community 8
    Convention 7, 52, 55, 58–9, 59n21, 61, 63, 75, 189–90
    law 55
    Office 7, 59–62, 67, 189
    Organisation 59n22
European Union 5, 7, 41, 43, 57, 101, 123, 125–7, 136, 146, 174, 184, 189–90
    Community trade mark 14, 18, 24, 37, 61
    countries 21, 32–3, 71, 117
    countries outside EU 32, 141

Court of Justice 127–8
EU-wide design 8
law 4
market 25, 129 181
Member States 59, 59n21, 62, 79, 107, 112, 130, 195–6, 198, 202
protection outside EU 36, 49, 106, 122, 139
provisions 113
territory 133
trade and imports 26
European Union Directive 109, 134, 189
E-Commerce Directive 27
exploitation 9–10, 47, 54, 89, 148, 167, 171, 187
assets 154, 165
commercial 140
confidential information 49
economic 98
of intellectual property 149, 156
invention 67–8, 70
IP 143–4, 176
market 134, 138
normal 120, 129
patent 173
performance 108
rights 1, 177, 184
works 9, 90, 92–3, 95, 159

F

fake 1, 105–6
brands 29
copies 205–6
fees 24, 33, 60, 67–8, 109, 132, 134, 156, 163, 168–72, 188
appropriate 22, 166
legal 62, 77, 153, 172
licence 70, 102, 199, 201, 205
maintenance 164
professional 175
renewal 14, 53, 59, 61, 69, 73–5, 138
royalty 8, 174, 203
France 7–9, 25, 41, 68, 70, 75, 83, 106, 134, 142, 145, 190–1
Champagne region 2
free riding 27, 29, 37

G

Germany 8, 24, 59, 68, 72, 75, 190–191
German 61, 118, 145

get-up 2, 33–5, 37, 39, 124–5, 152, 164, 168, 180, 181, 186
Gollin, M. 152
goodwill 3, 4–5, 6, 7, 10, 33–7, 39, 151–2, 157, 170, 180, 181, 184
business 2, 12, 34
Google 15, 27, 104, 144
Earth 190
search 23

H

Hague System for the International Registration of Industrial Designs 7–8, 139
harmonisation 41, 101, 134
see also Office of Harmonization
Harrison, S. 152
Henry product 33–5
Howell, C. 93
Human Rights Act 46–7

I

Iceland 7, 112, 117, 139
image 2, 15, 17, 19, 21, 47, 94–5, 103, 105, 110–11, 145, 152
brand 13, 26, 144, 151
computer screen 174
doctoring 35
iconic 97
luxury 27
moving 14, 88
presentation 36
text 87
visual 88, 142
immoral 17, 22, 24, 37, 55, 58, 103
India 32–3
industrial application 2, 5, 53, 55, 57–8, 63, 75, 77, 153
informal rights 3–4, 11
information 3, 13, 32, 50–1, 57, 60, 62, 64, 66, 69–70, 83, 85, 88–9, 103, 109, 113, 117, 132, 139, 163, 166, 173–4, 178, 186–7, 189, 198–9
access to 9, 27, 104
business 19, 47, 49, 185
confidential 6, 7, 9, 11, 40–7, 48–9, 106, 151, 168, 181
disclosed 160, 193, 196
false 28
financial 101

information *continued*
    good 155
    lack of 167
    protected by the law of confidence 180, 194
    relevant 157–8
    secret 2, 75, 202
    sensitive 145, 164–5, 197
    services 99n41
    valuable 51, 152
injunction 27, 34, 36, 44, 48, 50, 69–70, 74, 79, 99, 104–6, 110, 153, 161–2, 166, 193, 194–5, 199, 203–4, 206
    interim 31, 73, 188, 194, 196–7, 205
    permanent 196
    proprietary 200
innovation 1–2, 13, 46, 53–5, 102, 147–8, 152, 170
    agreement 156
    culture 155
    patents 75
    strategy 149, 158
Institute of Trade Mark Attorneys 23
intellectual property 1–2, 8, 10, 52, 138
    African Organisation 139
    Agreement on the Trade Related Aspects 107n62
    Awareness Survey 152n2
    portfolios 149
    protection 43
    soft 3, 4, 173, 179–80
    transactions 143
    value 11, 171
Intellectual Property Enterprise Court 162
Intellectual Property Office 16–17, 37, 64, 66, 69, 180
    African Regional 59n22
    national 132
    UK 2n1, 5n2, 7–8, 21–2, 24, 32–3, 46, 60–4, 66, 131–2, 134, 138–9, 152n2, 170n5, 172, 187–8, 191
intellectual property rights 1–3, 5–6, 52, 57, 69, 121, 128, 130, 148–9, 155, 157, 166–8, 181–3, 184, 196
    acquiring 175
    assignment of 172, 174
    criminal offences 205
    enforcement 193n1, 198, 200
    failed company 170
    failure to register 10

infringement 176, 197
    owners 177, 186, 203
    registered 11
    remedies for infringement 193, 194–5, 199
    scope 3–4
    selling 9, 170n5
    soft and hard 179–80
    of third parties 152–3, 156
    Trade-Related Aspects (TRIPS) 41, 79
    transfers 9
    value 171–2
internet 1, 34, 70, 79, 92, 95, 104, 116
    domain name 30, 36, 169
    downloading from 78
    policy 160
    Protocol 199
    search 66, 145, 161
    selling 25–6
    service 198
    service providers 27, 99, 116, 200
    software 4
    transmission 88
invalidity 70, 76, 168
    hearings 188
    proceedings 131, 170
    of registered Community design 133
inventions 2–3, 55, 57, 149–50, 158
    biotechnological 2, 58, 188
    disclosed 154, 159
    employees' 68
    hi-tech 174
    industrial 5, 10
    new 164
    overlapping 160
    patenting 151, 153, 155, 157, 170
    protection for 17, 52, 75
    written descriptions 75
Ipsum Online Patent Information and Document Inspection Service 60
Ireland 7–8
Isle of Man 112, 115, 117, 136, 139
Italy 41, 59, 62, 190
    Italian 24
    patent 7–8

J

Japan 32, 41, 58, 126

K

know-how 41, 145, 157, 164, 168, 171, 174
    ex-employees 44–5, 49
    licence 46
    secret 146
Kodak 15, 170

L

law 29, 48, 68, 88, 101, 157, 163, 180, 192, 196
    breach of confidence 3, 185
    case law 41, 119, 136, 193
    choice of law clause 49
    common 72, 182
    competition 8, 146
    of confidence 5, 40, 46
    contract 173, 173n3
    copyright 70, 107–8, 112–13, 120, 186, 197
    criminal 205
    design 85–6, 134, 188
    EEA state 117
    EU 189
    national 128
    of passing off 2, 3, 4, 181, 184
    patent 7, 10, 55, 171
    reports 202
    students 173n7
    trade mark 17, 126, 204–6
    UK 42, 73, 201
    unfair competition 7, 33
    see also legislation
lawyers 11, 58, 157, 162
    advice 166–7
    database 186
    foreign 178
    licensing 161
legislation 79–80, 95, 100–1, 142, 160, 180, 201, 203n13
    Bulgarian 119
    design 86
    relevant 198
    UK 31, 41, 52
licences 4, 10–11, 23, 32, 46, 53–5, 75, 98, 106, 110–11, 114, 121, 128, 132, 137–8, 164–70, 173, 180, 182–3, 184
    agreement 104, 116, 147, 160, 163, 191, 203
    appropriate 73, 153
    comparable 171, 177
    database 176
    deal 155, 161
    duration 146, 174
    exclusive 2, 8–9, 143–4, 186–7
    expiry 192
    fees 102, 199, 201, 205
    implied 91, 109
    music 99, 150
    negotiation 159
    patent 74
    of right 140, 183
    royalties 175
    terms 89, 101, 145
licensing agreements 13, 161, 170
    cross-licensing 54, 145, 151
Lidl 28
Liechtenstein 112, 117
literary work 4, 8, 79, 84–5, 87–8, 101, 111–12, 114, 116, 187
    Berne Convention 6, 92, 106, 118
    marketing 78
    original 80, 82
    trade 25
logos 2, 4, 10–12, 14, 18, 20, 25, 29, 35, 37, 39, 91, 132, 151–2, 158, 168, 184
L'Oréal 27, 31

M

Madrid Agreement for the International Registration of Marks 7, 21, 25n51, 36
    Romarin database 32
managers 150
    costs 172
    senior 11
market 13–14, 46, 59, 77, 79, 91, 98, 104, 110, 123, 126, 128–9, 131, 138–9, 146–8, 152, 154, 156–8, 168, 172, 183, 198
    black 29
    destroy 105, 144
    EU 129, 181
    expanding 151
    first to market 58, 63, 75
    flooded 162
    goods 21, 24
    goodwill 39
    insight 150
    leader 53
    lost 69, 159

market *continued*
    open 93
    overseas 184
    reach 147, 173
    research 61–2, 80, 171
    share 38, 160, 174
    single 25, 130
    stall 26, 205
    supermarkets 19, 28, 35
    sustainable 54
    UK 134, 136
marketing 1, 17, 22, 48, 62, 85, 93, 110, 145, 151, 157, 169, 176, 191
    advice 16
    costs 175
    department 37, 178
    direct 112
    first 136–7
    improved 57
    joint 144
    literature 78
    strategy 13, 40
    team 80, 167
    units 162
misrepresentation 4, 33–5, 39, 181, 184
monopoly 16, 18, 20, 30, 43, 53, 64, 82, 84, 97, 151–2, 159
    20 year 54
    advantage 150
    claimed 71
    complete 55, 57, 170
    created 156
    granted 58
    indefinite 17
    protection 10, 122, 140
    rights 3–5, 13, 53, 75, 124, 131, 174, 180, 203
    scope 70
morality 17, 58, 127, 133, 139
moral rights 79, 92–5, 103, 107, 109–10, 121, 182, 195
    breach of 201, 204
    performers 108
music industry 1, 89

N

newspapers 37, 43, 48, 88, 93, 95, 98, 118, 202
    archive 113
    Mirror Group 47
    News of the World 13
    the Sun 103
    The Times 83
New Zealand 136, 185
NICE classification system 13, 19, 37
non-disclosure agreement 41–4, 46, 48–9, 145, 168
Northern Ireland 189
Norway 7, 112, 117, 139
novelty 3, 10, 76, 123, 127, 131, 136, 174, 184
    destroy 46, 53, 55, 60–1, 64, 72, 75, 126, 156, 160
    lack 55, 72–3, 130, 188
        loss of 55, 58, 61, 64, 66
    prejudiced 128, 186
    requirements 125, 134, 139, 141

O

Office of Harmonization for the Internal Market (Trade Marks and Designs) (OHIM) 7–8, 17n16, 24, 32, 131, 189
    classification system 132
    see also harmonisation

P

packaging 13, 22, 25, 35, 124–5, 164
Paris Convention for the Protection of Industrial Property 1883 7, 130, 139
passing off 6, 13, 17n18, 30, 39, 166, 188–9, 203–4
    action 34–5
    law of 2, 3, 4, 7, 17, 180, 181, 184
    proceedings 38
    remedies 36, 194
    tort of 12, 33, 37, 201
patent 2, 3, 4, 6, 40, 43, 53–5, 60–3, 76, 80, 106, 125, 130, 136, 145–6, 151–3, 155, 157, 179–80, 181, 184, 187–8
    agent 11, 167, 172, 204
    application 57, 149, 158
    attorney 22–3, 42, 46, 67, 70, 77, 154
    bundle 160
    Comptroller 138
    costs 68, 172
    County Court 97, 191–2, 201
    Court 189, 192
    databases 64, 147
    design 75, 139
    examiner 63

expiry 53–4, 170
infringement 8, 161, 194, 203
monitoring service 69
national 7–8, 190
pharmaceutical 61n25, 173
pools 159–60
specifications 2n1, 5, 84
Teaching Kit 65n27
territorial 59, 72
third-party 73
trolls 58, 74, 199
UK 52, 191
UK Patent Office 10, 66
unitary 59, 61
Windsurfer 56
patent attorney 22, 42, 46, 62–3, 67, 70
    Chartered Institute of Patent
    Attorneys 23
    fees and costs 77, 153
    overseas 154
Patent Cooperation Treaty 58–9, 63, 75
    application 62, 66, 153
patent law 2, 7, 10, 171, 180, 204
    European 55
patent office 64, 174, 204
    European 7, 61, 189
    national 62, 75
    UK 10, 66
patent protection 1, 3, 5, 43, 54, 57, 74, 122, 159, 180, 191
    specifications 2n1 5, 84
Patents Act 1977 52, 66, 68, 188
pharmaceutical 172
    companies 1, 55, 167
    industry 54, 105
    licences 174
    patents 61, 173
photographer 47, 85, 94, 102, 105, 192
    copyright 80, 95, 97, 188
    permission 103
    professional 191, 202
photographs 3, 9–10, 14, 35, 40, 47, 57, 78, 80, 84–5, 94–5, 97, 103, 110–11, 140, 141
    copyright 105, 188, 190–1, 202
    domestic 93
    identical 96
    instant 158, 170
    published 201
    separate 102

police 29, 31, 37, 105, 161, 198, 206
proprietor 4, 8, 17, 20, 23, 27, 31, 34, 123, 170, 181
    first 134
    joint 69
    patent 138, 187–8, 203
    trade mark 32
public access 43, 48
    domain 9, 41, 43, 48–50, 59, 66–7, 69, 92, 114, 150, 159, 185, 199
    interest 23, 47–8, 103, 105, 180, 181–2
    policy 17, 58, 127, 133, 139

R

registered rights 3, 5, 9, 147, 166, 168, 175, 177, 191
registered trade mark 2, 4, 10, 14, 168, 179–80, 181, 191, 198, 204–5
    attorney 22
    infringing 29
    limitation 177
    oldest 12
    owner 36
    rights 184, 187
    UK 5, 7
    validity 190
registration 2–3, 111, 16–17, 30, 141, 151, 159, 163, 168–9, 172, 180, 190–1
    applications for 10, 130, 139
    in bad faith 18
    cannot be registered 4, 15
    certificate 22
    as Community design 8
    confusion 36
    costs 173, 184
    of designs 140
    formal 12, 179
    international 32–3, 139
    number 186
    opposed 23
    refusal 21, 25
    renewal 5, 6, 131
    single 7;
    see also Madrid Agreement
renewal fees 14, 24, 53, 59, 61, 67, 69, 73–5, 132, 138, 153, 172
reputation 1–2, 7, 12–13, 17–18, 20–1, 25, 27, 29, 34–5, 37–9, 53–4, 145–6, 151–2, 154, 162

reputation *continued*
    author's 94
    business 106
    company 76
    damage 166, 184
    enhanced 160
    organisation 151, 153
    performer's 108
    product 157, 160
reverse-engineering 42–3, 58, 75, 94, 104, 157, 161
revocation 6, 24, 32, 38, 54, 61, 72–3, 130, 144, 146, 159, 168
    hearings 188
    proceedings 23, 55
rights in performances 2, 3, 6, 106–9, 111, 180, 182–3, 204
Romarin database 32;
    see also Madrid Agreement
Rome Convention for the Protection of Performers, Producers of Phonograms and Broadcasting Organisations 1961 107n62
royalties 41, 79–80, 93, 98, 138, 160, 165, 173, 176, 201, 203
    audit 155
    figure 171, 177
    payments 8
    rates 144, 147, 174–5
    reduced 192

S

Scotland 9, 189, 193, 198
secret information 2, 48, 151, 202
    personal 41, 44
signatory countries 75, 92, 106
soft IP 3, 4, 173, 179–80
software 43, 58, 74, 84, 91, 101–2, 105, 121, 134, 150, 153, 157, 160, 164, 166, 169
    application 142
    code 82
    communications 174, 191
    companies 167
    computer 54, 78, 93, 104, 172, 187, 199
    copying 95
    copyright 110–11
    file 137–8
    fonts 124
    internet 4
    licensed 106, 145
    packages 8
sound recordings 6, 79, 83, 87–8, 99, 108–9
Spain 14, 24, 33, 41, 59, 62, 190
standards 18
    accounting 157
    patent 161;
    see also Trading Standards
Starbucks 158
Supplementary Protection Certificates 61n25
suppliers 11, 13, 24, 105–6, 151, 158

T

technical 57–8, 64, 127
    area 62
    changes 82
    disclosures 155
    drawing 89
    field 66, 69
    function 17, 139, 142
    inferiority 148
    people 157, 161
    plans 85
    problem 52
    reports 84
    resources 117, 119
    solutions 53, 75
    subject heading 60
    support 101–2
telecommunications 14–15, 74
    BT 99n42
territorial 179
    confidence 7
    limitations 6, 187
    patents 59, 72
    scope of protection 5, 174
    trade marks 24–5
thickets 55, 161
third parties 4, 42, 151–2, 169, 173, 185
    disclosure to 147, 164
    exploitation 138
    interests 200
    IP 165
    negotiations 49
    networks 116
    patents licensed 160, 184
    prevention of use 131
    rights infringed 162, 166
    selling to 93
    sharing secrets 46–7

INDEX

threat by 150
use 129
threats 73, 150, 159, 199, 205
    disclosure 43, 48
    groundless 31, 37, 72, 74, 187, 194, 202–3
    litigation 101, 166, 177, 193
    threatened opposition 33
trade mark attorney 21–2, 37
    Institute of Trade Mark Attorneys 23
trade marks 1, 3, 4–5, 5n2, 6, 7–8, 17, 20, 28–30, 35, 47, 82, 86, 91, 113, 130, 139, 149, 151–2, 154, 156, 160–3, 165, 167, 170–1, 181, 184, 186–7, 191, 203
    agents 172, 174
    application procedure 33
    attorney 21–2, 37
    community 14, 24
    databases 164, 166
    European Community 18, 61, 189–90
    infringement 26–7, 38, 105
    law 2, 17, 126, 188, 197–8, 201, 204–6
    licensing 144
    national 36
    owner 31
    protection 12–13
    registers 23, 158, 168
    registration 32, 34
    rights 16, 114
    UK 15, 25;
    see also registered trade mark;
    revocation
Trade Marks Act 1994 18, 21, 189n7, 194, 198
Trade Marks Registration Act 12
trade name 13, 16, 30, 184
    trading name 2, 10, 30, 80, 169
Trade-Related Aspects of Intellectual Property Rights agreement 41, 49
traders 12–18, 30, 37; registering marks 23, 36
trade secrets 2, 40–1, 49–51, 113, 146, 148, 151, 158, 164, 168
    employer 11
    ex-employer 44
Trading Standards 105
    Office 73, 105
    Officers 29, 31

U

UK 5, 7–9, 11–12, 16, 33–4, 36–7, 41
    copyright 6, 92
    customers 25
    economy 13, 101, 105
    Intellectual Property Office 2n1, 5n2, 21, 46, 60, 131, 152n2, 187–8
    legislation 31, 52
    patent 61, 69, 172, 191
    patent office 10, 66
    registered 18, 159, 174
    Trade Marks Act 1994 189n7
    unregistered design right 4, 123–4, 135, 137–8, 140, 142, 195
UK IPO 7–8, 21–2, 24, 32–3, 60, 62–3, 131–2, 134, 138–9
    booklet 170n5
    fees 172
    hearing officers 188
    mediation service 187
    services 191
    Supply Chain Toolkit 106n61
    website 46, 66
UK patents 7–8, 52, 61, 67, 69, 172, 190–1
    Office 10, 66
UK trade mark 15, 21–2, 24–5, 32, 172
    holder 26;
unfair competition 7, 33
    legislation 41
unitary mark 24, 32
unitary patent 59, 61
Universal Copyright Convention 92
unregistered design rights 2, 3, 5, 10, 131, 138–40, 152, 166, 180, 188, 191
    duration 137; UK 4, 6, 123–4, 130, 135–8, 140, 142, 195, 203, 205
unregistered rights 5, 142, 152, 166, 191
USA 7, 25, 32–3, 43, 58–9, 74, 98, 139, 155, 159, 162, 187

V

Virgin 16, 160

W

World Intellectual Property Organization 7, 32, 62, 139

Printed in Great Britain
by Amazon